WILLIAM GOLDING

DAVID ANDERSON

TED E. BOYLE

PHILIPPA TRISTRAM

PETER WOLFE

JEANNE DELBAERE-GARANT

ROBERT O. EVANS

ARNOLD JOHNSTON

JAY L. HALIO

E. C. BUFKIN

RICHARD S. CAMMAROTA

DAVID SKILTON

LEIGHTON HODSON

MAURICE McCULLEN

JACK I. BILES

William Golding

SOME CRITICAL CONSIDERATIONS

EDITED BY *Jack I. Biles* &

Robert O. Evans

THE UNIVERSITY PRESS OF KENTUCKY

ISBN: 0-8131-1362-8

Library of Congress Catalog Card Number: 77-73705

Copyright © 1978 by The University Press of Kentucky

A statewide cooperative scholarly publishing agency serving Berea College,
Centre College of Kentucky, Eastern Kentucky University,
The Filson Club, Georgetown College, Kentucky Historical Society,
Kentucky State University, Morehead State University,
Murray State University, Northern Kentucky University,
Transylvania University, University of Kentucky, University of Louisville,
and Western Kentucky University.

Editorial and Sales Offices: Lexington, Kentucky 40506

CONTENTS

ACKNOWLEDGMENTS

THE EDITORS ARE INDEBTED not only to the authors who worked so hard and so long to produce their essays but also to the many assistants who cut the manuscript, typed it, and finally prepared it for publication. We are indebted also to the University of Kentucky Research Fund, which paid for part of the preparation. We owe something as well to all the Golding critics who do not appear in these pages, even those who discouraged the project. And we acknowledge with as much gratitude as we can muster the invaluable efforts of Professor Robert D. Jacobs, Callaway Professor of English at Georgia State University, who carefully read and revised the original manuscript and offered innumerable suggestions for its improvement.

INTRODUCTION

LITERARY HISTORY TEACHES us that judgment of a contemporary writer must of necessity be tentative. Shakespeare was ranked by his contemporaries beneath Ben Jonson and Beaumont and Fletcher. Ann Radcliffe, considered a genius in her day, has passed from serious consideration, while George Eliot, who faded into eclipse after her death, has been revived by F. R. Leavis and Joan Bennett. Notwithstanding, the editors and essayists here, willing like Don Juan in Tirso de Molina's play *Burlador de Sevilla* to accept any challenge, will assert, if pressed, that Golding's reputation will outlive that of most of his contemporaries (excepting perhaps Graham Greene).

There are critics who have not forgiven Golding for the immense popularity of *Lord of the Flies*, the In book of an entire generation, but most would agree with Maurice McCullen that it is a modern classic. Admittedly its popularity tends to obscure the later works, though a number of critics have decided that *The Spire* is really Golding's masterpiece. That explains why there are two essays on that book in this collection.

Golding has worked a score of years receiving much praise and not a little denigration. Since critical opinions differ widely and he remains a difficult writer to assess, it seems time for a summation from a group of critics rather than another appraisal from a single point of view. All of the essays here are original, in keeping with that goal. Each deals with major themes or technical considerations, though many of these of course have already received some attention.

The first three essays address major considerations. In the beginning theologian David Anderson examines the question "Is Golding's theology Christian?" To answer he must rephrase: "Are the experiences enacted and communicated by Golding the kind . . . in which the Christian doctrine of man becomes existentially significant in terms of explanatory power?" He finds in the works a "collapse of bogus versions of reality and of the false religion which invents them." Golding's mythological enactments, he suggests, are a modern equivalent of the archetypal stories in Genesis—but let the reader judge for himself.

Ted Boyle examines Golding's existential vision, drawing upon Camus, Sartre, and Tillich. He finds Golding's most persistent theme the horror of life without restraints imposed by social order. Philippa Tristram's concern is with style, the "dubious" gift of speech itself, in an essay that sheds new light on Golding and provides a means of understanding his work.

The essays in the next section of the book take up individual works. First there is Peter Wolfe's essay on *The Brass Butterfly*, Golding's single excursion into drama. Examination of the fiction form of this work comes later in Leighton Hodson's essay on *The Scorpion God*. There follow essays on each of the published works excepting *The Hot Gates*. (The essays there, and the uncollected ones, incline to the personal and autobiographical; though interesting adjuncts to criticism, they differ in kind from the fiction on which Golding's literary reputation must rest and are therefore omitted from consideration here.) Jeanne Delbaere-Garant writes on *Lord of the Flies*, Robert O. Evans on *The Inheritors*, Arnold Johnston on *Pincher Martin*, Jay Halio on *Free Fall*, E. C. Bufkin and

Richard Cammarota on *The Spire*, David Skilton on *The Pyramid*, and Leighton Hodson on *The Scorpion God*.

The last part of the volume deals with special considerations. Maurice McCullen examines in detail the critical reception of *Lord of the Flies*, a work so popular it seems to deserve its own history. Then comes Jack I. Biles's bibliography, the most complete yet printed, a critical consideration in that it furnishes an indispensable tool for the critics of the future.

Perhaps the most difficult aspect of Golding's art is the demand he makes upon his readers, far greater than we are accustomed to expect in works of fiction. He prods our minds, forming our opinions by implications, ironies, glances, hints, and even sometimes deliberate omissions so that we have to work matters out for ourselves. He aims at sharpening our perceptions and our self-knowledge. If this collection helps us to understand what he is driving at, without of course detracting from his remarkable achievement (by making him easy where he wants to be hard), it will have served its purpose. It is with that hope we offer it.

David Anderson

IS GOLDING'S THEOLOGY
CHRISTIAN?

THE QUESTION POSED in this essay is more complex
than it may look. Golding's books are novels, with all the density, ambiguity, and concreteness of an art-form—far removed, it would seem, from the systematized abstractions
suggested by *theology*. Nevertheless, one critic has said the
novels do not make sense unless one remembers that Golding
is a Christian writer.[1] He was thinking in particular of the
failure of reviewers to recognize the shift from a naturalistic to
a theological perspective implied in the last line of *Pincher
Martin*. Reviewers thought the novel was about "the classic
predicament of man pitched against the elements," when in
fact it was about "the classic predicament of man pitched
against God even in death." Only the latter interpretation
takes the *whole* novel into account, and Golding has said that
in *Pincher Martin* he made the mistake of assuming greater
theological awareness among his readers than the majority
possessed.[2] Obviously, Golding's novels are not theology in
the academic sense, but it can hardly be disputed that they
are theologically oriented.

Some maintain that a theological novelist compromises his

integrity as an artist: he necessarily starts with foregone conclusions which make impossible the free exercise of the creative imagination. For the Christian, truth has already been
made manifest and there is nothing new to discover. So
characters tend to become mere exemplars of doctrine, pup-
pets whose actions reinforce a message which exists independently of them. Thus the Christian novelist is a polemicist.
Does Golding's work fall under this condemnation?

To say a writer has a theology need not mean he has
bowed before a set of doctrinal absolutes. His theology need
indicate no more than an understanding of man which takes
his experience of *transcendence* into account, which finds in-
adequate the positivist doctrine that the individual can be described in terms of the social and psychological structures in
which he exists. To have a theology in this sense is to assert
that man cannot be understood apart from his relationship to
transcendent reality and to draw out implications of that assertion. A tragic writer like Golding tends to explore the absence of God from the center of consciousness. He tries to
show what happens when man claims that reality is limited to
the area of his own mastery, and he exposes the demonism
that grips men when they interpret reality in terms of their
own greed and fear. He also wrestles with the baffling contraries his theology brings into focus: transcendence and im-
manence; freedom and necessity; being and becoming; good
and evil; innocence and guilt. Finally, he may imply the har-
monization of contraries in a divine act of reconciliation. His
success depends not upon the degree to which he engages us
in discussion of theological ideas, but upon the degree to
which he shocks us into recognition of forgotten elements in
the recesses of our awareness.

Golding is a maker of myths, not a debater of doctrines:
his concern is the creation of theologically significant experience rather than theological statement. He descries realities
of human behavior and consciousness which theological

statements indicate but do not enact. What is it like to experience the fall from innocence into sin? What is it like to experience damnation? To create an idolatrous god in the image of man or beast? To be stretched on the rack of such contraries as life and death, sacred and profane love, the self and the other? And, more tentatively, what would it be like to experience atonement and resurrection? These are some of the themes of Golding's novels, the stuff of existence upon which theological reflection operates. Doing theology does not mean spinning abstract formulations of nonempirical reality out of one's head. However remote and academic the theologian may seem, he asserts that his discourse has been prompted by events and experience judged to be of cosmic significance and giving access to the way things ultimately are. This process can also operate in reverse, when the creative imagination reenacts, in the form of myth, the immediate experience presupposed by doctrinal formulation. Such reversal can go further: it can enact experience which brings theological statement under reappraisal and challenges its assumptions (the early stories in Genesis and the Book of Job are biblical examples). Events and new knowledge can cause a disorientation calling for new theological solutions. How far a basic doctrine can be qualified and reinterpreted while remaining the same doctrine is a particularly perplexing question today. To give a specific example, which brings us near the center of Golding's concern, we may ask whether the traditional Christian doctrine of Original Sin is still the same doctrine when its basis in the story of the Fall is recognized as myth, not history, and when Original Sin is interpreted not as the result of a primal rebellious act, but as an inevitable concomitant of man's existential condition. It can be said that the doctrine is no longer the same if it leaves God out—if, for instance, human wickedness and misery are attributed to prerational drives deriving from man's animal ancestry which in time he will outgrow. The Christian doctrine of Original Sin is about the rupture of man's relationship with God; it is not about the incompleteness of evolutionary development. One factor that makes Golding a Christian writer is his recognition of the difference between these two anthropologies and his siding with the theological rather than the biological version, though he also recognizes that the terms in which the Christian doctrine becomes existentially significant today will require a reformulation of orthodoxy.

Although basic Christian doctrines may be held to be unchanging, what is more important is the ways they are stated, the extent to which their relevance to modern knowledge and awareness is displayed, and the strength and range of their explanatory power. Thus it may turn out that the best way of doing theology is to do what Golding and other Christian writers have done—that is, enact the kind of experience in which theological doctrines come to life and take on depth, so that they are lifted out of the context of arid academicism, where they can often be ignored.

Sartre is instructive here. He has offered novels and plays in which existentialism is conveyed not as a set of concepts, but as experience. Few professional theologians have tried to do for Christianity what Sartre has done for existentialism (an exception is Gabriel Marcel); yet the theologians who have spoken most compellingly in the last two generations have been men who, in Tillich's phrase, have sought to "correlate theological answers with existential questions"—who have understood the theological task not as the preservation and handing on of an orthodox tradition, but as a way of engaging with the dynamics of existence so as to clarify, in the light of Christian faith, the fullest range of human experience and consciousness.[3] In this endeavor, the theological value of the exploration of the human plight in contemporary art and literature has been recognized. Tillich's indebtedness is well known, and the work of Golding has attracted the interest of theologians.

If, however, theology is understood not simply as statement, but in the more humble terms of dialogue and exploration, standards of orthodoxy become harder to define and apply. This is not to say that Christian understanding has no distinguishing features: I have already asserted that there is a specifically Christian doctrine of man. But I suggest that the doctrine stands by virtue of its explanatory power and not its orthodoxy. Does the doctrine make better sense of human experience and awareness than its rivals? Does it bring within its compass a greater range of polarities and contradictions— that is, is it less reductionist than others? Does it offer solutions that measure up to problems more adequately than other doctrines? These questions for theological reflection arise out of Golding's work. In order to answer the question "Is Golding's theology Christian?" we must put it in more cumbersome but more accurate terms: "Are the experiences enacted and communicated by Golding the kind of experiences in which the Christian doctrine of man becomes existentially significant in terms of explanatory power?"

In Golding's novels the absence of God from the center of human consciousness is explored. Such absence can take two forms. In one, God is absent simply because he is unnecessary. The only meanings are those which man himself creates, and the puzzles and predicaments of existence are solved by human rationality scientifically applied. This view is represented by Piggy and by Nick Shales: "All day long trains run on rails. Eclipses are predictable. Penicillin cures pneumonia and the atom splits to order. All day long, year in, year out, the daylight explanation drives back the mystery and reveals a reality usable, understandable and detached. . . . Nick's universe is real."[4]

One reason Golding is a novelist rather than a polemicist is that he feels the attractiveness of this humanist claim. Ralph mourns the death of his "true, wise friend called Piggy" (Golding has denied that this is his own judgment, but it has its own level of authenticity in the novel), and Sammy admires Nick Shales for his humanity, his freedom from fanaticism, his generosity. If only man's autonomy were real! If only he *could* drive back the mystery until it disappeared and order his life by rational principles and techniques!

But with another form of the absence of God the rationalism of Piggy and Shales is powerless to deal. The true God is absent, but his place has been taken by a distorted, demonic image. Golding enacts experience which reveals that the rationalist hope is based upon a reductionist account of human awareness. Man is haunted by the supernatural, by a reality that transcends his own power of mastery and order and presents itself as a rival contender in the power game, requiring some kind of propitiation. The boys on the island and the new people in *The Inheritors* are afraid of devils; Pincher Martin is overwhelmed by "the black lightning"; Sammy Mountjoy experiences destruction of being by the forces of incoherence; Nick Shales's rationalism is silent before the final incoherence of death. The demons are the reason the attempt to live by law and reason is "no go," why things are what they are. The consequences are murder, cannibalism, madness, despair.

It is possible to argue, as Piggy does, that demons do not exist and that a cool rationalism will expose the deception. The impotence of this program is, Golding shows, due to the fact that man comes to cherish the demons because they endorse his own will to power. The demons are objectifications of lust masquerading as ultimate reality, and man needs the demons because they are the means by which he writes himself large upon the universe. Like Dean Jocelin in *The Spire*, he may address the demons as God and claim that his own hubris is service of the divine will. The demons *do* exist, but they exist as terrible perversions of transcendental reality.

The theological concept Golding has transmuted into

mythological form is known to us under the biblical term *idolatry*. The meaning of this term is analyzed in Ezekiel 14:1–11 and Romans 1:18–27. These passages may be summarized as follows:

(1) Men take their idols into their hearts. The meaning of an idol is the meaning man gives to it. The idolator constructs an objective counterpart of his desires with the purpose of legitimating them and enabling him to give them free rein uncontrolled by conscience. The gods of the idolator are projections that mold reality nearer to the heart's desire.

(2) Men put the stumbling block of their iniquity before their faces. Idol worship thus comes to be associated with violent physical stimulus, sexual excess and perversion, cruelty, violence, human sacrifice, and so forth. All this is a product of the distorted psyche, but it is cast onto a demonic reality which makes it far more terrible and destructive.

(3) The effect of idolatry is that men cut themselves off from God and no longer hear the divine word. That word is not an echo of human ambition; it is a critique, a judgment of man's moral distortion. God summons men to depart from iniquity and to align themselves with divine will.

(4) But man's false beliefs must be shattered—he must be brought into the cosmic night before the true light can shine upon him. There is no salvation in man's distorted nature. God comes to that nature as "a consuming fire" (Hebrews 12:29; cp. 10:31). Yet when men do seek the Lord, they find in him a reality beyond their dreaming.

The idea of God's negation of man constantly recurs in Christian thought. Man cannot receive divine grace until he recognizes the delusiveness of his idols and abandons the

claim that he is master of reality. The divine affirmation of
man is preceded by divine negation, by destruction of the
monstrous image of himself which he projects upon the universe. Perhaps no Christian writer of our time has expressed
this more uncompromisingly than Simone Weil. For her,
affliction (*malheur*) is the necessary tearing away of all attachments, the reduction of personality to the status of a
thing, to the point at which one becomes identified with the
forsakenness of the crucified Christ: "In affliction, the vital
instinct survives all the attachments which have been torn
away, and blindly fastens itself to everything which can provide it with support. . . . Affliction, from this point of view, is
hideous as life in its nakedness always is, like an amputated
stump, like the swarming of insects. Life without form. Survival is then the only attachment. That is where extreme
affliction begins—when all other attachments are replaced by
that of survival. Attachment appears then in its nakedness
without any other object but itself—Hell."[5]

The extreme limit of affliction is reached in the experience
Paul described as dying with Christ, for Calvary is the *locus
classicus* of God's negation of man, and there death becomes
the surrender of the human spirit into the hands of God.
Simone Weil continues: "To those in affliction life appears as
the one thing desirable, at the very time when their life is in
no way preferable to death" (p. 25). In this state, to accept
death is total detachment.

Perhaps Simone Weil was a saint, but the student of Golding can hardly read her words without being reminded of that
sinner Pincher Martin. His story is about "the technique of
dying into heaven," of accepting the divine negation of what
we now are so that divine affirmation may enter the void and
fill it with eternal life. Pincher Martin desperately needs to
learn this technique, because, as Nathaniel tells him, "in only
a few years [you will be dead]."[6] The statement of key significance in the novel (repeated more than once) is Nathaniel's

remark "Take us as we are now and heaven would be sheer negation. Without form and void. You see? A sort of black lightning destroying everything that we call life" (p. 70). Only those who have already learned to die into life can accept death's final negation and see in it an aspect of divine grace. But to those who have not so learned, God will appear as "black lightning." Pincher has not learned. He attempts to create his own reality beyond physical death, as he has done in life. The difference is that in life the delusion is able to feed upon other people. There is a reality which reflects the ego's projected image of itself; whereas, in death there is nothing objective at all, and the center of consciousness has to invent a circumference to locate its own existence. The circumference Pincher Martin invents is a rock in the Atlantic, and there he struggles grimly and even heroically for survival. The heaven he creates is hell—a naked attachment without any other object but itself.

In a sequence of photographic stills, we are given a synoptic view of Pincher's past. We see that he has tried to draw reality wholly into himself and to structure it in terms of his own lusts. Although Pincher is perhaps the most obnoxious of Golding's characters, he is also typical. He represents the theme of exploitation, which recurs in the novels: in the cherished demonism of Jack and the hunters; in the cannibalistic fetishism of the new people; in the exploitation of Beatrice Ifor by Sammy and of Evie Babbacombe by Oliver; in the ruthless obsession of Dean Jocelin. In each novel Golding reveals the collapse of bogus versions of reality and of the false religion which invents them. But nowhere does he do so more devastatingly than in *Pincher Martin*.

Pincher's rock, his invented reality, betrays occasional signs of its illusory nature, but it is not until the penultimate chapter that the illusion is shattered. Against the reality of absolute blackness, the rock "was proved to be as insubstantial as the painted water. Pieces went and there was no more than an island of papery stuff round the claws and everywhere else there was the mode that the centre knew as nothing." Finally, the lightning creeps towards Pincher's hands and towards the center: "The lightning came forward. Some of the lines pointed to the centre, waiting for the moment when they could pierce it. Others lay against the claws, playing over them, prying for a weakness, wearing them away in a compassion that was timeless and without mercy" (p. 201).

Before the black lightning strikes him, Pincher has a conversation with God. He tries to convince himself that the divine presence is a hallucination, but this belief crumbles under pressure of a reality that stands out against the rock and makes it seem "like cardboard, like a painted flat." He is now face to face with the one reality which cannot be consumed, which invites him to consider the hell he has created and to make a free surrender of his distorted identity. But Pincher will not surrender: he prefers his self-created hell to a divinely created heaven—"I shit on your heaven"—and so the absolute lightning moves in to penetrate his being, to burn up his invented self in the consuming fire of God's merciless compassion.

Pincher Martin can be viewed as a religious myth that enacts experience and demands reappraisal of established doctrine. The reappraisal demanded by *Pincher Martin* is not of traditional Christian dogma but of the reductionist versions of that dogma found in some modern theology. The theology implied by Golding's novels is in some respects rather old-fashioned. The novels invite us to experience humanness in terms of man's relationship to transcendent Being and to consider the demonic distortion of humanness which results when that relationship is ruptured. Golding's God thus appears as an authoritarian deity who demands surrender and obedience and negates human titanism. This is not popular theology today, when there is an emphasis on man's having come of age and God tends to be reduced to a mere inspirer and endorser of secular programs. Today the tendency is to discard everything in traditional Christianity which cannot be accommodated to prevailing secular values. This theology starts from a positivistic funding of all reality into the mundane and eliminates the doctrine of God's otherness, claiming to discover divinity in the highest human values and to leave room for human responsibility and freedom. There is, of course, insight in such theology: it defines a pole of theological truth which has badly needed new recognition. But it tends to become an inoffensive creed hardly worth an agnostic's disagreement. The opposite pole of theological truth is obscured, and one of the first things to go is the biblical doctrine of the wrath of God. Let us concede that the traditional picture of hell is morally repugnant; yet rejection of that picture need not leave us with a God whose concern for righteousness is minimal and whose love is only the affirmation of man as he now is. Golding creates a kind of extreme experience in which the wrath of God becomes existentially significant as a disruption of man's version of reality and a negation of the distorted ego which invents it. *Pincher Martin* could almost stand as a mythological rendering of Paul's words in Romans 1:18: "For the wrath of God is revealed from heaven against all ungodliness and unrighteousness of men, who hold the truth imprisoned in the chains of their unrighteousness." Karl Barth comments on this text: "The wrath of God is to unbelief the discovery of His righteousness, for God is not mocked."[7] No theologian of our century has more emphatically insisted on God's No to man than Barth, and he saw, as Golding also saw in *The Spire*, that this negation includes man at his best as well as at his worst.

Pincher Martin is certainly not man at his best. He is, one critic has said, an absolute bastard. He is a predator who could play the part of Greed in a morality play without wearing a mask. There is little doubt that Golding intends us to see in

Pincher a reflected image of twentieth-century man. There is
something titanic, almost sublime, in his determination to
cling to the reality he has invented and to defy the God who
offers him a prefabricated heaven as a reward for submission.
Pincher thinks God's dealings with man are contradictory and
unjust—he is condemned for using the very freedom God
himself bestowed. There is no answer to this contradiction in
Pincher's vocabulary: the terms in which he interprets freedom are those of grasping self-centeredness, and he is incapable of understanding or even of forming a concept of freedom that is a giving of the self to others and to God. Pincher's
damnation is the kind of experience that requires a shift of
perspective and new solutions: we are shocked into recognition of our own implication in his perversion of reality, and
the possibility of a radically new kind of awareness is opened.

However, Golding probably does not intend the total annihilation of Pincher by the black lightning of God's wrath.
What has to be burnt away is the invented self—the self that
is the creation of a misused freedom and a darkening of the
image of God in man. The lightning is pictured as lines of
energy which seek to prize open Pincher's predatory claws
and penetrate the fractured center of consciousness. In short,
Pincher's second death may be purgatorial rather than dam-
natory, leaving open the possibility that he may yet be saved.
Admittedly, there is no symbolization of a new life on the
other side of judgment, such as we find in *Free Fall* and *The
Spire:* there are no loud hosannas or burning bushes, no apple
tree to represent a grace that breaks in on us from transcendent reality and irradiates our vision. Yet there are hints
of possibilities beyond Pincher's second death. The action of
God is merciless but it is also compassionate—a paradox calling for resolution along the lines of the Christian doctrine of
redemption. "Behold then," said Paul, "the goodness and
severity of God" (Romans 11:22). It is no part of God's goodness to leave man in his terrible state of delusion; but his last

word to man is life, not death, for in Christ the contraries of God's severity and mercy are harmonized.

Golding once said that he had no solutions "ever," but he forces us into extreme forms of experience which give rise to a number of disturbing paradoxes.[8] Human consciousness seems to be split between opposing modes of reality: essence and existence, innocence and guilt, the absolute and the relative, the divine and the demonic, the self and the other. Sammy Mountjoy discovers that no conceptual scheme can harmonize the contraries. All systematizations of experience are reductionist, in that they fail to encompass the full distance between the poles of consciousness. Nick Shales, the humane rationalist, offers a determinist, predictable order in which sex is seen as a disruptive and even demonic intrusion; Rowena Pringle, the frustrated, visionary divinity teacher, offers religious ideals shockingly contradicted by her cruelty and insensitiveness; in the Communist party there is no guilt and therefore no forgiveness; the German interrogator's interpretation of moral duty is relativist and utilitarian and he does not know about people. But Sammy experiences extremes and knows that at opposite sides of the split in consciousness, they coexist. There is no bridge between the two worlds, but both worlds are equally real. Beatrice Ifor is both an incarnation of the eternal womanhood that leads us on high and an object of sexual desire to be possessed and humiliated. Sammy is an artist, whose eye penetrates to the glory behind appearance; but he is also a man, tortured by the incoherence of existence, the threat of nothingness at the center. He searches his life to find the point at which the split in consciousness occurred, the point at which he fell from innocence into guilt, from freedom into determinism. But perhaps there is no such point; perhaps reflection on experience simply discovers what has always been there.

Yet consciousness of the split must imply some residual awareness of a unitary reality, some knowledge of a prelapsarian state in which there was a single, unfractured vision. Such vision perhaps belongs to childhood, but in *The Inheritors* Golding locates it in an archetypal innocence he describes in mythological form. His Neanderthal is man before Adam's fall. Golding does not merely describe Neanderthalers from the outside, as an anthropologist would do; he attempts to enter their consciousness, to experience existence as they experience it. We respond to his skill by recognizing the recess in our own being where we remember that reality was once unfractured, and our minds fill with echoes of primal innocence and lost Edens.

It seems appropriate to describe *The Inheritors* in terms drawn from the Fall in Genesis. The "fall" is symbolized by a waterfall; and the split in consciousness, the expulsion from Paradise, finds representation in the physical gap that separates the new people from the Neanderthalers. *Homo sapiens* exists below the waterfall, and his attempt to climb above it is a disastrous failure. We are not told how man has become what he is; only his present state is described through the uncomprehending eyes of Lok and Fa. He has a developed language; he has discovered how to make tools and weapons and how to use mechanical techniques; he has achieved considerable mastery of his environment, and he has learned to coordinate effort. But with all this came sexual lust, violence, fetishism, fear of devils. The gods have become demons— projections of man's will to power, requiring propitiation by blood sacrifice. Golding suggests that the Fall of man is not the result of a sudden rebellious act, but the inevitable concomitant of the ability to progress from acceptance to mastery, from unreflective natural conformity to intelligent, self-conscious control.

The Genesis story has been modified to include modern knowledge of man's evolutionary development, but the essentials are not greatly different. The serpent in Eden is not a demonic reality external to man whose evil promptings penetrated an otherwise unchangeable innocence. The point about the serpent is, as von Rad has said, that it is cleverer than the rest of the animals and it is better understood as an image of man's developing intelligence.[9] Moreover, the knowledge of good and evil implies more than simply knowing: it suggests the much wider sense of experiencing and becoming acquainted with and even ability. Again, "good and evil" in biblical usage are much more than moral issues. The two categories include everything. "What the serpent's insinuation means is the possibility of an extension of human existence beyond the limits set . . . by God at creation, an increase of life not only in the sense of pure intellectual enrichment but also of familiarity with, and power over, the mysteries that lie beyond man."[10] The Fall is the story of human titanism, of man claiming total control over his existence and destiny and thereby going beyond the limits of his finitude. God's purpose is that man shall fill the earth and subdue it, but man goes further and claims mastery over the whole of reality.

Man enters maturity when he passes from "dreaming innocence" into "existential estrangement" (the terms are Tillich's), when he recognizes that his selfhood is not totally coincident with his present awareness nor with his environment, and he becomes capable of distancing himself from circumstance, of distinguishing between subjectivity and objectivity and of seeking to impose his will on the universe.[11] Yet in this process he forfeits the vision of the unity of all things in God and sooner or later murders his own brother. Golding's novel is not only a tale of the destruction of an innocent people by homicidal newcomers. It is an exploration of the paradox of man, vividly summarized in the final chapter under the symbol of Tuami's knife, whose blade is for murder but whose carved handle represents the love of Vivani for the last Neanderthaler. And the knife-haft, Tuami thinks, is much more important than the blade. We are left with the

possibility that somehow the split in consciousness will be
bridged by love and that man's final vision will be of a wider
and denser reality, uniting extremes of awareness beyond any
capability of innocence to imagine or attain. The Christian
reader is led to think of the uniting of those extremes at Calvary, though it was not until *The Spire* that Golding redis-
covered for us that dimension of faith.

Golding is not one of those simple-minded evangelists
who see religion as an easy solution to the puzzles of existence. Indeed, the official representatives of religion come off
badly in the novels. The choir-boys in *Lord of the Flies* become horrifying hunters. Miss Massey, the divinity teacher in
Free Fall, counterpoints her pronouncement "God is love"
with cuffs on her pupil's head; the curate is a pale-faced
pietist, and the clergyman who adopts Sammy is a conscience-
stricken homosexual. In *The Spire* Golding explores the
errors and delusions of one kind of *homo religiosus*. At first
sight, there could be no greater contrast than that between
Pincher Martin and Dean Jocelin. Pincher is a swine; Jocelin
is something of a saint. Yet the dean is shown to be no less
ruthless and self-centered than Pincher. The difference is that
whereas Pincher is at least an honest predator, the dean
wraps his own ambition in a cloak of religious duty.

Here is Karl Barth's comment on religious man, based on
Paul's words "The law worketh wrath" in Romans 5:15:

> In this context the word "law" embraces all who set out to
> experience the infinite, all who venture upon its contempla-
> tion or description or representation. This is always trans-
> gression. Whenever men suppose themselves conscious of the
> emotion of nearness to God, whenever they speak and write of
> divine things, whenever sermon-making and temple-building
> are thought of as an ultimate human occupation, whenever
> men are aware of divine appointment . . . , sin veritably
> abounds—unless the miracle of forgiveness accompanies such
> activity; unless, that is to say, the fear of the Lord maintains

the distance by which God is separated from men. No human
demeanour is more open to criticism, more doubtful, or more
dangerous, than religious demeanour.[12]

Men do terrible things when they act in the name of religion and claim divine authority for their programs. Precisely
because it points to a transcendent reality, religion can tempt
a man into the belief that he can himself attain transcendence, that he can climb out of the relativism and
finitude of his condition and attain absolute truth. Here, indeed, we find the deepest paradox of human consciousness:
that man touches the fringe of the eternal, that he glimpses
the infinite, and yet knows himself to be subject to temporal-
ity. So it is that he builds towers of Babel from which to survey his condition *sub specie aeternitatis* and claim equality
with God. But the towers are never high enough. Like the
original tower, they are unfinished, witnessing to the inevitable limitations of human endeavor and to the hubris which
has attempted to go beyond them. Jocelin's spire is a tower of
Babel. He has claimed absolute truth for what is only a finite
gesture, and the distorted spire bears witness to the distortion
of the religious consciousness that invented it.[13]
Human pride is one aspect of what Christian orthodoxy
means by Original Sin. The importance of this doctrine lies in
its recognition of evil in the best of human actions. We do not
require a doctrine to remind us of man's violence and barbarism; what we do need is a doctrine that questions his noblest
dreams and his most sublime inventions. Only man's recognition of his fallenness, of the distance that separates him from
God, can safeguard him from the attribution of absolute authority to his programs. Golding has shown what happens
when a man forgets his fallenness. Jocelin's vision of the spire
is a noble vision, symbolizing man's highest aspiration. Yet,
like all human visions, it is man's vision, not God's, and it is
tainted by motives springing from self-regard. The effect is to

unleash destructive forces that bring about almost unthink-
able disaster.

Yet in *The Spire* Golding explicitly represents an atonement, a reconciliation beyond the human tragedy. Jocelin
slowly arrives at awareness of the cost of his vision. Pangall
has been murdered and buried under the crossways as a ritual
sacrifice; Goody has died in agonizing childbirth as a result of
her sexual relationship with Roger Mason, which Jocelin has
condoned for the sake of the spire; Roger has become a
drunkard and ends up a helpless wreck after an attempt to
hang himself. In a moving scene, Golding describes Jocelin's
visit to Roger's house and his plea for the master-builder's
forgiveness. For a moment there is reconciliation, but Jocelin's continued talk drives Roger into frenzy and Jocelin is
thrown into the street. He is set upon by a mob as he lies
helpless in the gutter, but in an act of Christlike acceptance
he simply murmurs, "My children, my children." His back is
uncovered, and the mob recoils in horror from the sight of its
lesions. On his deathbed he is tended by his old colleague,
Father Adam, in whom he recognizes the mortality of all
mankind. What is heaven to us, if we cannot enter it hand in
hand with those we have wronged? Already Jocelin has had a
vision of Goody Pangall's red hair blazing among the stars and
of "the great club of his spire lifted towards it" (p. 221).
Perhaps after all sacred and profane love will be brought into a
harmony which affirms them both—a mode of life "where one
love can't compete with another but adds to it" (p. 214). And
in the final vision, like the momentary flash of a bluebird's
flight, the spire seems to burst into bloom, "laying hold of
earth and air, a fountain, a marvel, an appletree" (p. 205). The
spire has been built in sin—a symbol of man's desire to be as
God; yet, like the apple tree, it blossoms into a symbol of
resurrection, of life out of death, miraculous, gracious, and
compelling. Earth and heaven are shown to be united—not
by man's attempt to scale the heights, but by God's descent to

the depths. The tree of Adam's sin has become the tree of Christ's redemption; so perhaps the final paradox is that Jocelin was right to build his spire, because it is only when the extremes of human awareness have been experienced and fully defined that they can be encompassed in a harmonizing vision. *"O felix culpa quae talem ac tantum meruit habere redemptorem."*

Golding's novels are a great deal more than anything one can say about them. An essay that attempts to draw out meanings is bound to simplify, to ignore richness and density, to fasten on this part of the content rather than that, to treat the novels as problems to be solved rather than experiences to be entered. Inevitably, too, one's response is affected by one's own interpretation of life, and one tends to find what one expects. *The Spire* has been translated into Russian, and doubtless the good Marxist has no difficulty in seeing it as an exposure of religiocapitalist exploitation and bourgeois decadence. He would not be entirely mistaken in doing so, since a work of art, like experience itself, exists at many levels of meaning and can be matched to a variety of conceptual frames. I have tried to show that the Christian frame is more inclusive than its rivals, though this is not to say that every image and event has a counterpart in Christian doctrine. I have also suggested that Golding's work operates in some respects as a critique of Christian understanding, especially of those contemporary forms of it which discard the supernatural dimension of traditional belief and offer only a phenomenological version of reality. Golding gives us new ways of imaging Christian doctrine, mythological enactments which are also in an important sense the modern equivalents of the archetypal stories in Genesis. And what he reformulates is recognizably the mainstream of Christian tradition, not some reduction of it which is hardly distinguishable from its atheistic alternatives. At least Golding's doctrine of man is worth disagreeing with. What cannot be denied is the

depth and seriousness of his presentation and the sharp
reality of our response to it.

----

1. Dennis Keene, *William Golding and Jehovah* (Kyoto, Japan: University of Kyoto Press, 1963), 1.

2. Jack I. Biles, *Talk: Conversations with William Golding* (New York: Harcourt, 1970), 70.

3. Paul Tillich, *Systematic Theology* (Chicago: University of Chicago Press, 1957), 2:15.

4. *Free Fall* (London: Faber, 1959), 252.

5. *Gravity and Grace*, trans. Emma Craufurd (London: Routledge and Kegan Paul, 1952), 24–25.

6. *Pincher Martin* (London: Faber, 1956), 71.

7. *The Epistle to the Romans*, trans. Edwyn C. Hoskyns (London: Oxford University Press, 1950), 43.

8. Biles, *Talk*, 104.

9. G. von Rad, *Genesis* (London: SCM Press, 1961), 87. Cp. John Hick, *Evil and the God of Love* (New York: Harper, 1966), 320.

10. von Rad, *Genesis*, 87.

11. Tillich, *Systematic Theology*, 33, 38, and passim.

12. Barth, *Epistle to the Romans*, 136.

13. I have drawn this comparison at greater length in my *The Tragic Protest*. A classic exposition of the meaning of the tower of Babel is Reinhold Niebuhr's essay in his *Beyond Tragedy* (New York: Scribner's, 1938).

Ted E. Boyle

GOLDING'S EXISTENTIAL VISION

Existentialism, that is the great art, literature, and philosophy of the 20th century, reveals the courage to face things as they are and to express the anxiety of meaninglessness.

—Paul Tillich, *The Courage To Be*

The brilliance of our political vision and the profundity of our scientific knowledge had enabled us to dispense with . . . a kind of vital morality, not the relationship of a man to remote posterity nor even to a social system, but the relationship of individual man to individual man—once an irrelevance but now seen to be the forge on which all change, all value, all life is beaten out into a good or a bad shape.

—Samuel Mountjoy in *Free Fall*

TED HUGHES AND THOM GUNN, fascinated by the brute in man and nature, acquiesce to our historic barbarism. Sylvia Plath sublimated her psychosis but also acquiesced to the "boot in the face, the brute / Brute heart of a brute like you." Kingsley Amis makes jokes, but always the same jokes; John Fowles tells us literature is a parlor game because it makes no difference whether *The French Lieutenant's Woman* ends with a reconciliation or whether the lovers part forever. John Arden and David Storey give us untidy parables about how awful things are, and Harold Pinter insists on his athematic aperception tests. Only William Golding seems to possess the art and genius to confront the pain of a world without absolutes. That he has faltered in some works cannot diminish his achievements, for *Lord of the Flies*, *Free Fall*, *The Spire*, and *The Pyramid* are four of the best books of the twentieth century. They are based upon a simple idea: as Golding put it, "The only kind of real progress is the progress of the individual towards some kind of—I would describe it as *ethical*—integration."[1] Here Golding agrees with Camus, Sartre, and Tillich, who celebrate the human and eschew both the atavistic security of traditional theology and mechanistic replacements.

Golding is also like the existentialists in that his most powerful statements are instruction by negative example. Kierkegaard spoke of the faith of Abraham and as eloquently of Job's wife and her lack of faith; Kant was devastating in his critique of rational man, and Buber demonstrates the horror of the human being treated as an object. Sartre, Camus, and Beckett "appeal to the freedom of men so that they may realize and maintain the reign of human freedom"[2] by depicting the morbid solipsism of automatons. For Sartre's Garcin "hell is—other people"; Camus's Meursault is incapable of love and is excited only by the prospect of his own death; Vladimir and Estragon cannot act, contemplate hanging themselves to get an erection; and Krapp turns his back on life and listens to his tapes. Golding is also obsessed with suicidal impulses, inability to accept responsibility, the bad faith inherent in our love for systems, and our pliant acceptance of bestiality. Golding's novels are parables of caution and reflect his view that "the arbitrary checks . . . are nothing but . . . the bitter experience of people who are adult enough to realise, 'Well, I, I myself am vicious and would like to kill that man, and he is vicious and would like to kill me.' "[3]

The horror of existence without these arbitrary checks is the most consistent theme in Golding. He is intrigued by gimmicks, and he sometimes seems so embarrassed because his tales contain a moral that he confuses his readers.[4] Yet he is convinced that when man denies those checks that insure him freedom (his only ennoblement in an absurd universe), his existence is contemptible. This is Golding's major statement, and a consistent and existential point of view emerges when we pierce beyond the idiosyncrasies of his style.

Lord of the Flies is magnificent. No adults, no dead hand of society, no girls; yet the beast emerges; and if it doesn't come from causes we traditionally blame, "maybe it's only us."[5] But why not give in to the beast, why not accept the charge of the Lord of the Flies to Simon: "Run off and play with the others" (p. 132)? Why shouldn't the boys have fun, painting themselves and hunting pigs? The reason the Lord of the Flies must not be allowed to rule is evident. When Jack has established control of his hunting band and decides to enforce his authority by punishing Wilfred, two sentries, Roger and Robert, discuss their comrade:

> "He's going to beat Wilfred."
> "What for?"
> Robert shook his head doubtfully.
> "I don't know. He didn't say. He got angry and made us tie Wilfred up. He's been"—he giggled excitedly—"he's been tied for hours, waiting—"
> "But didn't the chief say why?" [p. 147]

This dialogue occurs after Simon's death and before Piggy's, and though it concerns a beating rather than a death, it seems a more powerful indictment of Jack and his hunters than the murders. Simon is killed in darkness, the final spasm of an orgy, and the murder is a collective act. Piggy is killed by Roger. In neither case was a decision made by the chief. The deaths of Simon and Piggy, horrid as they are, are primitive equivalents of manslaughter, crimes of passion. Wilfred's beating, however, is carried out at Jack's whim, for no reason except to demonstrate his control. It is not difficult to conceive of Jack's substituting ritual murder for ritual beating. In any case, the laws of the beast and his emissary, Jack, accept a limited definition of human possibility, and in accordance with this, the hunters restrict their own freedom and kill Simon and Piggy, and nearly kill Ralph. Simon, thinking of the beast, sees "the picture of a human at once heroic and sick" (p. 96). Ralph finds himself "understanding the wearisomeness of this life" (p. 70). But Ralph and Simon do not wish the beast to rule. They wish a society which, in respect for the conch and tending of the signal fire, reaches beyond the animal level.

Golding claims never to have read *Heart of Darkness*, but the similarity between the ethical views of *Lord of the Flies* and the Conrad story is striking, for both Conrad and Golding are convinced that without the restraint of social order the human being will sink below the level of the beast.[6] Says Golding, "On the whole, the fall off the straight and narrow tends to be a fall into something worse than one would be otherwise. So that society, taken whole, is a good thing. It enables us to use our bright side. When we fall off, we fall off into our dark side. . . . the straight road through the ordered universe enables people more easily to show their original virtue."[7] To Ralph's question "Are there ghosts, Piggy? Or beasts?" Piggy answers, "Course there aren't. . . . 'Cos things wouldn't make sense" (p. 85). Marlow makes a similar comment to explain Kurtz: "You can't understand. How could you?—with solid pavement under your feet, surrounded by kind neighbors ready to cheer you or to fall on you, stepping delicately between the butcher and the policeman, in the holy terror of scandal and gallows and lunatic asylums—how can you imagine what particular region of the first ages a man's untrammeled feet may take him into by the way of soli-

tude—utter solitude without a policeman—by the way of
silence—utter silence, where no warning voice can be
heard."[8] Marlow's comment is laced with irony beyond Piggy's reach, but both emphasize society as the means of making things work, of keeping the beast at bay.

Another parallel between the two works is revealing.
When Jack and his hunters steal Ralph and Piggy's fire, Ralph
says, "The fire's the important thing. Without the fire we can't
be rescued. I'd like to put on war-paint and be a savage. But
we must keep the fire burning" (p. 131). In speaking of the
savages on the riverbank, Marlow asks, "You wonder I didn't
go ashore for a howl and a dance? Well, no—I didn't. . . . I
had to watch the steering, and circumvent those snags, and
get the tin-pot along by hook or crook" (p. 97). Both Golding
and Conrad acknowledge the appeal of the beast, but both are
aware that rescue, the striving of man to excel himself and a
reverence for the restraint inherent in ordered society, is the
only means by which man can avoid the fate the jungle thrusts
upon him. Ralph will not join Jack's hunters, for he realizes he
would cease to exist except as a savage; Marlow lies to Kurtz's
Intended and thus affirms that man, in spite of his sickness, is
heroic. Otherwise, "It would have been too dark—too dark
altogether" (p. 162).

In *The Inheritors*, Golding appears to affirm original
virtue, which the reader can only infer in *Lord of the Flies*.
After all, without the unexpected rescue Jack and his hunters
would have killed Ralph as they had Simon and Piggy, and the
qualities these boys represent would have passed from the
island society and, by implication, from the macrocosmic one
which we inherit. It is difficult to sympathize, however, with
Mal, Ha, Fa, Nil, Lok, Liku, and the "old woman," for their
plight is not ours and their pictures are irrelevant. Golding's
primitives are gentle; we are not. They abhor killing; we do
not. They live in the present, with little conception of past or
future; we are different. Camus says it better: "What can a

meaning outside my condition mean to me? I can understand only in human terms. . . . If I were a tree among trees, a cat among animals, this life would have a meaning, or rather this problem would not arise, for I should belong to this world. I should *be* this world to which I am now opposed by my whole consciousness and my whole insistence upon familiarity."[9] No talent, either Golding's or his critics', can correct the sentimental misconception of *The Inheritors*. I believe Golding when he says, "I got desperate—I thought I *must* write a book; so I more or less sat down and wrote *The Inheritors* in three weeks."[10]

Pincher Martin is also flawed, for Golding never quite projects the viciousness of Martin's ego except by the desperate device of asking us to transmute our loathing for maggots into our loathing for the character. Martin is a lecher, but hardly a distinguished one; selfish, but not cosmically so; and his "An Occurrence at Owl Creek Bridge" death depends on an amateur plot device. A few touches compel, as when Martin builds his rock figure to attract passing ships: "I cannot shout to them if they pass. I must make a man to stand here for me. If they see anything like a man they will come closer."[11] Here, with inspired symbolism, Golding succinctly demonstrates that Martin is anything but a man—a heap of rocks has more humanity. The evil with which Martin plots the death of Nat nearly convinces us that Golding's "pincher" is evil enough to be fascinating. Nat says his prayers at the ship's rail. When Martin has the helm he gives an order to change the course of the ship abruptly, and thus throws Nat into the sea. Why? Because Martin covets Nat's beloved, Mary. How do we know? Because Martin has threatened to kill himself and Mary by driving his car off the road if she will not allow him to ravish her. Yet Golding fails to convince us that Martin's frantic clutching at life is evil, is different from Dylan Thomas's shout to his father, "Rage, rage against the dying of the light." And the God who visits Martin's rock near the conclusion is simply ridiculous. Of course, this presence is a projection of Martin's addled mind, but it is still difficult to accept God in seaboots, sou'wester, and turtleneck sweater.

Golding's impulse in *Pincher Martin* is clear, however, and the conversation Martin has with his God almost manages to make coherent the mass of boring detail the story contains. Never able to blame himself, Martin accuses God: "You gave me the power to choose and all my life you led me carefully to this suffering because my choice was my own. . . . Yet, suppose I climbed away from the cellar over the bodies of used and defeated people, broke them to make steps on the road away from you, why should you torture me?" (p. 197). Martin, adamant to the end, never employs his original virtue, never attempts to transcend the absurd. He is brother to Camus's Meursault, of whom Tillich says: "He is a stranger because he nowhere achieves an existential relation to himself or to his world. Whatever happens to him has no reality and meaning. . . . There is neither guilt nor forgiveness, neither despair nor courage in him. He is described not as a person but as a psychological process which is completely conditioned, whether he works or loves or kills or eats or sleeps. He is an object among objects, without meaning for himself and therefore unable to find meaning in his world."[12]

Perhaps Golding realized that *Pincher Martin* is only partially successful, for Sammy Mountjoy, in *Free Fall*, is remarkably similar to Martin. Both are supreme egotists. Both, in their passion for possession, destroy others. Both are artists—Martin an actor, Mountjoy a painter. Golding has imbued both with that fabricating vision necessary for an individual to achieve an existential relationship with his universe. Neither will accept the responsibilities of his perception, and each realizes his imprisoned state. Golding has done a much more accomplished job, however, with *Free Fall* than with *Pincher Martin*.[13] The protagonist of *Pincher Martin* is sketchily drawn, but in *Free Fall*, even the minor characters possess memorable vibrancy. Ma, Evie, Johnny, Philip, and the rest are a remarkable pantheon, and each is coherently defined. Sammy's Ma, bursting out of her Rotten Row privy, is a vivid example:

> Her skirts are huddled up round her waist and she holds her vast grey bloomers in two purple hands just above her knees. I see her voice, a jagged shape of scarlet and bronze, shatter into the air till it hangs there under the sky, a deed of conquest and terror.
>   "You bloody whore! Keep your clap for your own bastards!"[14]

The war in *Pincher Martin* seems incidental to bringing Martin to his rock. But in *Free Fall* the war is an outgrowth of collective action by the Mountjoys of the world. Sammy knows this: "There is no peace for the wicked but war with its waste and lust and irresponsibility is a very good substitute" (p. 132); "I could see this war as the ghastly and ferocious play of children" (p. 150). And this is why *Free Fall* is a more rewarding book than *Pincher Martin*. Sammy, like Jocelin in *The Spire*, discovers that human existence is the end of human existence, that "the relationship of individual man to individual man" is all that matters. Pincher Martin never does.

Samuel Mountjoy does not make his discovery easily. Before his enlightening imprisonment in Halde's broom closet, he escaped responsibility by placing his freedom at the disposal of various systems. At school, Sammy had two views of the universe presented to him—the spiritual view preached by the almost sadistic Miss Pringle, and the rationalist view of the physics teacher, Nick Shales. Sammy chose the rationalist view and complemented his rationalism with a fierce sensual-ity and a lukewarm communism. Golding's Sammy is always running—from his freedom.

The central passages in this reading of the novel are Sammy's seduction of Beatrice and Halde's interrogation of Sammy. After finding Beatrice sexually disappointing, Sammy asks, "Don't you feel anything?" She answers, "I don't know. Maybe" (p. 119). After Halde tells Sammy of the death of his fellow prisoners, Sammy stares at their photographs and wonders, "Do you feel nothing then?" He answers himself, "Maybe" (p. 142). Sammy, in the midst of his campaign to seduce Beatrice, says to her: "I want to be with you and on you and round you—I want fusion and identity—I want to understand and be understood—Oh God, Beatrice, Beatrice, I love you—I want to be you!" (p. 105). As Sammy wishes to *be* Beatrice, so Halde wishes to *be* Sammy. Halde says: "I've been studying you. Putting myself in your place" (p. 141) and "I loathe myself, Sammy, and I admire you" (p. 152). Both Sammy and Halde are clearly dissatisfied with their conceptions of themselves. Both wish to identify with the spiritual facet of existence, which they have tried to deny—Sammy through Beatrice and Halde through Sammy.

Sammy's Beatrice is identical with Dante's—a visionary ideal; her surname, Ifor, confirms what Sammy says about wanting to *be* Beatrice. Sammy wishes to substitute his "I" "for" hers. Halde also wishes to escape from himself, though his desire to substitute the identity of another for his own is perhaps not so strong as Sammy's. In Beatrice, Sammy imagines there exists a spiritual presence of which he has denied the possibility in himself. In Sammy, Halde imagines the existence of abstract qualities of loyalty which as a Nazi he has decided do not exist. If Sammy possesses knowledge useful to the Nazis, as Halde believes, then Sammy's refusal to communicate it is an affirmation of a quite impractical loyalty, an affirmation of the irrational and the spiritual—those qualities Halde desperately wants to affirm even as he denies them:

"Are you telling the truth, Sammy, or must I admire you. . . . because I dare not believe you. . . . I loathe myself, Sammy, and I admire you. If necessary I will kill you" (pp. 151–52).

In Sammy, Halde sees the qualities of spirit he himself lacks, just as Sammy has created in Beatrice a projection of his spiritual deficiencies. Sammy becomes less than a human being to Halde. He becomes an object through which Halde attempts both to affirm and to degrade the spiritual qualities of the human being. Halde nearly drives Sammy mad; Sammy does drive Beatrice mad. To Halde and Sammy, each in control of a system which denies the spirit, human beings are not ends in themselves but only means. Both these rationalists employ human beings as objects to enlarge their conceptions of themselves, all the while denying that human existence can be interpreted other than rationalistically.

When Halde throws Sammy into solitary confinement, the terror-stricken Sammy is forced to look inward. His sensual painter's eye cannot function in darkness. Something beyond the physical exists, however, and will not be denied. Shrinking from the power of the spirit—the power he denies—Sammy cries out, "Help me! Help me!" (p. 184). With this cry, even though it stems from his hollowness and despair, Sammy affirms the world of the spirit.

The young Sammy had been a collector of cigarette cards featuring the proud faces of the kings of Egypt. Now he sees with an eye beyond the sensual; he sees the human being as more than object or machine. A fellow prisoner approaches him; Sammy is overwhelmed: "He was a being of great glory on whom a whole body had been lavished, a lieutenant, his wonderful brain floating in its own sea, the fuel of the world working down transmuted through his belly. I saw him coming, and the marvel of him and these undisguised trees and mountains and this dust and music wrung a silent cry from me" (p. 187). Sammy has grown beyond Halde, who says, "I made my choice with much difficulty but I have made it.

Perhaps it was the last choice I shall ever make. . . . I am in the power of my machine" (p. 140).

Finally, Samuel Mountjoy is responsible—for himself and those he has touched, notably Beatrice. And Golding has brought Mountjoy to the existential discovery that in man's tormented ability to decide his own fate exist his freedom and his victory over the absurd.

Despite the forceful clarity of theme and the geometric beauty of structure, *The Spire* is an irritating novel, for Golding strains to the limit our tolerance for stylistic idiosyncrasies. He does too little, and he asks too much of his readers. From a sprig of holly and a wisp of red hair, we are to conclude that Pangall has been murdered, that Dean Jocelin lusts for Goody. That Jocelin sees everything except his spire very unsteadily cannot redeem the spare style. If things are seen only from Jocelin's point of view, and his limited vision is meant to reinforce the sterility of his obsession, the narrative still cries out for a normative, contrasting point of view. We feel cheated, especially if we remember the handling of realistic detail in *Lord of the Flies*, *Free Fall*, and *The Pyramid*.

Still, the evil, sterile inhumanity of Jocelin's project imbues every page. As Jack and his hunters lose their freedom out of fear of the beast, and as Christopher Martin and Samuel Mountjoy escape responsibility in their allegiance to solipsistic rationalism, so Jocelin loses his freedom and denies responsibility in his obsession.

Driven by his angel, a manifestation of his sickness and of satanic force, he ignores the needs of his parishioners. Pangall is aped and mocked by the workmen. Roger Mason, the master builder, and Goody, Pangall's wife, are drawn into adultery. Jocelin is dumbly aware, "But still he said: 'I am about my Father's business!' "[15] Goody's "shame squeezed his heart," but he does not help her. When he does speak to her, he denies her need for him: "I must put aside all small things.

. . . If they are part of the cost, why so be it. And if I cannot help, what is the point of all this brooding? I have too great a work on hand" (p. 95).

Goody is not the only one Jocelin drives away; the entire congregation deserts the cathedral because of the noise and mess Mason's workmen create. The pillars supporting the roof sing because of the stress placed on them by the enormous weight of the spire: "The news filtered through to Jocelin . . . that they were the only things that sang in the whole building. The services had moved out and were held indignantly in the bishop's palace" (p. 138).

Still, Jocelin insists he is listening to his angel. That his angel is in Satan's service is made clear by the imagery of Jocelin's immediate physical contact with the spire. Before the spire is well under way, Jocelin must content himself with a model: "He detached the spire with difficulty, because the wood was swollen, and held the thing devoutly, like a relic. He caressed it gently . . . as a mother might examine her baby" (pp. 50–51). Whether the spire is his child or his phallus, Jocelin's passion is sterile and selfish. Soon he finds it "easier to ignore ground level; and this was necessary because, with the bending of the pillars, people at ground level tended to interrupt him" (p. 147). When Jocelin climbs the spire the sun seems to him to shine brighter, and he is overwhelmed in pride at his God-like view: "He looked down. . . . He watched an old man go heavily into a privy, and, secure between his walls, leave the door wide open. Three houses away was a woman . . . preparing to go from house to house. She had two wooden pails and the yoke lay near against the wall. Screwing up his eyes, he could make out that the pails contained milk; and he smiled grimly to himself as he watched her top up each pail with water" (p. 103).

The spire stands, but hardly as a monument to God's grace. Jocelin's folly is a reminder of the subversion of humanity inherent in devotion to abstractions. Unfortunately, Jocelin realizes only in his dying vision the putridity he has made of his life. In his aberrant passion, he has not only destroyed himself, but has expended his love on the spire and has allowed Roger Mason and his wife, Rachel, and Goody Pangall and her husband to sink into the same muck as that on which the spire is built. Excruciatingly late—and it is a tribute to Golding's art that we call Jocelin a fool almost immediately—Jocelin says, "I would take God as lying between people and to be found there" (p. 212) and "I traded a stone hammer for four people" (p. 214). Golding has cogently defined the evil of an imagination gone mad, an imagination so denatured that it tells the ultimate lie—that there is an end which is not human life itself.

Denial of life, of responsibility, of freedom is also the theme of *The Pyramid*, a novel cantankerous in its avoidance of the issues it raises. Perhaps this story is too close to Golding's own adolescence. Golding turned from science to literature. Olly is pressured by his parents to give up music for chemistry. I assume Golding won his freedom and consequently his humanity by choosing as he did; Olly, quite clearly, becomes a machine.

The Pyramid is a brilliant analysis of the prison of English village life, and its brilliancy is evident in its universality. Golding's Stilbourne is indistinguishable, except for minor details, from any small town in Britain or America. Olly loves Imogen, too rich and too pretty for him; she marries Claymore, the newspaper publisher, one of the richer, right sort. Olly envies Bobbie Ewan, for Bobbie has a red motorbike and the favors of Evie Babbacombe, daughter of the Stilbourne town crier. Olly also envies Bobbie's social position, for Bobbie is the son of the doctor, and Olly's father is a pharmacist. It is this envy, and his consequent climb up the materialistic ladder of middle-class success, that control Olly's life. He is free to choose even after he leaves Stilbourne, and his choice of a life that is an extension of the values of his small town is an index to his failure as a human being.

Olly is by no means as vicious and selfish as Martin or Sammy, nor does he destroy other people's lives with the satanic abandon of Jocelin. Yet he does treat people, especially Evie, as objects. Olly decides he must possess Evie, much as Mountjoy decides he must make love to Beatrice. He plans his campaign carefully: "There was no doubt about it. I should simply have to be subtle, devious, diplomatic—in a word, clever. Otherwise the only way I was going to *have* a girl was by using a club."[16] And have her he does, but in their sexual encounter there is no hint of tenderness: "As I beat my hasty tattoo in boyish eagerness, I was lost among the undulations. . . . She would not consent to any quick rhythm; only the long, deep ocean swell in which her man, her boy, was an object, no more" (p. 62). Evie is, of course, no innocent. She has been involved with Bobbie Ewan before Olly, and Golding gives us some laconic clues that she has had a sexual relationship with at least three others including her own father, Sergeant Babbacombe. Olly's crime is his subversion of even the little feeling he has for Evie to the sterile judgment of Stilbourne. Afraid that Evie may be pregnant, Olly views the consequences with horror: "My father . . . my mother. . . . To be related, even if only by marriage, to *Sergeant Babbacombe!* I saw their social world, so delicately poised and carefully maintained, so fiercely defended, crash into the gutter" (p. 65). Olly is very young, however, and will have other opportunities to choose to become a human being rather than a fragment of the Stilbourne machine.

Evie leaves Stilbourne and becomes the mistress-secretary of a rich industrialist. Olly goes to Oxford to study chemistry, but he never really leaves Stilbourne, as is evident when he returns home on a holiday and is coerced by his

mother into performing in a production of the Stilbourne
Operatic Society. Olly is to play a gipsy-beefeater, a violin-
playing, halberd-toting retainer to the main character. The
opera is the creation of Mr. Evelyn de Tracy, Golding's English equivalent of Professor Harold Hill. Olly's mother gush-
ingly describes one of the scenes: "I think it's in Hungary
or Ruritania or somewhere. It's a restaurant, you see. *She*
doesn't know he's the king in disguise and *he* doesn't know
she's the princess of Paphlagonia in disguise. It's very clever
as an idea" (p. 97). As plans for the operetta progress, Golding's satire becomes more biting, though never misanthropic.
The comic scenes are so well written that readers familiar with
Golding must wish he had not waited until *The Pyramid* to
unveil the full power of his talent. But Golding is after more
than laughter. Olly's absurd garb and his participation in the
comic and pathetic performance are symbolic of his de-
humanization. He knows the operetta is a horrid caricature,
not entertaining even for those participating. Yet he submits,
not so much out of filial loyalty as out of fear of breaking the
code.

The third section of *The Pyramid* is hardly comic, save in
the black sense. Here Golding, through Olly, tells the story
of Clara Cecilia Dawlish, the music teacher known as Bounce.
Her father, a failed musician who believed in "the New
Woman, Wagner and Sterndale Bennett," had made a sexless
automaton of his daughter. Golding describes her this way:
"There was no pink or white in her face, only pale yellow,
which, combined with her high cheekbones, lashless eyes and
hairless brows, gave her an appearance Chinese rather than
European, indeterminate rather than female" (p. 139). She is
awakened to her femininity when she meets Henry Williams,
a young mechanic, and when her father dies, Bounce outfits
Henry's new garage. But Henry is already married. In what
seems a reversal of Faulkner's "A Rose for Emily," Bounce

denies what pride she still possesses and allows Henry and his
family to move in with her. As Henry becomes more successful, he needs Bounce less, and finally the family moves out.
She suddenly becomes accident-prone, having several nearly
fatal mishaps with the car she bought from Henry. Finally,
Stilbourne has its victory: "Bounce pacing along the pavement
with her massive bosom, thick stomach and rolling ungainly
haunches; Bounce wearing her calm smile, her hat and gloves
and flat shoes—and wearing nothing else whatsoever" (p.
175).

Years later Olly, steeped in middle-class success, returns
to Stilbourne in his expensive car: "The glass windows of my
car made a picture postcard of the place. I could roll through
it, detached, defended by steel, rubber, leather, glass" (p.
132). He stops at the cemetery and views Bounce's grave
marker. Below her name he reads the inscription placed there
by Henry, "Heaven is Music," an ironic and insensitive epi-
taph, for Bounce had needed so much more—if not Henry's
love, at least more affection than is suggested by the phrase on
her tombstone. Nor had Bounce received affection from Olly,
though she had with great labor made him an accomplished
violinist. Olly and Henry are alike in their fear, their selfishness, their disrespect for another human being, who needed
so little and got nothing. Olly realizes his criminal kinship
with Henry when he stops at Williams's garage for gasoline:

> He took my money and went to change it. I stood, looking
> down at the worn pavement, so minutely and illegibly in-
> scribed; and I saw the feet, my own among them, pass and
> repass. . . . and suddenly I felt that if I might only lend my
> own sound, my own flesh, my own power of choosing the fu-
> ture, to those invisible feet, I would pay anything—*anything:*
> but knew in the same instant that, like Henry, I would never
> pay more than a reasonable price.
> "—and ninepence is three pounds. Thank you, sir."
> I looked him in the eye; and saw my own face. [pp. 182–83]

Olly, then, has failed, as have most of Golding's other heroes, though Mountjoy and Jocelin pass ever so slightly beyond the threshold of accepting responsibility for their freedom. In his meticulous demonstrations of responsibility not accepted, Golding has made a powerful statement, even though he moves only hesitatingly into the realm where he might show his characters living by the values they have defined. If Golding's attitudes are existential, his art, devoted to exemplifying death-in-life, stimulates us to assume responsibility for our own lives out of repulsion for Jack, Martin, Jocelin, Olly. When Halde is questioning Sammy, he says, "I am in the power of my machine" (p. 140), and it is to the destruction of dehumanizing machines that Golding's art is dedicated. His best works are imprecations against bad faith, the automatic, fearful, selfish response Sartre defines with uncharacteristic clarity in *Being and Nothingness*.

1. Jack I. Biles, *Talk: Conversations with William Golding* (New York: Harcourt, 1970), 41.

2. Jean-Paul Sartre, *Literature and Existentialism*, trans. Bernard Frechtman (New York: Citadel Press, 1965), 160.

3. Frank Kermode, "The Meaning of It All," *Books and Bookmen*, 5 (October 1959), 9.

4. Golding describes the endings of some of his novels as gimmicks, and James Gindin employs the term as an indication of Golding's limitations. See *Postwar British Fiction: New Accents and Attitudes* (Berkeley: University of California Press, 1962), 196–206.

5. *Lord of the Flies*, casebook ed. (New York: Putnam, 1964), 82.

6. James Keating, "Interview with William Golding," casebook ed., 194.

7. Biles, *Talk*, 43–44.

8. Joseph Conrad, *Heart of Darkness* (London: Dent, 1961), 116.

9. Albert Camus, *The Myth of Sisyphus and Other Essays*, trans. Justin O'Brien (New York: Knopf, 1955), 51.

10. Biles, *Talk*, 61.

11. *The Two Deaths of Christopher Martin* (New York: Harcourt, 1956), 61.

12. Paul Tillich, *The Courage To Be* (New Haven: Yale University Press), 144–45.

13. But see Ian Gregor and Mark Kinkead-Weekes, "The Strange Case of Mr. Golding and His Critics," *Twentieth Century*, 167 (February 1960), 124–25.

14. *Free Fall* (New York: Harcourt, 1959), 21.

15. *The Spire* (New York: Harcourt, 1964), 64.

16. *The Pyramid* (New York: Harcourt, 1966), 38.

Philippa Tristram
GOLDING AND THE LANGUAGE OF CALIBAN

IN THE FIRST ACT of *The Tempest* Prospero rebukes brutish Caliban for ingratitude:

> I pitied thee,
> Took pains to make thee speak, taught thee each hour
> One thing or other. When thou didst not, savage,
> Know thine own meaning, but wouldst gabble like
> A thing most brutish, I endowed thy purposes
> With words that made them known.[1]

In the perspective in which speech is the distinction between man and beast, Caliban is rightly rebuked. He has been granted, and has misused, a gift that could have raised him a rung in the ladder of evolution. His response confirms the accusation of ingratitude:

> You taught me language, and my profit on't
> Is, I know how to curse. The red plague rid you
> For learning me your language. [1. 2. 363–65]

In another perspective which Golding understands well, Caliban is in the right, not Prospero. From this point of view language is not an unequivocal good that the civilized, in generosity, confer upon the barbarous. Instead, the gift of speech is dubious, a sign of imperfection, evidence of a corrupt and fallen nature. Perhaps unintentionally, Prospero concedes the possibility: "When thou didst not, savage, / Know thine own meaning . . . I endowed thy purposes / With words that made them known." In Prospero's account, Caliban's purpose has been the rape of Miranda, and in Prospero's definition language has not only enabled the dumb beast to articulate: it has brought to conception a deed of which the beast would otherwise have been innocent. Words may relieve Caliban of a frustrating incapacity, but, in consequence of those actions following possession of speech, they also reduce him to the status of slave, "Deservedly confined into this rock" [1. 2. 361].

Golding not only shares Caliban's point of view; in *The Inheritors* he exalts it. Shakespeare does not idealize the simplicity of Caliban's existence before the arrival of Prospero. Golding, however, regards his prehuman creatures as unfallen and the possessors of a happiness their inheritors can never enjoy. Religious tradition, in which speech is associated with the Fall, gives his attitude authority. Genesis first mentions speech in the Temptation. "According to what we read in the beginning . . . we find that a woman spoke before all others. I mean that most presumptuous Eve . . . in answer to the enquiry of the devil."[2] Dante regarded language as the capacity which set men below angels rather than above brutes. Angelic conversation (like that of Lok's people), was, he assumed, intuitive, and it did not need words as human discourse, "held back by the . . . mortal body," did. Dante was measuring the distance between angels and men; that between man and beast he considered to be a further profound descent. It would, he argued, be rational to assume that speech was a gift granted to the unfallen Adam and first employed in converse with God. But he could not escape the evidence of Genesis—woman spoke first, not man; and she spoke with the devil.

There is a great distance between Dante and Golding; yet Golding might well regard this reading of Genesis as anything but naïve literalism. His imagination is drawn to the simplicities of primal myths, and it is through their rediscovery that he seeks to arrive at the truths of his contemporary world. In all his novels he has been concerned with man's fallen nature and with the relation of the Fall to the blighting self-consciousness of which language is a product. The myth of Eden, an aspect of *The Tempest*, can be glimpsed in *Lord of the Flies* and *The Inheritors;* in different ways both novels reenact the history of the Fall. In *Pincher Martin* and *Free Fall*, on the other hand, the loss of innocence is seen as an individual catastrophe; these novels work back, not forward, to the evil in each man's heart. Here language is the sign of loss of innocence and of the longing for redemption to which the loss gives rise.

Golding's interest in language is not of course identical with his own language or style. But to some extent the two are inseparable. *The Spire* and *The Pyramid*, for example, are not preoccupied with language, but their central figures are, like all Golding's heroes, in a sense artists. Jocelin is a builder, Oliver a musician, Tuami a carver, Sammy a painter, Jack and Simon choristers, Pincher Martin an actor. If Golding, in *The Inheritors*, finds language a dubious gift, if in *Pincher Martin* he shows its profit as being knowing how to curse, he nevertheless regards language as redemptive. His heroes are artists because artists make the maximum demand upon the medium. The questions that preoccupy Golding relate finally to the process of artistic creation, for creativity may prove redemptive and furnish a return to innocence. The relation between the concerns of the novels and the style, between the artifact and the sense in which the artifact is a comment upon itself, is very close. The dialect of Caliban and the dialogue of Caliban with himself become one.

The Inheritors, Pincher Martin, and Free Fall inscribe a spiritual history of man and his language, of his innocence, his fall, and his redemption. Of these The Inheritors, centered upon the unfallen world, is most explicitly concerned with language and guilt. Eleven of its twelve chapters describe the prearticulate condition of the predecessors of Homo sapiens. Lok's people, just beyond the evolutionary bar, are not entirely without language or reason; they have a little of both, but rely upon neither. To the new people, they are animal, partly because they cannot really talk, partly because they exhibit an animal's immersion in sensual experience. The first men, in consequence, regard their predecessors with that amused patronage and hostility which we exhibit towards apes, feelings that result from our perception of similarity as well as difference. Prospero's treatment of Caliban, though it has more of the humane pretension of the colonial governor, is not dissimilar.

Yet that total reliance upon the senses, which makes Lok's people brutes, implies an attitude toward life which is the antithesis of brutality. It is Tuami's people, not Lok's, who are bestial. Because they respond to immediate demands of the senses, Lok's people inhabit a world free from notions of past and future and innocent of apprehension or possession. They search for food and fuel collaboratively in response to hunger and cold, and they seek to satisfy no more than those needs. "The people were silent. Life was fulfilled, there was no need to look farther for food, to-morrow was secure and the day after that so remote that no one would bother to think of it" (p. 61).[3] Provision for more than the morrow, characteristic of his successors, baffles primitive Lok: "He inspected the logs, his mouth hanging open and a free hand pressed flat on top of his head. Why should the people bring all this food—he could see the pale fungi clear across the river—and the useless wood with it?" (p. 103).

The new people have speech, but no pictures, whilst Golding's primitives, like Dante's angels, do not need words to understand each other. They share pictures, and the capacity to see and to make others see them has little to do with speech. When Lok says that the new people are "without pictures in their heads," it is because their sense of possession, with its relation to past and future, seems to him a denial of community. He is more richly endowed with words than the rest of his kind, but at the cost of pictures. "Ha has many pictures and few words," Fa remarks. "Lok has a mouthful of words and no pictures" (p. 38). Ha, as a result, is a better leader than Lok, whose words rarely correspond to what he sees in imagination. Words, in fact, are for Lok's people virtually objects of fear: "When the word had been said it was as though the action was already alive in performance and they worried" (p. 37). Like Caliban, they sense the ominous relation between word and act: articulation engenders commission. Their intuitions are another matter, for their pictures can only be communicated where intuitions are shared. Language, on the other hand, can coerce where communal conviction is lacking. Thus the pictures of Lok's people are not primitive forms of concept but something different. They reveal communal impulse; they do not impose an imperative.

As this distinction between picture and concept implies, Lok's people allow the world more independent being than their conceptualizing successors will. Ha reflects: "If the log had crawled off on business of its own then the people would have to trek a day's journey round the swamp and that meant danger or even more discomfort than usual" (p. 14). Nothing in the natural world is denied individuality, its right to live according to its own law. Even parts of the body may possess independence reflecting their sensual being.

> Lok's ears spoke to Lok.
> "?"
> So concerned was he with the island that he paid no atten-
> tion to his ears for a time. [p. 104]

This responsiveness to the distinctive being of things pre-
serves an innocent world. Lok's people do not kill. When they
devour the body of a doe, they sense "a kind of darkness in
the air."

> Lok spoke loudly, acknowledging the darkness.
> "This is very bad. Oa brought the doe out of her belly. . . .
> But a cat killed you so there is no blame." [p. 54]

The new people do not share this respect for the natural
world; on the contrary, they exploit it. The natural world, in
consequence, becomes a place they fear; and their gentle
predecessors, whom they destroy, are the demons of their
disturbed conscience. The final chapter of *The Inheritors*,
representing the consciousness of the new race, is sequential
as the rest of the novel is not. Motives are rationally connected; there is a sense of past and future; the syntax flows.
The final paragraph exemplifies this: "Holding the ivory
firmly in his hands, feeling the onset of sleep, Tuami looked at
the line of darkness. It was far away and there was plenty of
water in between. He peered forward past the sail to see what
lay at the other end of the lake, but it was so long, and there
was such flashing from the water that he could not see if the
line of darkness had an ending" (p. 233). The prose of Lok's
people is expressive in a different way: "Lok was running as
fast as he could. His head was down and he carried his thorn
bush horizontally for balance and smacked the drifts of vivid
buds aside with his free hand. Liku rode him laughing, one
hand clutched in the chestnut curls that lay on his neck and
down his spine, the other holding the little Oa tucked under
his chin. Lok's feet were clever. They saw" (p. 11). Like Lok's

experience, the prose is disjointed. Events are registered as they occur; the mind does not cause them to happen. The life of the innocent is instant and sensual. The language of the fallen is more literary; the control of its syntax expresses a poetry of its own. But it is the self-conscious creation of imagination and mind; its events do not occur, except in the haunted consciousness of the head.

Only in *The Inheritors* does Golding present the experience of innocence as a prelapsarian condition. Yet the innocent can be found elsewhere in his novels, amongst those who, though subject to a cosmic fall, have not succumbed to a personal one. This is not a prerogative of childhood. The adult may retain his innocence, as Nick Shales does in *Free Fall* or Nat in *Pincher Martin*, whilst the child may already be fallen, like Jack in *Lord of the Flies*. Such innocence is not inarticulate, but it tends to share with Lok's people that quality of immersion in the moment so total that the imagination is freed from limitations of rational reflection.

This innocence may be readily illustrated from a passage from *Free Fall*, where Sammy Mountjoy asks:

> When did I lose my freedom? For once, I was free. I had power to choose. The mechanics of cause and effect is statistical probability yet surely sometimes we operate below or beyond that threshold. Free-will cannot be debated but only experienced. . . . I remember one such experience. I was very small and I was sitting on the stone surround of the pool. . . . There was no guilt but only the plash and splatter of the fountain. . . . I had bathed and drunk and now I was sitting on the warm stone edge placidly considering what I should do next. The gravelled paths of the park radiated from me: and all at once I was overcome by a new knowledge. I could take whichever I would of these paths. . . . I was free. [pp. 5–6]

Where adult consciousness debates—"The mechanics of cause and effect is statistical probability"—the child, so like and yet so remote from that adult, is wholly immersed in the moment. The sensuous textures of that day return with a totality having nothing to do with reasoned connection. The child does not, in the usual sense, choose which path to take; spontaneously, he dances down one and thus chooses. In terms of the mind, Sammy chooses Beatrice Ifor, but he is by then the slave of acquisitive passion and has lost that election through dance in which the freedom of the child consists.

Sammy's language, though it has a poetry analogous with Tuami's, is, like Pincher Martin's, expressive of a nature chained by its fall. The fallen of Golding's novels, particularly Pincher, have more to do with the contemporary world than do his innocents, for the fallen seem to represent what civilization has become. Pincher undergoes the miseries of a consciousness abandoned to the pitiful spiritual resources of that civilization, on which his innocent friend Nat is an oblique comment, as an image both of what it abuses and what it has lost. Where Nat's language is sparing in both senses, Pincher could well exclaim with Caliban: "You taught me language, and my profit on't / Is, I know how to curse." Moreover, like Caliban, Pincher is deservedly confined upon his rock, for the language he has learned, because of the values it expresses, has brought his sins to commission.

In a sense, the rock of *Pincher Martin* is a reversed Eden, and the rituals that Pincher enacts are parodies of Adam in Genesis. As Adam names the animals, so Pincher names the parts of the rock, but where Adam's baptisms are recognitions of the rich diversity of creation, Pincher's are an endeavor to assert the supremacy of his intelligence and thus to retain his sanity. Clearly, there is no poetry in such name-giving: "I call this place the Look-out. . . . The rock out there under the sun where I came swimming is Safety Rock. The place where I get mussels and stuff is Food Cliff" (p. 84). The relation between naming and controlling can be sensed in this passage, for the names express no recognitions of otherness but merely the relevance of the parts of the rock to Pincher's needs. A little later he makes this connection between language and dominion explicit: "I am busy surviving. I am netting down this rock with names and taming it. . . . What is given a name is given a seal, a chain. If this rock tries to adapt me to its ways I will refuse and adapt it to mine. I will impose my routine on it, my geography. I will tie it down with names. . . . I will use my brain as a delicate machine-tool to produce the results I want. Comfort. Safety. Rescue" (pp. 86–87).

It is significant that comfort, safety, and rescue can only be achieved in opposition to the natural world. Thus, to alert aircraft to his presence on the rock, Pincher must make it evident that something out of nature is stranded there.

> Men make patterns and superimpose them on nature. At ten thousand feet the rock would be a pebble; but suppose the pebble were striped? He looked at the trenches. The pebble was striped already. The upended layers would be grey with darker lines of trench between them.
> He held his head in his hands.
> A chequer. Stripes. Words. S.O.S. . . .
> Seaweed, to impose an unnatural pattern on nature, a pattern that would cry to any rational beholder—Look! Here is thought. Here is man! [pp. 108–9]

The pattern and the word are related; both are impositions of the will, endeavors to make the being and its environment subject to the rational mind. This is Pincher's definition of sanity. His exposure to the sea is exposure of the civilized being to the conditions of its primitive origins. It is an experience that returns him to the reactions of Lok's people. The prose here is packed with verbs, mimetic of instantaneous action. The parts of his body have their own life: "His mouth was clever. It opened and shut for the air and against the water. His body understood too. Every now and then it would clench its stomach into a hard knot and sea water would burst out over his tongue" (p. 10). But to allow physical reactions autonomous intelligence is to abandon the rational control of the brain, and Pincher's consciousness soon rallies to remedy the situation.

> But inside, where the snores were external, the consciousness was moving and poking about among the pictures and revelations . . . like an animal ceaselessly examining its cage. It . . . ignored the pains and the insistence of the shaking body. It was looking for a thought. It found the thought, separated it from the junk, lifted it and used the apparatus of the body to give it force and importance.
> "I am intelligent." [pp. 31–32]

If this endeavor of the consciousness to assert itself is the distinction of individuality and rationality, it is also their torment. The body has resigned itself to death, but the mind cannot let go, and its struggle to survive is its misery. Because Pincher fears "losing definition," he has to invent the rock and all he endures upon it. But even that does not suffice. He requires the presence of others in which to spy "and assess the impact of Christopher Hadley Martin on the world" (p. 132). He does not want someone to love, but someone who would love him in order to describe him to himself. Someone to hate would do equally well. As one of his friends points out, Pincher is the personification of greed: "He takes the best part, the best seat, the most money, the best notice, the best woman. He was born with his mouth and his flies open and both hands out to grab" (p. 120). Pincher's torment is to have nothing left to seize. But his reason, and the language which is its instrument, creates in his mind a world, a rock, out of words, on which he endures long after the body has perished. Before it finally dissolves, Pincher's consciousness expresses its dilemma:

"On the sixth day he created God. Therefore I permit you
to use nothing but my own vocabulary. In his own image
created he Him." . . .

. . . "You gave me the power to choose and all my life you
led me carefully to this suffering because my choice was my
own. Oh, yes! I understand the pattern." [pp. 196–97]

Pincher Martin's language traps him in a cage from which
there is no escape, for a man is confined by the concepts, the
words, that his consciousness offers him. The language Pincher learned will offer him no solace and no solution. This is not
to suggest that the serenity of the good derives merely from a
different vocabulary. Goodness is a state of being, rather than
reflection, and the good do not express what they are in
words. Thus Pincher describes Mary's eyes as "large and wise
with a wisdom that never reached the surface to be expressed
in speech" (p. 148); and the words of Nick Shales in *Free Fall*
often contrast with the goodness of his essential being. In a
literal sense the good people in Golding's novels give life to
the cliché that actions speak louder than words, but this is
because true action is a product of unselfconscious being. It is
those who rely most upon words—Pincher, Halde, Sammy—whose self-consciousness torments them, and whose actions are often brutish. Like Caliban's, the world their speech
constructs is dark and full of blasphemy; moreover, they are
denied Caliban's comfort—they have no Prospero to curse.
There is no personal God in the world of Golding's novels.
They do not exclude the possibility that God exists; rather,
they imply that God, as language conceives him, cannot exist.
Rowena Pringle in *Free Fall* speaks the language of religion,
but there is far less of its spirit to be found in her than in the
atheist Nick. Words, one might say, are essentially tautologi-
cal, and the man who thinks he can signify God in speech is
the prisoner of tautology.

Yet the speech of Caliban would be judged with less than

justice if his statement that he used it merely to curse were
taken as the whole truth. Some of the most beautiful lines in
The Tempest belong to Caliban, and they are expressions of
aspiration:

> Be not afeard. The isle is full of noises,
> Sounds and sweet airs, that give delight and hurt not:
> Sometimes a thousand twangling instruments
> Will hum about mine ears, and sometimes voices
> That, if I then had waked after long sleep,
> Will make me sleep again. [4. 2. 144–49]

The fallen nature, which knows it is fallen, has a range of
longing and of loss, of aspiration, that unfallen nature cannot
express because it is privileged to be ignorant of such emotions. It is from that sense of deprivation that poetry as well as
blasphemy is born.

The song, as well as the scream or curse, emanates from
the new people of *The Inheritors*. When the innocent scream
it is purely a reflex:

> Then among the laugh-sound on this side of the river Liku
> began to scream. She was not screaming in anger or in fear or
> in pain, but screaming with that mindless and dreadful panic
> she might have shown at the slow advance of a snake. Lok
> spurted, his hair bristling. . . . The screaming tore him inside.
> It was not like the screaming of Fa when she was bearing the
> baby that died . . . ; it was like the noise the horse makes
> when the cat sinks its curved teeth into the neck and hangs
> there, sucking blood. Lok was screaming himself without
> knowing it and fighting with thorns. [p. 105]

Lok's devotion to Liku is as wordless as his panic; and to be
without a name is, in a sense, to be without a value. Perhaps it
is only the fallen who need to recognize value, but there is a
sad inexpressiveness in the animal acquiescence of Lok's
people in their own destruction, an inexpressiveness perhaps
unavoidable in those who have no concept of past or future.

The final image of the abandoned Lok is full of pathos, but it lacks the dignity of tragedy: "The creature wrestled with a rock that was lying on a mound of earth but was too weak to move it. At last it gave up and crawled round the hollow by the remains of a fire. It came close to the ashes and lay on its side. It pulled its legs up, knees against the chest. . . . It made no noise, but seemed to be growing into the earth" (p. 221). The language of Tuami is sharply in contrast with that of his predecessor. It is rife with suspicion, lamentably devoid of tenderness, and given to cursing, but it can express a range of emotions that are beyond the reach of Lok: "Tuami, his head full of swirling sand, tried to think of the time when the devil would be full grown. In this upland country, safe from pursuit by the tribe but shut off from men by the devil-haunted mountains, what sacrifice would they be forced to perform to a world of confusion? . . . Restlessly he turned the ivory in his hands. What was the use of sharpening it against a man? Who would sharpen a point against the darkness of the world?" (p. 231). If words necessitate a certain kind of sin; if, in Dante's terms, an inarticulate Eve could have had no commerce with the serpent; it is also true that without words certain emotions that we value highly could not be felt. Lok is not only incapable of articulating "Who would sharpen a point against the darkness of the world?"; he is also incapable of feeling that emotion. If before the coming of Prospero man knew little of evil, he also knew little of those voices which made him cry to dream again. If Eve had not fallen, the Incarnation would not have occurred. Like the myth of Genesis, the notion that the Fall was a *felix culpa* is imaginative as well as religious truth.

If Golding's heroes are almost always artists, it is surely because the creative imagination is most deeply responsive to the torment of the Fall, and its aspirations to perfection are consequently the most intense. That Sammy's medium is paint and Jocelin's is stone makes little difference, since the novels present both media as speech. The deficiencies men seek to remedy in art have much in common, whatever the medium. It is Tuami, not Lok, who needs to complement his deficient and reflective nature with artifacts, to register his sense of past and future with memorials. Without this sense of time, primitive man produces no art. Having acquired that sense, man is perpetually dissatisfied and creates in order to assuage his dissatisfaction.

At one extreme the artist is the guiltiest of human beings, for the range of his insights and emotions is the most comprehensive. Certain of Golding's characters—Halde and Philip in *Free Fall*, for example—are much less admirable than men such as Sammy, more evil indeed, if that term is acceptable. But the rationality of Halde and Philip has become so isolated as to be almost instinctual; they seem to obey a law of their nature, and because they know no other, less is required of them. But Jack in *Lord of the Flies*, who uses song as a weapon; Jocelin, whose prayer in stone is erected at so much cost to the human spirit; Pincher and Sammy, both of whom use their art to gain their ends—these cannot be readily forgiven, and the torment of all but Jack is closely related to this realization.

Both *Pincher Martin* and *Free Fall* take the relation of human guilt, language, and art a step further, for both are written fictively as well as actually from a conviction that art is the monument to man's Fall. Pincher's experience of the rock makes this explicit, since the narrative, as the ending reveals, has no existence outside the mind. The refusal of the brain to accept annihilation has created the geography and history of its purgatorial torment, and the prose of the novel is a sustained mimesis of the effort that sustains such a fiction.

But Pincher, second-rate actor and would-be writer, is less an artist than Sammy, and if his story is a victory for art it is an unwitting one. Pincher's narrative is full of curses, for he

refuses to understand that the torment of making his fiction is
one for which he alone is responsible. Sammy's narrative has
Caliban's curse upon it, too, but also more of his poetry.
From its inception, Sammy understands the nature of his
story—that it is an examination by a fallen conscience for the
point at which consciousness fell.

The prose of *Free Fall* contains, in consequence, as much
singing as cursing, as much recognition as rejection. The passage in which the adult Sammy recalls the hospital in which
the child was cured of mastoiditis is an example: "I have
searched like all men for a coherent picture of life and the
world, but I cannot write the last word on that ward without
giving it my adult testimony. The walls were held up by
sheer, careful human compassion. I was on the receiving end
and I know. When I make my black pictures, when I inspect
chaos, I must remember that such places are as real as Belsen.
They, too, exist, they are part of this enigma, this living" (p.
77). Because he is concerned to understand his own nature,
Sammy can perceive the extremes of virtue and depravity.
Pincher, never self-critical, is confined to a narrower spectrum of response. Sammy's world is more alive and vivid than
the grayly abrasive world of Pincher. The verb-filled prose of
Pincher Martin produces the idiom to be expected from a man
"born with his mouth and his flies open and both hands out to
grab." *Free Fall*, on the other hand, is adjectival rather than
verbal, for it constantly tries to relate the gray world of
Pincher to the luminous planet of innocent vision. The coexis-
tence of these two visions can be sensed in its first paragraph:

> I have walked by stalls in the market-place where books,
> dog-eared and faded from their purple, have burst with a
> white hosanna. I have seen people crowned with a double
> crown, holding in either hand the crook and the flail, the
> power and the glory. I have understood how the scar becomes
> a star, I have felt the flake of fire fall, miraculous and pentecos-

tal. . . . I live on Paradise Hill, ten minutes from the station,
thirty seconds from the shops and the local. Yet I am a burning
amateur, torn by the irrational and incoherent, violently
searching and self-condemned. [p. 5]

Language can enable experience as well as inhibit it. The
diurnal idiom of "I live on Paradise Hill, ten minutes from the
station," inhibits vision. It is a way, resembling that of
Pincher, of refusing to see or respond. But the language of
the earlier sentences redeems that of the marketplace: "I
have understood how the scar becomes a star, I have felt the
flake of fire fall, miraculous and pentecostal."[4] It is interesting that Golding should so often have recourse to the language
of religion, and particularly in the two novels that have most
to do with vision, *Free Fall* and *The Spire*. There is nothing
disconnected in the syntax of such prose, but its movement is
rhythmic rather than rational; its certainties are those of emotion rather than of reason. The relation of things to words is in
consequence metaphoric; it is no longer a question of possessing, but of liberating. In religious context, meaning accretes
richly about such simple words as *scar*, *fire*, and *star*, and the
poetry and awe of a communal consciousness exchange definition for mystery.

While Dante realized that language distinguished men
from angels, he nevertheless wished to set a high value upon
it. It was for him the noble instrument of man's conversation
with God, rather than woman's gossip with the devil. As a
writer, Golding inclines in the opposite direction. Yet he
might be ready to agree with Dante that the Fall was, after all,
a *felix culpa*, for without the sin of Adam, God would not have
become man in order that men might be redeemed. Golding's
writings allow words to renew themselves, just as Caliban's
language can issue in poetry. A conviction that Caliban would
have done better without words permeates the writing of

Golding; yet the novels themselves are evidence to the contrary.

---

1. The folio attributes this speech (1. 2. 353–58) to Miranda, but most editors have preferred, for obvious reasons, to give the lines to Prospero.

2. Dante discusses the issue in *De Vulgari Eloquentia*, chapters 3 and 4.

3. All references are to the Faber paper-covered editions.

4. It has been pointed out to me that, in the first hard-cover edition of *Free Fall*, *star* was printed, not *scar*. But the transformation of *scar* into *star* answers both to physical and metaphysical experience, a resource of meaning which accords with the tenor of the passage.

Peter Wolfe

THE BRASS BUTTERFLY:
FORMULA FOR SLOW CHANGE

WITH ALASTAIR SIM in mind, Golding adapted for
the stage his 1956 novella, *Envoy Extraordinary*, changing
the title to *The Brass Butterfly*.[1] The adaptation is no mere
recasting in dialogue form. Golding understands the difference between narrative and dramatic technique; differences
between story and play reveal a keen theatrical instinct and a
sure grasp of dramatic conventions.

Both typical and, as his only published play, atypical of
Golding, *The Brass Butterfly* has a dubious standing with
readers and playgoers. Dick calls it "an anthologist's heir-
loom, like Joyce's *Exiles*," and Golding himself terms it "a
very imperfect play."[2] This disclaimer has kept critics from
studying its artistry. The criticism the play has attracted cen-
ters on idea and lesson rather than on technique. By allowing
their concept of Golding the moralist to block their perception of the dramatic artist, critics have scamped their work.
The Brass Butterfly is the only long work in the Golding
canon whose aesthetic worth has not been assessed.[3] In this
essay I examine technique, but rather than bypassing the

moral lesson, I try to channel it into the play's imaginative and historical contexts. To show a group of characters generating a lesson and then to channel that lesson through a shaft of political history should reveal any writer's moral stance more clearly than a bald rehearsal of idea.

Like Golding's description of the play as "very imperfect," *The Brass Butterfly*'s scrappy stage history discourages study. Whatever stage success the play enjoyed belongs to its infancy. After a successful premiere, with Alastair Sim directing and acting the lead role at Oxford in February 1958, it played to friendly audiences in Edinburgh and elsewhere. *The Scotsman* praised it, but no such reception greeted the London production. Richard Findlater called the work "a humdrum bid at writing other people's [viz., Bernard Shaw's] plays"; Philip Hope-Wallace listed its faults: "No weight behind the narrative; no hammer and tongues [*sic*] in the dialogue; too many aphorisms, too little action." Nor did the work please the reviewers when it played at the Brooklyn Academy of Music in January 1970. Stewart H. Benedict called it "hollow at the center"; Clive Barnes qualified his praise of the production by concluding, "The play remains oddly elusive."[4]

These remarks are unfair. Golding did infuse *The Brass Butterfly* with drive, continuity, and a well-built plot. And while the charge of elusiveness makes some sense, it leads nowhere. Golding's novels are also often attacked, wrongheadedly, for obscurity and elusiveness. But *The Brass Butterfly* is easier to grasp than the novels, and it stands close philosophically to the fiction. The play's island setting—Capri in the third century of our era—conveys in a comic-historic way the same sense of being stranded as the island setting of *Lord of the Flies*. The clash of science and humanism looks ahead to *Free Fall*. The play's obsessive characters recall both the power-hungry chorister, Jack Merridew, and Dean Joce-

lin's obsessive vision in *The Spire*. The dying empire occurs as
anthropological drama in *The Inheritors*, and the play's military atmosphere calls to mind *Pincher Martin* and *Free Fall*.

Golding's real subject in *The Brass Butterfly* is pre-
socialized man—what man is rather than what he does. The
main target of his satire is science, particularly science's smug
assumption that it can bring about the Golden Age. In "On
the Crest of the Wave," Golding argues that science can
neither change man's nature nor touch the truths man lives
by: "Our humanity rests in the capacity to make value judg-
ments, unscientific assessments, the power to decide that this
is right, that wrong, this ugly, that beautiful, this just, that
unjust. Yet these are precisely the questions which 'Science'
is not qualified to answer with its measurement and
analysis."[5] The play contrasts the reasonable nature of science and the unreasonable nature of man. Science has little
application beyond itself; its gifts, though useful, Golding sees
as toys or hobbies. Men prefer food, fun, and pretty girls to
scientific lessons.

A summary of the action shows that the play sets out to
delight, instruct, and frighten its audience rather than lay
bare man's depravity. Though the danger bred by the action is
real, it dissolves too quickly to suggest man's fallen nature. On
the other hand, the play's mood is not cheerful. The blasted
hopes, missed connections, and overturned plans question
man's ability to save himself. Futility and exhaustion assert
themselves at the outset. The first sound in *Envoy Extraordinary*, which features impotence as vividly as *The Brass
Butterfly*, is the song of a eunuch. Rome's glories have
passed, and the setting is not the busy seat of government
but the emperor's pleasure-palace on Capri. Both setting and
character express the tiredness of the era. The "exquisite
good taste" of the royal villa is "perhaps . . . the least bit too
good." The aging, sybaritic emperor is a debased Caesar;

Postumus, the unimaginative man of military action, a degraded Alexander. His foil, Phanocles, inventor of the steamship, explosives, the printing-press, and the compass, is a Prometheus *manqué*.

Characterizing the dry-rot of the age, the play opens with Mamillius, the emperor's bastard grandson, lying on his stomach and writing a poetic invitation to death: "Darken the five bright windows of my mind. . . . Admit the corpse within." Introduced as "a man-boy?" and given a womanish name, the supine Mamillius reminds us of fashionably world-weary Oxbridge aesthetes, bored, aimless, and cheaply cynical. He says later in the act: "There is nothing new under the sun. Everything has been invented, everything has been written, everything has been done." His conversation with a captain of guards is broken by the stormy entry of Postumus, a "superb man of action" and the heir designate of the empire.

Postumus is chafing because three Christians he sentenced to death have escaped prison and fled Capri. His rage is soon quelled—but not by the ineffectual Mamillius. Entering with his retinue, the emperor uses political wisdom and honeyed words to quiet Postumus's wrath and sends him to plunder Africa in the name of civilization. After Postumus leaves the stage, Caesar grants an audience to Phanocles, the inventor, and his beautiful sister, Euphrosyne. Although Phanocles has come to describe his latest invention, the steamship, Caesar wants to hear about another of his devices, the pressure-cooker. Phanocles, who lives in the airless, bloodless realm of mechanical cause-and-effect, finds himself overturned several times by human inconstancy before the act ends. Not only does his pressure-cooker, and not his prized steamship, take Caesar's fancy; he also learns that Euphrosyne's beauty, rather than his own inventive genius, prompted Caesar to extend the audience to three times normal length. Yet his down-spiraling spirits reverse course when, at act's end, he is named director-general of experimental studies.

Act 2 introduces a clamor of movement, most of it disruptive. The note of danger sounds early, as four slaves carry onto the stage a rocket that Phanocles has invented In the stage directions, Golding calls the rocket's container "a horrible box" and adds that it should look "as much like a coffin as the cast and public will take." Absent from *Envoy Extraordinary*, the coffinlike box has theatrical value that would be lost in a narrative. The projectile inside the box exerts the same force. "Black and yellow . . . [and] standing on its stalk," it resembles both a phallus and a guided missile: "It is the size of a man and more. It is very nasty."

The missile is called "a malicious finger," and it remains on stage during Mamillius's wooing of Euphrosyne. Mamillius's touching of the rocket while he courts Euphrosyne provides one of the act's best effects, reaching beyond the characters to comment on all courtship. As the conjunction of missile and casket expresses the conjunction of vitality and death, so does Mamillius's handling of the incendiary missile express the dynamics of creation. Reason and restraint bring nothing new into the world. One must forfeit control in favor of the blood; yet the blood is blind. What is more important, any surging-out of raw passions creates risks. So while the discharge of vigor renews life, it can also kill. The rocket wins a big victory for Caesar in act 2, but in the world's crazy way: although it puts down a rebellion—with a misfire—it kills over two hundred Roman troops.

The display of the missile and the courting scene give way quickly to the return of Postumus. The missile, the steamship that Phanocles is building, and Mamillius's new view of himself as a lover *and* a soldier have shaken Postumus's dynastic hopes. Rather than risk the emperor's altering the succession in Mamillius's favor, he declares a regency, puts the emperor under house arrest, and makes ready to kill Mamillius. But the act ends on a calm note, as the emperor, instead of panicking, prepares to eat dinner.

A backward look to the end of act 1 shows that the quiet finish of act 2 accords with, rather than violates, dramatic unity. The chain of reversals ending act 1, while clashing with the serenity created by Postumus's departure from Capri, sets the tone for the wildness that runs through act 2. Accordingly, the emperor's decision to eat looks ahead to the partial restoration of order that comes in act 3. The third act finds Mamillius, Phanocles, and the emperor held prisoner in the royal villa. Postumus has taken charge of the army and means to take over the government. Having burned Phanocles's steamship, he makes ready to blow up the royal villa with the rocket. But in the flurry, Euphrosyne upsets his plans by removing the arming vane. In keeping with the animist imagination of pagan cultures, the vane is the brass butterfly of the title. It came into the play dramatically in act 2 when Phanocles warned the man mounting the rocket, "On no account touch the butterfly." Euphrosyne's touching the butterfly saves Caesar's life and reign, for removal of the safety device makes the missile backfire when ignited. So instead of destroying the royal villa, Postumus blows up himself and his troops. The backfire is typical. It happens while the emperor is praying to the Thunderer, Euphrosyne is petitioning Christ, and Phanocles is rhapsodizing about the supremacy of reason. To begin with, fear that his political hopes had dimmed sent Postumus back to Capri, but, instead of brightening these hopes, his return extinguishes them. Reversals like this abound. Euphrosyne never planned to sabotage the rocket, but the raw fact of death—the sight of corpses floating in the harbor—strengthens her hold on life. Not only does her filching of the safety device save the empire, but also helps her see that she loves and wants to marry Mamillius.

But Euphrosyne is a Christian. Because Rome worships

Jupiter, her ascendancy to Rome's ruling house would change
the religious life of the state. Caesar laments his inability to
fight this change. His lamentations are interrupted by Phanocles, who announces his latest invention—the printing-press.
The emperor is at first thrilled; then he realizes that the self-
expression printing fosters can cause chaos. Desiring to post-
pone this fret and fever, he sends Phanocles to China as his
envoy extraordinary.

The curve of the action is both fluid and fixed. Great
changes have taken place in the Roman state since act 1. Yet
in another, more Chekhovian sense, the public drama has
come back to its starting point: an important holding action
has been managed, and Postumus's brief moment of glory is
dwarfed by the inglorious state it but temporarily disrupts. In
act 1 Caesar sent Postumus on a mission of imperial conquest.
The play ends with Phanocles also drummed out of the empire under the guise of service. Both appointments are veiled
banishments. The stuff of kingship may be desirable in an
heir designate, but the presence of kingliness in the shadow
of an occupied throne foments disorder; no state can thrive
with more than one king. Likewise, Caesar knows that Phanocles's inventiveness can only be diverted and not stopped. By
sending him to China, on "a *slow* boat," he safeguards the
repose of his person and his kingdom for the balance of his
reign. Government serves the many. Phanocles and Postumus are fierce individualists. If genius inheres in the ability
to turn all of one's efforts to a single task, then they are
geniuses. But while ultimately useful to the state, they fret
their leaders and inflame their fellow citizens. As the emperor
says, "The universe does not seem to give something for nothing." The emperor acts like any other governor who has read
his Plato when he treats Phanocles and Postumus as public
menaces.

Menaces they are. Impatient with reality, Phanocles
wants nothing less than to change the world. He boasts, "My

aim is to reshape the whole future of humanity." Like all saviors, though, he must fail. He is a strict rationalist adrift in an irrational world. He worships reason unreasonably. Although he uses the Socratic method, his rational system lacks human reference. The emperor rightly accuses him of working with perfect elements. During his audience with Caesar, Phanocles claims to "move easily in the world of substance and force." What he has overlooked is the world of men, where his movements are fitful and halting. When we meet him, he is dirty and hungry. He cannot even express himself well. Although the emperor listens to him for the equivalent of three normal audiences, he cannot understand Phanocles's explanation of his invention. Postumus, too, finds Phanocles baffling, and Mamillius considers him a bore. Nor does he make good his boasts. When Caesar asks him, "Where is all your logic when the gods take a hand?" and "You were going to change the universe. Will you improve it?" he cannot answer. His failure, like his inability to explain the world by mechanical laws, goes beyond conviction and choice. He has inherited a legacy of lost causes and failed schemes.

The best summary of Phanocles's failure in perception comes in the introduction to the play by Sylvan Barnet, Morton Berman, and William Burto:

> Golding's technologist, Phanocles . . . is the comically imperceptive fool who looks so single-mindedly at one thing . . . that his folly is evident. . . . He does not understand mankind. He cannot understand why men are interested in beautiful women ("the bedding of individuals," he calls it) when "there is such an ocean at our feet of eternal relationships to examine or confirm." By eternal relationships he does not mean man's relationship to eternal things, but the relationships of things to things. . . . The emperor finds him hubristic. And Phanocles is something of a comic version of Aeschylus's Prometheus, now not sublimely but comically unaware of man's capabilities.[6]

Like that of Phanocles, Postumus's role has been changed for the stage. While he does not appear in *Envoy Extraordinary* until past the halfway mark, he enters the play early in the first act, bringing with him dramatic and ideological conflict. Harsh, humorless, and controlled, he craves power so much that he violates due process to get it. Mamillius mistakenly calls him "an insensitive bruiser." Postumus uses spies and informers to create opportunities. Once he sees his chance, he moves quickly; in command, he practices the philosophy of might makes right. Ironically, his lust for power makes him powerless. So aggressive is his personality that he misunderstands the nature of love. There is no love in him, and thus he fails to see how it works in others. Lacking faith and imagination, he thinks that Caesar's love for Mamillius will betray the emperor into making Mamillius his heir. This misjudgment costs Postumus his life.

It also betrays a chronic short-sightedness, for the emperor is the play's outstanding figure. Golding makes him the vessel of political wisdom and the driving force behind the political theme. No mere *raisonneur*, Caesar acquires dignity through his deeds as well as through his words. He has a fine moral balance to match his quick mind. His humanity outstrips that of his counterparts. Mamillius avoids humanity; Phanocles's science, Postumus's reign-of-terror politics, and Euphrosyne's evangelism ("We Christians must remake the world") all try to change it. Caesar accepts it and wants to make the best of it. Life's most ordinary moments he finds full of wonder and joy: "How exquisite beyond expression is the beauty of the common world!" he says. His belief that life is not organized to make people happy does not stifle his search for happiness. An Apollonian realist, he does not equate change with progress; change, he knows, does not always improve life. Given man's unreasonable nature, peace is too rare and good to be put to the test by every new discovery or invention. Even though he thwarts science, he does not betray society.

We do not meet him at the height of his powers. Worn down by years of statecraft, he has grown tired of ruling. But he still carries out his duties with energy and wisdom and regards himself as "the servant of all men." Like any good ruler, he knows he cannot enjoy a normal human relationship; he knows, too, that power makes a mockery of morals. Responsibility for his subjects gauges his conduct. When the public good clashes with moral or personal choice, he acts for his people every time. Nor are his actions rash. His nation's political leader as well as its spiritual leader, he takes his job seriously. He considers statecraft a sacred trust, and he brings to it a high degree of skill and dedication. He knows how to inspire people and hold their loyalty. Adaptable and alert, he knows the limits and the privileges of power. For instance, he corrects Mamillius when his grandson accuses Postumus of hiring spies: "No, no, Mamillius," he says, "A man with prospects as brilliant as the Heir Designate does not need to pay cash for anything."

Wit like this always serves Caesar's ruling purpose—to bring peace and plenty to his countrymen. Thinking quickly, he makes the backfiring missile that kills Postumus an occasion to stabilize his reign: "Captain, go down to the misguided and—irreligious soldiers who are coming in to the quay. Tell them that Jupiter, the All Father, has destroyed the Heir Designate before their very eyes, for the sin of open rebellion against the Emperor." Later, he talks about the explosion in broader terms. He still values the mishap for preserving Rome's dynastic order; the importance of restoring the legitimate succession cannot be overemphasized. The nation itself hangs in the balance, because any insurrectionist regime, scorning process in government, invites others. An endless chain of juntas discredits a throne and leads to a permanent police state. But the restoration of order in act 3, necessary as it is, costs dear. Even human nature, the emperor points out, seldom gives something for nothing: "It [the missile] has cost the world a merciless ruler who would have murdered half a dozen people and given justice to a hundred million. The world has lost a bargain."

Caesar's conservatism arises partly from his office. Rulers always distrust change. Change shifts the balance of power and stirs up the lower classes. By temperament and choice, then, Caesar seats himself in the past. He joins the other characters in his tendency to look to the Golden Age. But whereas Euphrosyne, Phanocles, and Postumus put it in the future, he finds it in the past. A gastronome rather than a glutton, he revisits it through the faculty of taste: "I have always been a primitive where meat is concerned. To taste meat in its exquisite simplicity would be a return to those experiences of youth that time has blunted." Good food quickens his blood, fuels his imagination, and tightens his grip on reality. Like Brecht's Galileo, another big eater, his love of food confirms his rage for experience.

Any discussion of *The Brass Butterfly*'s technique should start with the play's debt to classical drama. Dick lists "the unified action, the Terentian double plot, [and] the messenger's report of the off-stage violence."[7] To this may be added the single setting, the small cast, and the absent divinity. The romantic subplot works better as idea than as drama. Euphrosyne and Mamillius are paper-thin. Their falling in love virtually at first sight violates psychological realism. It is also bad theater. Golding does not give his audience time to commit themselves to the young couple because he does not give the couple a chance to get acquainted. Euphrosyne and Mamillius are both so self-centered that their love is not plausible. And because their implausible love causes so many changes, the play grows top-heavy with improbability. But Golding did as much as he could with his materials. The Euphrosyne of *Envoy Extraordinary* would have been even less able to carry her share of romantic interest. In the story she never talks and always keeps her face veiled. The play gives her more to do and say. It retains her job of removing the brass butterfly from Phanocles's rocket and adds to her role by making her a proselytizing Christian.

Ironically, her virtues are not dramatic. Mamillius falls in love with her before she says a word to him. A few minutes of conversation with her changes his flat, stale world to "wonderful undiscovered country." After rousing him from his jaded pseudosophistication, she promptly makes a man, a soldier, a Christian, and an embryo monarch of him. This violent change fuels Golding's satire on technology: though scientific change works but slowly into the historical process, both profane and holy love change life immediately. (Phanocles tells the emperor, "What am I to say, Caesar? She is my sister. Her beauty has come up, as it were, overnight.") The psychic revelations that create a spiritual revolution fit well with Golding's portrayal of life's unreasonableness. But they do not work well theatrically, lacking the integrity to give the play immediacy and animal vigor.

Some vigor animates the dialogue, though. Barnet, Berman, and Burto say that Golding "takes the past and lets it speak in the idiom of the present."[8] The point is well taken. Most of the dialogue is cadenced in the relaxed conversational mode of today, though Golding modulates the play's contemporary voice. He alludes to modern maxims, as when Mamillius asks, "The sword is mightier than the pen?" He re-creates some of the military stiffness of old Rome. He dresses the characters in togas and sandals and has them refer to practices of antiquity. The antique formality of imperial Rome clashes with the updated speech. This clash, making relaxation difficult, produces a Brechtian sharpness. Meanwhile, the often-mentioned heat-haze, the trancelike state in which Euphrosyne removes the brass butterfly, and the general

humiliation of reason all jolt the play out of the realm of cognition. Logic and order cannot thrive amid such confusion.
The backfiring of Phanocles's missile caps a riot of broken
appointments, canceled demonstrations, overturned hopes,
misjudgments, and crimes.

Golding uses structure to hold this riot in check. The
play's design, it needs to be said, reveals technical skill far
beyond that found in most first plays. Golding shapes his
drama so that he can get the most out of his materials. Contrast or opposition is the mainspring, and the first act introduces sharp contrast straightaway as an organizing principle.
The luxurious appointments of the royal villa in Capri clash
with a prominently displayed bust depicting "a brutal-looking
man" who evokes "an exterior world where life is earnest,
real, and rather bloody-minded." Accordingly, the flaccid
Mamillius clashes with the heel-clicking captain of guards.
Then Postumus enters, introducing more contrast with his
slothful cousin, whose soft, white arm he twists, and also with
the captain, who takes rather than gives orders. The storm
whipped up by Postumus's anger and impatience subsides
when the emperor comes on stage: "Ah, there you are,
Postumus," he says right away, "Come and sit for a moment,
and drink wine with me." After Caesar's imperial serenity
smoothes Postumus's wrath, another malcontent enters. But
Phanocles, unlike Postumus, is no actionist. His labor-saving
inventions redirect other people's energies. And his ambition
to extend man's scope contrasts both with Postumus's to-
talitarianism, which aims to limit man, and with Mamillius's
avoidance of men.

Act 1 is trim, tight, and fast-moving. Along with dramatic
conflict, it introduces ideas about power, and it shows how
technological change struggles to enter the historical process.
The act closes with Phanocles's appointment as director-general of experimental studies. This provisional climax, the plot's
first major development, marks a peak in the action. It also

accords with the political motif carried over from the outset, for another climax, more spectacular, is still building. Although Postumus has been sent away, he has shown enough of his personality and ambitions to make dramatically feasible his junta late in act 2.

The emperor's impeccable diplomacy, Mamillius's sloth, and the removal of Postumus from Italy all bathe act 1 in a late-afternoon glow of harmony and slow ease. But act 2 is dominated by brokenness and frustration. Though nobody except Caesar backs the status quo, any attempt at change causes havoc. Nothing goes as planned. Euphrosyne breaks her vow of silence. The emperor first fails to show up for the demonstration of the rocket; then he cancels the demonstration altogether. Postumus disrupts civil order by arresting Mamillius and Caesar and declaring himself Regent. No wonder Phanocles and Caesar call the junta a nightmare. Earlier, Caesar spoke of the inadequacy of "normal . . . human communication." The heat-haze beating up from the harbor creates a climate of unreality, where reason, order, and process have little chance to survive. Befitting this midsummer madness, men drown and burn at the same time when Phanocles's steamship blazes in the harbor.

Act 3 partly repairs the wreckage strewn about by the madness. What remains to be told is the artistry with which reintegration is managed. *The Brass Butterfly* marches crisply to its end. Philosophically, the events of acts 1 and 2 make the state's mixed victory a fitting climax. Dramatically, all the play's forces fuse to drive the inevitability home with impact and clarity. All the major characters except Postumus, we remember, are being held captive in the royal villa. The fear of imminent death that grips them not only promotes suspense but also encourages them to speak directly—that is, regardless either of rank or fear of reprisal. They say exactly what they feel. The emperor, meanwhile, must inspire loyalty and generate honor from his person rather than from his office.

His dual success promises well for the state. It also counter-
weights the shrillness bred by Postumus's junta.

This happy balance of control and forward drive, besides
expressing form and theme, declares Golding a playwright of
stature. *The Brass Butterfly* combines the merits of unity and
depth. No mere tour de force, it is a carefully planned, well-
knit work. William Golding is not only wise; he has a trained,
theoretical mind and, an artist to his fingertips, knows the
theoretical uses of artistic form. As in his novels, the form of
The Brass Butterfly balances, refreshes, and criticizes its
powerfully imagined theme. Its freshness and power make
the play topical and eternal. The conjunction of these
strengths also makes it a civilizing force.

---

1. The story is in *Sometime, Never: Three Tales of Imagination by
William Golding, John Wyndham, Mervyn Peake*, 1–60. [*Sometime, Never*
was published originally in London by Eyre & Spottiswoode in 1956. There
was no hardcover edition in the United States; the Ballantine paperback
(published July 1957) was reprinted in September 1957, November 1962,
and November 1971. Since 1967, "A Note to Teachers and Parents" by
Richard H. Tyre has been included. *Envoy Extraordinary* has been reis-
sued in hardcover in Golding's *The Scorpion God: Three Short Novels*
(London: Faber, 1971, and New York: Harcourt, 1972), 115–78.—Eds.]

2. Bernard F. Dick, *William Golding* (New York: Twayne, 1967), 63;
Golding quoted by James R. Baker, *William Golding: A Critical Study*
(New York: St. Martin's, 1965), 48.

3. *Envoy Extraordinary* should be understood as sharing this neglect.
But, see Helen Nethercutt Parker, "William Golding's *The Brass Butterfly*:
An Analysis" (M.A. thesis, University of North Carolina at Chapel Hill,
1970) and Denise Cross Dickens, "Success and Failure: 'Envoy Extraordinary' and *The Brass Butterfly*" (M.A. thesis, Georgia State University,
1975.)—Eds.

4. Ronald Mavor, "Alastair Sim Returns: Beautiful New Comedy,"
Scotsman, 25 March 1958, 8; [Richard Findlater] "Richard Findlater at
the Theatre," *Sunday Dispatch* (London), 20 April 1958, 31; Philip Hope-
Wallace, "Theatre," *Time and Tide*, 26 April 1958, 520; Stewart H. Ben-
edict, " 'Butterfly' Flaps Wings Successfully," *The Jersey [City] Journal*, 31
January 1970, 26; Clive Barnes, "Theater: A Smooth and Elegant 'Brass
Butterfly,' " *New York Times*, 31 January 1970, 34.

5. *The Hot Gates and Other Occasional Pieces* (New York: Harcourt, 1966), 130.

6. Sylvan Barnet, Morton Berman, and William Burto, *The Genius of the Later English Theater* (New York: Mentor, 1962), 440.

7. Dick, *William Golding*, 64.

8. Barnet, Berman, and Burto, *Genius*, 439.

Jeanne Delbaere-Garant

RHYTHM AND EXPANSION IN *LORD OF THE FLIES*

WATER AND ROCKS, ebb and flow, angles and circles, microcosm and macrocosm, reason and intuition, good
and evil, flies and butterflies: rhythm beats in *Lord of the
Flies*, sometimes loud, sometimes with "an undertone less
perceptible than the susurration of the blood," but always
with the regularity of waves against the reef.[1] This continual
back-and-forth motion, the rhythm of life, is complemented
by a rhythmic use of gradation suggesting the constant progress of evil. The killing of pigs and the throwing of rocks, two
important activities of the boys on the island, provide a metaphorical structure for the illustration of the author's theme.

In the description of the setting is a basic opposition between sea and island, liquidity and hardness, flux and fixity,
roundness and angularity. The "circular horizon of water"
contains the "square motif of the landscape." This pattern,
however, is not closed upon itself. It expands upwards, outwards, inwards in a never-ceasing reproduction. Sea and sky,
islands and stars answer each other: the sky mirrors itself in
the water together with the "angular bright constellations." At
a mile's distance from the island and parallel to it lies a coral

reef, against which waves break so that the beach is duplicated in the sea, "as though a giant had bent down to reproduce the shape of the island in a flowing, chalk line but tired before he had finished" (p. 38). Finally, there is a reminder of the water motif in the island, a reminder of the rock motif in the sea. As in the yin and yang of the Chinese, there is a black patch in the white surface and a white patch in the black, a piece of squareness in the liquid element and a pool in the island: "There, where the island petered out in water, was another island; a rock, almost detached, standing like a fort, facing them across the green" (p. 38). Likewise "Some act of God—a typhoon perhaps—had banked sand inside the lagoon so that there was a long, deep pool in the beach" (pp. 17–18), a pool which is only invaded by the sea at high tide.

There is rhythm also in the abrupt succession of night and day and even in the configuration of the island itself. The boys, having come with their rhythmic changes set to the time of the clock and of their European tradition, must now adapt to the physical cycles of their new abode: "The first rhythm that they became used to was the slow swing from dawn to quick dusk" (p. 73). Time is no longer measured by the clock but by the regular movement of sunlight from the horizontal at dawn to the perpendicular at noon and back to the horizontal in the evening. On the island the sandy beach is interrupted by the "square motif" of the mountain: "The most usual feature of the rock was a pink cliff surmounted by a skewed block; and that again surmounted, and that again, till the pinkness became a stack of balanced rock projecting through the looped fantasy of the forest creepers" (p. 34). As this rhythmical alternation of vertical and horizontal planes measures the tropical day and underlies the structure of the island, so contrastive and repetitive patterns govern the structure of the novel, which is built on a contrapuntal balance of opposites and on repetitions, echoes, parallels, which blend and culminate in the last chapter.

The action starts smoothly. The first chapter consists of an alternation of pictures and scenes according to whether Golding describes the place or presents the characters. From the beginning we are aware of correspondences: a bird's cry on the first page is answered by Piggy's voice, and the noise emitted by Ralph's blowing of the conch is echoed by the mountain. Even the fundamental patterns of the geophysical world will be unconsciously imitated by the boys in their activities: the contrast between the circular horizon of the sea and the angular shape of the island is reproduced in the circles and triangles into which they fall when they come together. When they hold meetings the boys form a triangle which eventually deteriorates into a sketchy and empty shape. When they hunt, Jack's choir-boys form a circle around the pig, and this pattern becomes neater as the boys revert to savagery. On the evening of Simon's death the circling movement has become so regular that it begins "to beat like a steady pulse." The conch, reconciling roundness and angularity, the irrational and the rational, in its "slight spiral twist" is a symbol of wholeness. The boys do not know this but take it as a talisman and feel that it is precious and rare.

The basic opposition between sea and reef corresponds to a contrast between the two groups of boys. Ralph's group—the democratic one—is characterized from the start by its heterogeneity, Jack's—the authoritarian one—by its organization. The boys of the first group come one by one, adding individual face to individual face: "There were badges, mottoes even, stripes of colour in stockings and pullovers. Their heads clustered above the trunks in the green shade; heads brown, fair, black, chestnut, sandy, mouse-coloured; heads muttering, whispering, heads full of eyes" (p. 25). The choir-boys, however, are first perceived as "something dark," a creature whose blackness interrupts the clear sand as the square motif of the mountain interrupts the beach. The geometrical elements suggest strict organization: "The creature was a party of boys, marching approximately in step *in two parallel lines* and dressed in strangely eccentric clothing. Shorts, shirts, and different garments they carried in their hands: but each boy wore *a square black cap* with a silver badge in it. Their bodies, from throat to ankle, were hidden by black cloaks which bore *a long silver cross*" (p. 126, italics mine).

As a rock stands detached amid the water and a pool stretches on the island, a boy is singled out on each side: Simon and Piggy do not really belong to their groups. They are first noticed because of physical particularity which sets them apart and is commented on by the other boys: Simon because of his fainting fits, Piggy because of his obesity. They are outsiders: Piggy is laughed at and rejected; Simon goes off to meditate in the jungle. These two boys play a more important part in the novel than Ralph and Jack, who are most often set against each other. Indeed, in their opposition and complementariness Piggy and Simon epitomize all that exists in the universe: Simon is the passive element; like the candle-buds in his shelter opening their white flowers to meet the night air, he is always open, ready to let the world enter his soul and fill it. Piggy's protruding belly is the image of his affirmation, of his determination to change the world instead of accepting it. He is the rational mind opposed to intuition and insight. The two boys die significant deaths: Piggy's skull breaks into pieces against the rock which stands apart at the other end of the island, a symbol of himself keeping forever outside the triangle of the other boys' meetings or the circle of their ritual dances. Simon's body is lifted gently by the tide that fills the pool—an empty receptacle like himself—and takes him away to the open sea. The event manifests a larger rhythm into which it is integrated: "Somewhere over the darkened curve of the world the sun and moon were pulling; and the film of water on the earth planet was held, bulging slightly on one side while the solid core turned. The great wave of the tide moved further along the island and the water lifted. Softly, surrounded by a fringe of inquisitive bright creatures, itself a silver shape beneath the steadfast constellations, Simon's dead body moved out towards the open sea" (p. 190).

By introducing correspondences between setting and characters Golding intimates that the same law governs the geophysical world and the world of man. Human nature is an aspect of nature at large. Man is neither worse nor better than nature: the same evil principle permeates and harms both. Before the boys came to the island "some unknown force" had split the rocks and given the place its present aspect. When the boys scramble up these rocks they notice a scar across the landscape, probably made by the fuselage of their plane when it crashed. They smash a deep hole in the canopy of the forest by dislodging a boulder in order to reach the top of the mountain. The place is wounded successively by "some unknown force," by the civilized world of grown-ups, and by the boys themselves. At the end of the novel Ralph, with his bruised flesh and a "swollen and bloody scar where the spear had hit him" is identified with the island. The metaphorical scar of the first chapter was real after all.

In chapter 4 Golding concentrates on this rhythm of life in which each living creature is the victim of a force larger than itself. The littluns are on the beach, building castles in the sand. Two bigger boys, Roger and Maurice, look for a while at the castles and start kicking them over. The littluns do not protest any more than a grown-up would if his town had been suddenly destroyed by a typhoon. One of them, Henry, leaves the place and goes to the edge of the water. There his attention is caught by little organisms which come scavenging over the beach, and he starts poking about "with a bit of stick *that itself was wave-worn and whitened and a vagrant*" (italics mine). He is fascinated because he can exercise control over these tiny transparencies which, though embryonic, are endowed with life. Absorbed in his play he fails to notice Roger, who has remained near the scattered castles and observes him with the same attention as the littlun observes the scavengers. Suddenly a breeze shakes a palm tree sixty feet above Roger's head and nuts fall like stones about him. Roger is not touched but looks "from the nuts to Henry and back again": "The subsoil beneath the palm tree was a raised beach; and generations of palms had worked loose in this *the stones that had lain on the sands of another shore*. Roger stooped, picked up a stone, aimed, and threw it at Henry—threw it to miss. The stone, *that token of preposterous time*, bounced five yards to Henry's right and fell in the water" (p. 78; italics mine). Man and nature are in turns victims and victimizers. It is this confused new knowledge that Jack brings back from the hunt: you "feel as if you're not hunting, but—being hunted; as if something's behind you all the time in the jungle" (p. 67). The same blind force moves Henry's hand when he destroys the work of the scavengers on the beach, Maurice's when he scatters the sandcastles, Roger's when he throws stones at Henry, the wind's when it looses nuts around Roger, and the afternoon sun's when it "emptied down invisible arrows" on Henry's head. The fact that the stick is wave-worn and that the stones have lain on the sands of another shore situates the whole process in a larger perspective not limited in time or space.

To remind us of this general rhythm, of which the action of *Lord of the Flies* is only a miniature manifestation, Golding selected his material with care and reduced the episodes of the book to two types of opposite activities developing inversely. On the positive, rational side are expeditions and assemblies; on the negative, irrational side, throwing rocks and killing pigs. Keeping the fire is not for the boys a regular activity since they soon neglect it. A symbol of man's reason and intelligence (there could be no fire without Piggy's glasses), the fire can be either positive or negative according to how it is used. Meant as a signal fire for passing ships or planes it becomes, through misuse, a wild beast with a life of its own which invades the whole place, kills the little boy with the mulberry-colored birthmark, and threatens to destroy them all. What happens by accident in the second chapter is done deliberately at the end by the boys turned savages.

Each of the three expeditions on the island is made by a three-boy party: successively, Ralph, Jack, Simon; Ralph, Jack, Roger; Jack, Maurice, Roger. Jack, the red-haired devil figure, is present in each. The first aims at exploring the place to make sure it is an island. The worlds of common sense (Ralph wants to draw a map of the island), of action (Jack wants to kill a pig), and of imagination (Simon sees candle-buds among the bushes) are united in the joy of common discovery and experience. About the middle of the book a second group of boys decides to climb the mountain to look for the beast. Ralph and Jack remember their first exploration, and "consciousness of the bad times in between came to them both" (p. 132). Ralph senses the rising antagonism between himself and Jack. Roger now replaces Simon; hatred replaces love. The third expedition takes place after Jack has formed his own group and has decided to steal Piggy's glasses to light their own fire. The forces of evil (Roger, Maurice) gradually replace love and common sense (Simon, Ralph). The constructive aim degenerates into robbery and destruction. At the end Ralph is alone against an expedition made by savages and conducted against himself.

The first assembly gathers in the afternoon following the first expedition. Ralph sits on a fallen trunk with the choir boys on his right, the larger boys on his left, and the littluns in front. He finds he can speak fluently and has the self-confidence of a real chief. The question about the snake-thing asked by the boy with the mulberry-colored birthmark casts a gloom over the general optimism and is a premonition of evil.

The second meeting is described at length. It occurs after the fire has gone out. Ralph is in a grim mood and, looking at the other boys with new eyes, he begins to adjust his views and to fall into a mood of speculation foreign to him ("If faces were different when lit from above or below—what was a face? What was anything?" [p. 97]). The third assembly is called by Jack after the second expedition. Jack tells the others that Ralph ran away when he saw the beast and that they should now choose him, Jack, as chief. As nobody answers he goes off by himself, leaving order and reason behind (p. 158). Ralph is vaguely aware of the situation but seems powerless to change anything: it is as though the great force that split the rocks was now splitting their group; the sky, "as if in sympathy with the great changes among them," is different and the air is stifling. Piggy blows the conch after the third expedition, when his glasses have been stolen. But the beach is deserted and only "the shape of the old assembly, trodden in the grass" answers the call. Ralph can no longer find words, cannot think properly, and Piggy must help him remember what to say.

Those meetings indicate the gradual deterioration of the civilized element, as Ralph's confident talk turns into a lamentable stuttering and the neat geometrical pattern of the first assembly wears off into a sketchy triangle before becoming a mere shape emptied of people. The meetings are in direct connection with the explorations, which are presented directly and then commented upon in the assemblies, so that the same event is seen from two different angles. Besides, each new meeting accretes new meaning by being charged, in Ralph's mind, with memories of the previous ones, which gradually awaken him to the consciousness of something he did not know before. He becomes more and more silent, conscious of the increasing evil but unable to stop it.

With the throwing of rocks and the killing of pigs the movement is first confused and only gradually asserts itself as

the boys lose control of the rational in themselves. The memory of punishment received for throwing sand in a younger
boy's eyes holds back Maurice's hand on the beach. The
interdictions from his former life keep Roger from throwing
stones at Henry: "There was a space round Henry, perhaps six
yards in diameter, into which he dare not throw. Here, invisible yet strong, was the taboo of the old life. Round the
squatting child was the protection of parents and school and
policemen and the law. Roger's arm was conditioned by a civilization that . . . was in ruins" (p. 78). When Jack raises his
hand to kill his first pig, "There came a pause, a hiatus, the pig
continued to scream and the creepers to jerk, and the blade
continued to flash at the end of a bony arm. The pause was
only long enough for them to understand what an enormity
the downward stroke would be" (p. 40). At the end of the
novel the same boys, Maurice, Roger, and Jack, have become
real forces of evil, intoxicated with their own power and impatient to exercise it.

Indeed, the throwing of rocks begins with Roger's first
stone in the sea, which is a perfect diagram of Golding's technique to depict the progress of evil. The same act recurs with
an amplification similar to that of waves spreading in larger
and larger circles around a stone thrown in the water. When
he kills Piggy, Roger makes the same gesture as when he
threw stones at Henry. Only the stone has become a "monstrous red thing" and Roger a murderer. Yet at the beginning
the boys mean no harm. If they roll a rock through the forest,
it is because it bars their progress; they join efforts to move it
and are happy when they succeed:

> "Heave!"
> Sway back and forth, catch the rhythm.
> "Heave!" . . .
> The great rock loitered, poised on one toe, decided not to

return, moved through the air, fell, struck, turned over, leapt
droning through the air and smashed a deep hole in the
canopy of the forest. . . .
"Wacco!"
"Like a bomb!" [pp. 36–37]

After that, the way to the top is easy. Although this is only
a first step in deterioration, the boys' exclamations point to
the future and a further expansion of evil which, like the rock,
will gather pace as it tumbles down. From the start the boys
are aware of their power ("Eyes shining, mouths open,
triumphant, they savoured the right of domination" [p. 39])
and look with exhilaration at the platform beneath with
"insect-like figures moving near it" (p. 38). The second throw- *Rocks*
ing of rocks takes place in chapter 6 when the hunters decide
to look for the beast. The antagonism between the chiefs
makes them think of war and see the pink bastion as a fort.
Jack suggests that a palm trunk might be shoved as a lever
under the last broken rock so that it can be launched more
easily at an imaginary invader. Meanwhile the hunters are
heaving and pushing rocks for fun. Under them the grass is
"dotted with heads" (p. 132).
    Once they have imagined a weapon, the hunters are not
satisfied until they use it against a real enemy. They do so as
soon as the opportunity offers: Roger, leaning all his weight on
the lever, lifts the big rock and propels it at Piggy. A change
of perspective takes place at the end, when the throwing of
rocks is seen from the point of view of one of the insectlike
figures. Because he is now one of them, Ralph knows that
nothing will stop the tumbling monster. He can make out the
familiar "Heave! Heave! Heave!" as the hunters try to catch
the rhythm, and he knows that the rock, "half as big as a
cottage, big as a car, a tank" is aimed at him.
    There is the same tidelike amplification in the killing of

pigs. After he has overcome his repulsion, Jack thrusts his knife into the living flesh of his victim. The reader does not witness the scene directly; it is related by the hunters when they come back from the forest. Ralph is waiting for them, furious and helpless on the ashes of the signal fire which they have let go out. They are so excited they fail to notice his anger and speak all at once:

> "We got in a circle—"
> "We crept up—"
> "The pig squealed—" [p. 86]

Again, as after the throwing of the first rock, there is perfect harmony between the boys who have been caught in the same rhythm ("so then the circle could close in and beat and beat—"), who have shared the same experience and are now rich with the same knowledge and memories. But the world of Jack ("of hunting, tactics, fierce exhilaration, skill") and the world of Ralph ("of longing and baffled common sense") part here. Envious and resentful, Ralph watches them while Maurice acts the pig and runs squealing to the center of the circle made by the hunters who mimic the killing and dance around him.

The mock hunt is repeated in chapter 7. The hunters have just missed a boar and console themselves by organizing a game in which Robert enacts the pig while other boys dance and chant around him. As in the second throwing of rocks, the hunters are disappointed because it is just a game: the desire to spill blood possesses them, and they see this as only a surrogate for the real thing. Once more Jack is the instigator of evil when he suggests that a boy might be used as a substitute for the pig:

> "You want a pig," said Roger, "like in a real hunt."
> "Or someone to pretend," said Jack. "You could get some-

one to dress up as a pig and then he could act—you know,
pretend to knock me over and all that—"

"You want a real pig," said Robert, still caressing his
rump. . . .

"Use a littlun," said Jack, and everybody laughed. [pp.
142–43]

Again what Jack conceives in imagination and presents as a
joke will become reality. When they hunt the third time (the
reader now witnesses the scene directly), the game turns into
murder. It begins with the killing of a sow surrounded by her
young piglets. The hunters pursue her to the open space
where Simon, concealed by the leaves, has retired to meditate. The violence of the hunt contrasts with the fragile
beauty of the butterflies which, as usual, occupy the center of
Simon's clearing. Jack orders Roger to "Sharpen a stick at
both ends" so that they can impale the sow's head and leave it
as an offering to the beast. It is some time before the butterflies desert the open space and are replaced by flies that
alight on the sow's dripping head and Simon's sweating face.
Identification with the sacrificial victim foreshadows his fate.
After the hunt the boys' excitement is increased by the stifling
heat and the menace of an approaching storm, and they fall
back on their ritual dances to protect themselves: "Some of
the littluns started a ring on their own; and the complemen-
tary circles went round and round as though repetition would
achieve safety of itself" (p. 187). Even Ralph and Piggy,
"under the threat of the sky, found themselves eager to take a
place in this demented but partly secure society." The tension
grows, the need to kill becomes urgent, and when Simon
comes out of the forest to tell them that the beast is a dead
parachutist he is assaulted and slain.

In the last chapter, everything is seen from Ralph's point
of view. He hears the chant that accompanies the killing of a

pig and is told by the twins that Roger has "sharpened a stick at both ends" (p. 234). It takes him some time to make sense of this enigmatic sentence, which the reader immediately understands; he then remembers that the hunters needed such a stick to impale the sow's head and that they now want another for his own.

The throwing of stones and the killing of pigs develop in similar ways: both pursuits are initiated out of necessity, repeated for fun, turned against a human being (significantly, Piggy and Simon, who represent the two poles of the human mind) and finally against Ralph, who has become the center of consciousness and learns to decipher, now that he is its victim, the darkness of the human heart. The change of perspective takes place at the beginning of the last chapter, when the action—which had been up to then observed from the outside—is seen entirely through the eyes of the main character. In *Pincher Martin* Golding drops the external presentation of the action altogether and writes a whole novel on what takes place inside the mind of a character, leaving it to the reader to reassemble disconnected pieces of the jigsaw. Here we are both outside and inside, witnessing the hunt and sharing the thoughts of the hunted. This gives the novel an apparent simplicity, which is misleading. Because its surface offers no real resistance many critics have tended to ignore the complexity of *Lord of the Flies*, though this novel is no less subtle than *The Inheritors* or *Pincher Martin*.

After making clear, through a rhythmical balance of opposites recalling the waves of the ocean, that all things, animate and inanimate, are governed by the same law, that evil does not spare man any more than it does nature, that each living creature is in turn hunter and hunted, Golding shows, through a series of repetitions expanding like the movement of the tides, that there is no stopping evil. When he shifts the focus of the novel in the last chapter, he anticipates a device used later in *The Inheritors* and *Pincher Martin*. In the last chapter of *The Inheritors* there is a switch in point of view; the action is no longer seen through the eyes of Lok but through those of a new man. In *Pincher Martin* the sudden intrusion of the naval officer—a duplicate of the one that rescues the boys—gives a twist to the novel and generalizes its effect. These gimmicks are combined in Golding's first novel: after focusing on Ralph to present the action through the boy's consciousness, the author focuses on infinity and universalizes his theme. Not only is this contraction-expansion in keeping with the movement of the novel, but the metaphorical structure itself is borrowed from the two main activities through which the progress of evil has been illustrated.

The killing of the pigs provides Golding with his first metaphor: all the concentric circles of the novel now close in on Ralph—identified with the pig and the place—in a climactic high tide of evil that threatens to engulf him and the island alike. He has become the prey of the evil force which he had so far observed from the outside: he is the boar tracked by the hunters and considers the possibility of bursting the line; he is Piggy menaced by the great block above his head; he is Simon used as a sacrificial victim by the savages; he is the littlun who perished in the fire at the beginning of the story ("There was another noise to attend to now—a deep grumbling noise, as though the forest itself were angry with him. . . . He knew he had heard it before somewhere, but had no time to remember" [pp. 241–42]). Finally he is the island itself, "scorched up like dead wood." And then, when the scar is no longer a metaphor but is felt in his own bruised flesh, he weeps for the end of innocence.

This contraction is immediately followed by an expansion when the officer appears. His "fun and games" echoes Ralph's words at the beginning of the novel and suggests, like the white beach line reproducing the contour of the island in the sea, a further duplication of the whole story. This time it is the throwing of stones that provides Golding with his metaphor: the movement is no longer centripetal but expands from the center outwards, from the world of the children to the world of the grown-ups, from the island to the world at large. The island is a microcosmic stone thrown in the middle of the ocean with waves of evil radiating around it in larger and larger circles. The events witnessed in *Lord of the Flies* do not end when the book does. If Roger's first stone leads to his murderous gesture, there is no reason why the rock thrown at Piggy should not also lead to the bomb launched against an enemy's country and ultimately to the atomic bomb that will destroy mankind. At this stage not only Ralph but the reader himself is aware that once the process has started there is no stopping the enraged monster.

---

1. *Lord of the Flies* (London: Faber, 1962), 72.

Robert O. Evans

THE INHERITORS: SOME INVERSIONS

GOLDING OFTEN TURNS ordinary matters inside out and observes them from a startling point of view. This technique dominates the style of the first three novels and is especially prominent in the second. Golding hints at the basis of the technique in an interview with Frank Kermode: "I have a view which you haven't got and I would like you to see this from my point of view." Some critics seem to notice it (for example, Baker speaking of H. G. Wells says, "In Golding's story the formula is reversed").[1]

At its simplest *Lord of the Flies* is an inversion of the Ballantyne novel on which it was loosely based as well as a reversal of the cosmic optimism of *Robinson Crusoe, The Swiss Family Robinson,* or Wells's theory of progress. There are other self-imposed limitations. The action of *Lord of the Flies* is performed almost entirely by children. *The Inheritors* shares that limitation, for until the final portion of the book events are related through the minds and senses of Neanderthals, childlike in their simplicity. Two critics have spoken of this technique as an "upside-downness" and have partly traced how it relates to point of view and, in lesser degree, to the philosophical meaning of the narrative.[2] "We become," they say, "sharply aware of how upside-downness is related to the deep water of the river and the fall," symbols upon which the story turns.

Lord of the Flies and *The Inheritors* then are deliberate distortions of works on which they were based: the former, Ballantyne's *The Coral Island;* the latter, various works of H. G. Wells.[3] Perhaps Golding's starting point was familiar popular literature. Thus Golding may be open to a charge of attempting to make serious literature from light materials, but if he was aware of any risk he ignored it and went on with the job. Nor did he attempt to conceal what he was doing. In *The Inheritors* Golding provides a clue from the start. He begins with a modified quotation from *The Outline of History*.[4] No matter how much he may have had "The Grisly Folk" or *A Story of the Stone Age* in the back of his mind, *The Outline of History* provides the anthropological skeleton upon which the tale is draped.

Even so, the Wells quotation is suspect, for it is never stated that the incident the story depicts is the final, decisive conflict between *Homo neanderthalensis* and *Homo sapiens*, though that implication provides the novel with depth and seriousness (and most critics have jumped at it). Still, it may not matter how specific the implications are, for the novel is not science fiction. It deals with a confrontation between members of an extinct race called the People and our own prehistoric ancestors, the New Men (or simply the Men or the Others). Most of the anthropology in the book seems to be in good order, and Golding has said he read deeply in the subject, but he had little reason to seek beyond *The Outline of History* for what he needed.[5] Indeed, though we have rearranged chronology in the past fifty years, we still know precious little about *Homo neanderthalensis;* what Golding needed beyond Wells he invented.

How closely he relied on his source may be seen from

some comparisons. For example, Wells wrote, "Finally, between 40,000 and 25,000 years ago, as the Fourth Glacial Age
softened towards more temperate conditions . . . a different
human type came upon the scene, and, it would seem, exterminated *Homo neanderthalensis.*" In a footnote he agrees
with Professor Osborn that Neanderthal Man is an extinct
species—a species which "did not interbreed with the true
men."[6]

Golding took only what he wanted from the passage. First,
he inverted the geological event. It was not when the age
softened and grew warmer that Mal, the leader, brought the
People to the Mountain, for the age is growing colder—either
the People migrated too early in the season or the glacier is
descending instead of receding. Golding is deliberately ambiguous. Mal is old and knows he is about to die; thus he
started the migration from the seashore earlier in the year
than usual; the Ice Women have not melted when the People
arrive at the Overhang. But, has he not run a risk of starving
the tribe? What has become of his instinct to preserve the
race? Then, in terms of plot, what need is there for a confrontation with the New Men? Or has the glacial season somehow
changed? If so, the axiom the People live by—"Today is like
yesterday and tomorrow"—is no longer true.[7] Conditions are
changing and the People are changing too. The point may be
very important to the story. But whatever the explanation,
the reader is faced with an inability of his logic to sort out and
interpret events.

Fa's emotions present us with another ambiguity. During
the story all of the People are exterminated except the baby,
and by implication the race becomes extinct. Both primeval
fear of extinction and inversion of man's sexual desire to per-
petuate himself appear in those passages where Fa attempts
to persuade Lok to recapture the baby (the New One) from
the New Men. The baby, however, is Nil's, probably fathered
by Ha. Fa herself, despite maternal instincts, is unable to

bear children, and in any case, "She was not a woman to lie
with. Something of the Old Woman was invisibly present in
the air around her head" (p. 27). The New Men have also
kidnapped Liku, Lok's daughter by Nil, and there Lok exhibits both a paternal feeling in his wish to recapture the child
and a desire to preserve the race. Some critics have made
much of the communal, family relationship of the People,
using Lok's feelings towards Liku for illustration. I suggest
Golding is mostly concerned here with sorting out basic instincts.

Fa is interested only in recovery of the baby. She cares
nothing about Liku, though the reasons for her feelings are
obscure. Perhaps she is jealous of the child her mate fathered
upon Nil, but certainly we should not jump to that conclusion.
It may be she is protecting Lok's feelings, for she knows, as
Lok does not, that the New Men ate Liku. The People are like
the Men, but they are also in mysterious ways different from
them. The reader cannot afford to forget that it is the Men,
not the People, who are his forebears, whose emotional patterns are predecessors of his own. It may be possible to sort
out all the ambiguities in the tale into an inexorable logic, but
for the moment it is enough to note that Golding leaves the
baby alive in the hands of the Men. Perhaps he found himself
in less than full agreement with Wells's footnote and wished
to leave a remote possibility for interbreeding between the
races.

There is reason for doing so in Golding's story, for as we
discover how the People live and communicate we recognize
echoes from our own past. True, we are the inheritors from
the fierce New Men, but there is also a corner of us that descends from the People. At the point Golding is examining
them they are largely incapable of reason, though they are in
process of discovering the intellectual tools necessary to reason. No doubt had they been left unmolested on Golding's
earth they, too, would in time have learned to reason, for

today is not really like yesterday and tomorrow—excepting cosmic accident for which the People already allowed.

The People communicate partly by sharing mental pictures. They have extrasensory perception to complement keen sense perception, more animal than ours and more accurate. One way of looking at their perceptions is to consider our own (or those of the New Men) as dulled or inverted versions of the perceptual ability of the People. Thus in the beginning senses were well enough developed to permit Lok and Fa to follow spoors, like dogs, as well as to communicate in pictures shared from one mind to another. Both skills have been lost, but Golding is trading on our faith in extrasensory perception as he presents his primitive epistemology. Thus, symbolically the roots of our nonrational ways of knowing and communicating may rest with this New One, the baby fathered by Lok and kidnapped to be fed at the breast of Vivani, the central female figure among the New Men.

Other inversions of technique (surely in Golding related to Aristotle's doctrine of reversal and discovery), once recognized, may deepen our understanding of the story, for *The Inheritors* is a moral fable, telling us not only something of our ancestry but something as well about how we should behave. As Kinkead-Weekes and Gregor put it, the novel "is an adventure, and we are the Inheritors."[8]

Some of Golding's inversions of ordinary material are ironic. Sometimes his irony is accomplished by forcing the mind of the reader into recognizable patterns, even formulaic expressions (another debt from the Greeks?). The process is rhetorical. For example, the People are meek while their conquerors are fierce. By an enthymemelike process we are led to see the statement "The meek shall inherit the earth" as an inversion of the hard truth.

Golding conditions the minds of his readers by reference to their religious background (as perhaps Aeschylus and Sophocles did by calling upon Homer and the myths), but with Golding this technique is more than a matter of biblical reference. Not only has he the Bible to assist him but classical and modern literature as well. In this respect, though details differ, he is employing a technique used by Spenser, Shakespeare, Milton and many other poets. Here the problem for Golding was to transfer a pre-Christian story into ethical terms related to Christianity. Compare, for example, Shakespeare in *Antony and Cleopatra*, where the problem is similar: a pre-Christian story has to be related in ethical terms understandable to a Christian audience. So successful was Shakespeare that he managed to convince many readers (and not a few critics) that Enobarbus, who plays a Judas role in the play, hanged himself though actually he died of a broken heart.

The religion of the People in *The Inheritors* is matriarchal, the government patriarchal. Mal is the political leader, the decision maker, but the Old Woman is the spiritual leader. Mal explains their religion in his account of their genesis: "There was the great Oa. She brought forth the earth from her belly. She gave suck. The earth brought forth woman and the woman brought forth the first man out of her belly" (p. 35). So Golding presents an inversion of God-the-Father–oriented Christianity. He may be more original than he at first seems, for his account in its simplicity almost appears to antedate early vegetation myths found in antiquity or reworked by such modern writers as Joyce or Beckett. Golding seems to speculate on the root of myths and imply that before the beginning of the race (*Homo sapiens*) God existed. Oa is a feminine synonym for God, and the whole recitation bears primitive relations to other genesis stories.

In any matriarchal religion there is an inversion of our preconceptions, but Golding does not concern himself much with this twist of thought. Under the primitive conditions he described, the importance of transferring the racial line through the female was paramount. There may, however, be another inversion in the mysterious word he selected for deity, Oa. God has many names. On thousands of Christian altars he is described as the beginning and the end, Alpha and Omega, and the name Golding chose for the deity of the People is a reversal of those initials, in keeping with the way the author has manipulated our attention throughout the story. (This ability to force readers through partial recognition of formulaic terms has so far, I believe, gone unnoted.)[9] Oa is the end and the beginning: the Omega and the Alpha.

It is not possible to be certain that Golding did this deliberately, but it is appropriate to his conception of the People, who have no clear idea of causality nor much conception of time. To them Alpha-Omega and Omega-Alpha would amount to the same thing, though their innocence is drawing to a close. Even had there been no confrontation with the New Men, the People would soon have begun some sort of primitive reasoning, and, Golding implies, their keenly developed sense perceptions and extrasensory powers would have declined.

These implications are vague, but the fact is explicit. Near the end of the novel Lok discovers *like*—that is, the process of analogy (though as the most innocent or childlike member of the tribe he is unable to employ it very far). Fa can already make simple causal connections. For Lok the poisoned arrow shot by the Men is just another flying twig, but Fa knows better. If this brief summary were completely accurate we might draw several conclusions, but again the ideas Golding presents are clothed in ambiguity, arising from the nature of the style and the immensity of the task he has set himself. Lok had already begun to rationalize early in the book in the passage concerning doe's meat (or perhaps that was an example of specious reasoning).

The apparent contradiction concerning the doe's meat could also have arisen from Wells. In *The Outline of History* he wrote, "Primeval man would not be particular about hav-

ing his food overfresh. He would constantly find it in a dead
state . . . an unpleasant odor would not be objected to; it is
not objected to now in many continental hotels" (pp. 62–63).
Golding ignored Wells's joke, but made much of the idea of
primitive man partaking of meat he found. Our logic infers
that before man had tools to kill he must have developed a
taste for meat. Thus, he must have found meat dead from one
cause or another. This idea is a rationalization without evidence to support it: indeed, prehistoric man might have developed a taste for meat from eating small creatures he slew
with his bare hands. Our ideas on such matters (and Wells's)
are bound by centuries of preconceptions unknown to primitive man and seem logical only to us. In any case, Lok and Fa
find a dead doe and provide Golding with material for religious speculation. It is permissible for them to eat meat for
sustenance when they are not guilty of killing, but a sense of
shame and foreboding lingers. The passage, involving still
another inversion—for surely a sense of the forbidden must
have arisen fairly late in primitive man, after a rudimentary
social structure had been accepted—is one of the most impressive in the novel (and central to the exegesis of many critics).

As Lok and Fa tear into the doe, driven by hunger and a
primitive instinct for survival, their animal nature takes prec-
edence over their social (or spiritual) nature. At this point Lok
rationalizes. The meat is not really for them, even though
they devour it as they dismember the animal. It is for Mal, the
patriarch, who is ill. This is a complicated, sophisticated rationalization, seeming at first far beyond the ability of the
characters. But viewed in terms of the Wells passage, the
complications are eased. Wells suggested that primitive man
may also have been cannibalistic: "If driven by hunger and
hard pressed, he would perhaps sometimes eat his compan-
ions or unhealthy children" (p. 63). Again Golding has inverted the source. Lok and Fa would never have slain the

doe; they would have starved first. Nor would they ever slay another hominoid, though the New Men would not hesitate to do so. The People are natural vegetarians with a keenly developed sense of religious values. If they do not live in a Garden of Eden (Golding again drives us to the formula), they do occupy a state of prelapsarian innocence. They live without Original Sin, and there lies the basic difference between the People and the Men. Golding is treating Wells's conceptions about progress ironically.

It was, I think, to make this point that he decided to treat sexual relations as he did. In the story the People consist of three loosely formed couples and two children: Mal, the patriarch, and the Old Woman; Ha and Nil; Lok and Fa; the maiden Liku and the new baby. Liku is the child of Lok and Nil, for the People have no sense of sexual constancy. What urges they feel, they express shamelessly. Kinkead-Weekes and Gregor emphasize the communal aspects of this society while ignoring literary and aesthetic reasons for such communality. These relationships help prepare the reader for Fa's interest in saving the new baby, but not Liku. Her feelings about Liku appear to be motivated by ordinary jealousy when we translate them into modern terms (which Golding does not quite permit). He is not presenting his Neanderthals as wife swappers nor recommending inconstancy; we need to seek deeper for an explanation of the sexual communality in the novel. Golding might have used his People to formulate an attack on the institution of marriage had he wished, but there is no hint in the novel that the communality of sexual activity conceals any criticism of modern institutions. It was necessary to his task to separate Original Sin from sexual activity— hence another inversion, a sort of free sexuality with no social onus. The People are free of Original Sin; the Men are not. There is simply neither sin nor crime in the world the People inhabit.

The People are treated here in a fashion analogous to the

treatment of the children in *Lord of the Flies*. There also Golding deals with the Fall, separating it from sexual practice by making all the actors children under the age of puberty. In that portrait, Original Sin is nevertheless present. In *The Inheritors* he inverts the subject, pushing the moral frontiers back into prehistory; in neither book is there any moral treatment of sexual conduct. That must wait for *Free Fall*.

It is difficult to conceive from the novels how Golding presumes depravity arose. He does not subscribe to orthodox explanations. In *The Inheritors* the reader is permitted to speculate on the subject only after more than half the book is finished, for Golding keeps back the confrontation between the People and the Men until the reader has learned to experience in his own imagination the perceptions of the People. As they are largely incapable of reason, it may be tempting for some readers to explain depravity in terms of the development of rationality.[10] Perhaps that is a fair conclusion to draw from what Golding presents, but it is a connection he never makes.

He does not imply that reason brought about sin but rather that the two arose mysteriously at about the same time. The People are innocent, though the Fall is always symbolically in the background. They have come from the seashore to the mountain to live in the shadow and sound of a waterfall. The Men are already depraved when smoke on the horizon makes their presence known in this strange glacial world. The People think only in primitive fashion, and the apparatus they use—visualization in pictures—is based on memory. Only rarely does it seem to contain some prescience. Men on the other hand are engineers, capable of harnessing causality. They can build stockades, travel by canoe, take preventive measures—in their primitive fashion do most of the things modern man does. But if reason were responsible for their depravity, would not Lok's early struggles have doomed him at once? Again Golding has inverted a commonplace, that

man is a rational animal, with all that implies. He even
suggests that reason may in some natural way accompany depravity.

His source may once more be *The Outline of History:*
"Man at that time was not a *degraded* animal, for he had
never been higher; he was therefore an exalted animal, and,
low as we esteem him now, he yet represented the highest
stage of development of the animal kingdom of his time."[11]
Thus when *Homo neanderthalensis* appears in the novel in a
highly developed moral state compared to *Homo sapiens*, this
involves an inversion of the ordinary way of looking at evolutionary progress. Golding, however, was not indulging in sentimental primitivism. How then are we to explain the moral
superiority of People over Men? The question is not an easy
one, but it is central to our interpretation.

There is of course a serious way of being interested in the
primitive without being sentimental. Anthropologists exhibit
this kind of interest, and certain critics have made a good deal
of Golding's supposedly impeccable anthropology. But the
book is not a treatise on anthropology or religion. It is after all
a novel, and its roots are literary. Graham Greene suggests
something of the same view of primitive man in *Journey
without Maps*, where he tried to explain his dissatisfaction
with the seediness of modern life by saying that at some point
in prehistory man may have taken a wrong turning. He explained his journey into the Heart of Darkness as a quest for
the turning point. But Greene was no more successful than
Malinowski in his study of the Trobriand islanders, for the
anthropological approach to such matters has serious short-
comings. No matter how primitive the living examples, they
are never primitive enough. In *Heart of Darkness* Conrad
evaded this issue by concentrating on Europeans (but Golding
has claimed he never read Conrad's book). Perhaps he has
never read Aldous Huxley's *The Devils of Loudun* either, but
one can go a long way towards explaining his view of the Peo-

ple through some of the treatiselike passages in Huxley: "We
are born with Original Sin; but we are also born with Original
Virtue—with a capacity for grace . . . a 'spark,' a 'fine point of
the soul,' a fragment of unfallen consciousness, surviving from
the state of primal innocence and technically known as *syn-
teresis.*"[12] It would seem, then, that a literary milieu may
have interested Golding rather than an anthropological one, a
milieu which deals imaginatively with philosophic-theological
questions under a thin skin of science largely borrowed from a
few quotations from *The Outline of History.*

The Inheritors might have turned into something quite
different, a vehicle, for instance, for satirizing modern conceptions of progress, but Golding shows no interest in that
subject. Instead he seems to say that innocence is generally
doomed because of Original Sin, though a spark of Original
Virtue remains (the baby saved by the kidnappers) as an outside possibility. The inheritors are ourselves, who have inherited the worst qualities of the Men, though there is something
in us left over from the bygone age of the People. And there
are enough hints in the book to permit some readers to believe that Golding does imply man has made some progress in
his struggle upward from the Fall. The book tends to conceal
this view because it deals with a major evolutionary event, the
passing of one species and the emergence of another.

Deeply involved in the course of evolution is man's growing degradation. At every turn we are faced with an anomaly.
As his engineering knowledge develops, man loses powers of
sense perception. He can no longer turn his ears to isolate a
sound (as dogs still do). As speech develops, verbalization begets further verbalization. Lok can verbalize to some extent,
and the New Men are birdlike in their conversations. But
speech, the handmaiden of reason, begets violence and evil.
The New Men indulge in orgies, and their religion (symbolized by the drawing of a stag upon the earth—Golding has
ignored Neanderthal drawings on cave walls) is a perversion

of the simple religion of the People. They do not worship Oa nor are they in touch with the eternal; instead they construct graven images.

At first the reader (who may not have read the late Huxley) feels himself in unfamiliar territory. Can Golding's view of rational man be that of one who despises his fellow creatures? Should we consider him akin to Swift? The problem in understanding the novel lies, I believe, in its remoteness from a familiar milieu, an ordinary frame of reference. Golding does not find rationality abhorrent. True, he loves the People (as Christians are told to love virtue) and despises the New Men, who stand for the savagery that is part of our inheritance. But Golding does not find the modern condition hopeless. [13]

A frame of reference for the novel may be constructed from such writers as Conrad, Greene, and Huxley—whether Golding has read them or not. The philosophical questions he deals with are those forced upon us by the modern condition. A kind of theological-scientific frame may be found in the work of Teilhard de Chardin in his teleological explanation of evolution in the universe (and perhaps in his view of special creation). Man arose, Teilhard argues, not in a direct evolutionary line but through several modes of hominization (the existentialist might call them *sautes*). On his phylogenetic tree the prehominoids constitute one evolutionary thrust in a predetermined pattern, the Neanderthals another, and *Homo sapiens* the final version in a teleological universe in which reason is the highest evolutionary development, though Teilhard was no more misled by false reason than Golding. And Teilhard clearly suggests that Neanderthal Man existed into the era of *Homo sapiens*—on grounds much firmer than Wells had and equally pertinent to Golding's myth.

No one can be sure that the species ever met. For Wells's speculation there is no evidence at all. Neanderthal Man may simply have starved to death or been unable to adapt to changes in his environment. Or he may have been destroyed through cosmic accident (plague perhaps). But the possibility provides the narrative event that attracted Golding, and the idea (as Teilhard suggests) that it was all part of the divine scheme saves Golding from cynicism.

Had an encounter really occurred the New Men might have proved superior in ways other than reason. We tend to equate intelligence with superiority of every kind, but in truth, as Golding says, moral or spiritual superiority is some-times the province of very simple creatures, even in our own day. In Golding's fable modern man has lost many desirable characteristics. Teilhard, thinking along similar lines, sug-gests in reverse much the same thing. The late Neanderthals, he says, may have been a "progressive branch, sleeping, one might say, waiting for the coming dawn."[14]

Such a view may be of help in understanding Golding's tragic myth. Original Sin was a terrible price to pay, but, though Golding does not say so, it is necessary for salvation. Thus in the last chapter Golding turns his attention to the New Men, after the Neanderthals have returned to the belly of Oa, whence they emerged. Golding describes the end of Neanderthal Man: "The creature wrestled with a rock that was lying on a mound of earth but was too weak to move it. At last it gave up and crawled round the hollow by the remains of a fire. . . . It made no noise, but seemed to be growing into the earth, drawing the soft flesh of its body into contact so close that the movements of pulse and breathing were inhib-ited" (p. 221). Golding brought his strange creatures full cir-cle before switching his attention—and again we are re-minded of a formulaic phrase, this time from the burial ser-vice: earth to earth, ashes to ashes, dust to dust!

A few other points are pertinent. Baker, writing of *Lord of the Flies*, though in a statement that could as well apply to *The Inheritors*, makes a good deal of Golding's debt to Euripides' *The Bacchae*. The play's purpose, as he interprets

Euripides, was "to trace the defects of society back to the defects of human nature."[15] Whether that was Euripides' purpose is not the question, for it was certainly Golding's, nor can one question the influence classical drama had on the writer. But Golding is not rehashing a classical theme. He is directly involved with modern philosophical and theological concerns, and though his means differ from those of most writers he may be related to a frame of reference that is important in modern literature. (Iris Murdoch's repeated references to the Pelagian heresy are another way of examining the same questions.)

The irony of the title *The Inheritors* helps explain the structure of the work (that is, the shift in the last portion to the New Men). It is not the savages who are inheritors from the age of innocence, but rather we ourselves who inherit many of the worst characteristics of the savages. It is this introspection that moves the novel out of the realm of science fiction and into that of moral speculation. Golding destroys preconceptions and calls into question many current ideas. *The Inheritors*, then, is a book with serious significance, a tragedy constructed not to make cynics of its readers but with an Aristotelian purpose—to purge emotions and in subtle ways alter character and conduct. One might claim it is an exercise in catharsis (much needed in the aftermath of World War II).

---

1. Kermode, "The Meaning of It all," *Books and Bookmen*, 5 (October 1959), 9–10; Baker, *William Golding: A Critical Study* (New York: St. Martin's, 1965), 22.

2. Mark Kinkead-Weekes and Ian Gregor, *William Golding: A Critical Study* (New York: Harcourt, 1968), 91.

3. Peter Green, "The World of William Golding," *Review of English Literature*, 1 (1960), 62–72.

4. GOLDING: "We know *very little* of the appearance of the Neanderthal man. . . ."; WELLS: "We know *nothing*. . . ." (italics mine).

5. Jack I. Biles, *Talk: Conversations with William Golding* (New York: Harcourt, 1970), 106–7.

6. *The Outline of History* (New York: Macmillan, 1921), 65.

7. *The Inheritors* (London: Faber, 1955), 46.

8. *William Golding*, 74.

9. Baker makes much of the influence of the Greeks on Golding, particularly Euripides' *The Bacchae* on *Lord of the Flies*, but Golding's dependence on formulaic recognition seems much more closely related to Homer than to any of the dramatists.

10. For Golding's remarks on the topic, see Biles, *Talk*, 109–11.

11. Wells, *Outline*, 62. It is sometimes difficult to tell exactly whom Wells is quoting: this passage seems to be from Worthing Smith, *Man the Primeval Savage*.

12. *The Devils of Loudun* (New York: Harper, 1971), 98.

13. During an NBC "Today" program interview in November 1963, Hugh Downs asked Golding, "Is there any hope for any of us?" Golding replied that civilization is "not in the least bit hopeless," else we wouldn't continually ask questions about hopelessness.

14. Pierre Teilhard de Chardin, *The Phenomenon of Man*, trans. Bernard Wall (London: Collins, 1959), 198.

15. Baker, *William Golding*, 7. In the quoted phrase, Baker uses a Golding statement about *Lord of the Flies*.

Arnold Johnston

THE MISCASTING OF
PINCHER MARTIN

WITH *Pincher Martin* (1956), Golding attempted to clarify his philosophical position, which critics of his first two novels had found either patently obvious or willfully obscure. Critics also had suggested that Golding's approach was eccentric and looked askance at what seemed to them elements of science-fiction.[1] Hoping that *Pincher Martin* would answer such charges, Golding saw the book as "a blow on behalf of the ordinary universe," written "so vividly and so accurately and with such an exact programme that nobody can possibly mistake what I mean."[2]

Pincher Martin redefines several aspects of Golding's philosophy and makes concessions to critics of his unorthodox methods. The novel is also a defense of Golding's vision and an assertion of his artistic integrity, which perhaps explains why *Pincher Martin* drew more critical fire than *Lord of the Flies* or *The Inheritors*.

The plot is simple: Christopher Hadley Martin, an officer in the Royal Navy, is marooned on a tiny island in mid-Atlantic when his ship is torpedoed; the novel deals with his struggle to survive until rescue comes. Though retaining the survival theme, *Pincher Martin* differs from its predecessors, particularly in its individual focus. Both *Lord of the Flies* and *The Inheritors*, while concerned with individuals, work largely through group dynamics and interactions, with each novel's basic actions and themes developing from the juxtaposition of opposing groups. As Kinkead-Weekes and Gregor observe, *Pincher Martin* "is the first Golding novel to bear for its title the name of an individual . . . the first to have an adult, contemporary protagonist, drawn at length, and concerned . . . with sexual and social relationships in a modern world."[3]

Thus the novel emerges as an amalgam of elements common to Golding's previous novels and also seems responsive to the charge that his fictional world is removed from contemporary reality: here are the isolation, desperate struggle for existence, brilliant description, and moral intensity of the earlier books; yet here too, in flashbacks, are contemporary society and a typical protagonist.

The initially harsh response to *Pincher Martin* focused, however, on another familiar Golding touch: the novel's final few pages make clear—in a startling turnabout—that Martin's ordeal occurs *after* his death, thus demanding that it be treated as a metaphysical experience rather than a physical one. Reviewers assailed the conclusion as another Golding gimmick, recalling Ambrose Bierce's "An Occurrence at Owl Creek Bridge."[4] Although later commentators recognized the unifying role of the ending, those early reactions add an instructive dimension to consideration of the book. But perhaps the best way to demonstrate the significance of the ending— and the confusion of the early critics—is to look first at the ways Christopher Martin confuses and miscasts himself in the drama of his life and death.

In his first two novels Golding examined the essential proposition that man's rational, creative powers may be applied with devastating effect to ways of avoiding, as well as of pursuing, truth. In *Lord of the Flies* Golding deals with the

consequences of that proposition, showing the destruction
that may be unleashed when man turns from his own nature.
In *The Inheritors* the proposition is examined in more detail,
comprehending not only consequences, but also first causes,
culminating in the moment when Tuami recognizes that the
potential for creation and destruction lives within man, and
implying that the urge to survive is supported by an intellect
that may delude as well as save. *Pincher Martin* is an exhaus-
tive demonstration of the original proposition, illustrating the
delusive and egotistical length to which man's creative powers
may take him in the name of survival.

Pincher Martin begins abruptly, with the chaotic perceptions of a drowning man: "He was struggling in every direction, he was the centre of the writhing and kicking knot of his
own body. There was no up or down, no light and no air. He
felt his mouth open of itself and the shrieked word burst out.
'Help!' "[5]

There is no help. But the reader is plunged at once into
Martin's desperate fight against death. The first calming note
in this frantic scene is Martin's formation of a lucid image, an
analogy for survival (pp. 8–9). As Biles and Kropf point out,
this image of a Cartesian diver in a jam jar, which reminds
Martin of his lifebelt, is at the heart of the novel's theme.[6]
Like Descartes, Martin takes for his guiding principle the
phrase "Cogito, ergo sum" and attempts to create "a little
world . . . quite separate but which one could control."

The battle lines are drawn between Martin and the universe. As he declares later: "I don't claim to be a hero. But
I've got health and education and intelligence. I'll beat you"
(p. 77). The situation is archetypal, and when Martin chooses
as the stage for his drama a barren rock, the Promethean
image suggests the metaphysical dimensions that develop in
the novel.

The words *stage* and *drama* are appropriate here. As one
learns in the final chapter, Martin's rock is a construction of

his mind, the part that "was so nakedly the centre of every-thing that it could not even examine itself" (p. 45). The "centre," using the raw materials of recollection, creates the rock out of "the memory of an aching tooth" and tries to sur-round Martin with a world that will shut out the reality of death. The theater for this play is the *globe* of Martin's skull (one may assume that the word, used frequently, is indeed a pun). Bufkin, in "*Pincher Martin:* William Golding's Morality Play," shows how theatrical terms pervade the novel and how Martin, whose peacetime profession was acting, continually casts himself in dramatic roles.[7] But both as actor and as sur-vivor, he is subject to external pressures.

In a crucial flashback to his acting career, Martin, cast as a shepherd in a morality play, is forced to double as one of the Seven Deadly Sins. Pete, the producer, whom Martin is cuckolding, is delighted by the actor's discomfort. As they walk downstairs to the costumer's workroom, or crypt, to choose Martin's second role, Pete remarks to the director, "Curious feeling to the feet this carpet over stone, George. Something thick and costly, just allowing your senses to feel the basic stuff beneath," immediately after which he gestures at the costumes: "There they are, Chris, all in a row. What about it?" Though Chris tries to pick a part irrelevant to his personality, Pete assigns him the role of Greed—"Darling, it's simply *you!*" (p. 119)—and introduces him to the mask he will wear: "This painted bastard here takes anything he can lay his hands on. . . . He takes the best part, the best seat, the most money, the best notice, the best woman. He was born with his mouth and his flies open and both hands out to grab. He's a cosmic case of the bugger who gets his penny and someone else's bun" (p. 120). The point is clear: in the cos-tumer's crypt Martin's producer strips him to "the basic stuff beneath," just as God will do at the moment of death.

This scene introduces a symbolic pattern. Pete, the pro-ducer, identified here both with God and with imminent death, appears throughout the novel in scenes analogous to Martin's "present" on the rock. In these fragments Martin the actor attempts to evade the roles that suit him and to usurp those that match his ambitions. His refusal to accept death is merely the culmination of a long process.

Bufkin points out that "Martin's particular vice—greed— stems, as does all sin, from the original sin of pride, *super- bia*."[8] And Martin's solitary defiance of death, of God's will, certainly argues pride. But the mask of Greed fits him best. Pictured in flashbacks as a man whose pride is manifest in small-minded grasping, Martin is far removed from the tragic hero that he plays on his rocky stage. Golding has said of Martin: "He's fallen more than most. In fact I went out of my way to damn Pincher as much as I could by making him the nastiest type I could think of, and I was very interested to see how critics all over the place said, 'Well, yes, we are like that.' "[9] Well acquainted with the heroes of the Greek trage- dians, Golding is striving for something different. Try as he may to usurp the role, Martin is no more Everyman in Gold- ing's morality play than in Pete's.

The most to be said for Martin as an actor, with his smooth looks, is that he is his company's "best bloody juvenile"— hardly an image adequate to tragic heroism. Chris hears and sees the tragic hero only obliquely, whether from the wings or onstage; thus, his concept of such a role is disjointed and frag- mentary. An actor, already at one remove from the creative process, Martin tries to seize not only the role of tragic hero, but also of playwright, of creator himself. Indeed, Martin challenges perhaps the greatest human creator-actor of all, Shakespeare—from his first echo of that other doomed usurper, Hotspur (p. 80), to his last despairing pose as the mad Lear (p. 197). The result is parody—Martin is both par- odic hero and parodic creator.

Martin's efforts to sustain the dual role of hero and creator are underlined—and diminished—by parallels to religion,

myth, and literature. Kinkead-Weekes and Gregor show that
Martin's sojourn on the rock is an ironic parallel to the Bible's
seven days of creation, during which Martin tries to stave off
the nothingness of death by manufacturing his own world,
first creating light and air, then the rock, to the moment when
he "creates" God in his own image.[10] First, submerging the
dangerous admission of competition with God, Martin sees
himself as a latter-day Crusoe, surveying his estate, listing
methodically the requisites for survival, and generally "netting down this rock with names and taming it" (p. 86).[11] But
the world of Crusoe is too prosaic and substantial to remain
related for long to Martin's illusionary island. He is forced to
switch to simpler roles, less dependent on the order of the
natural world, but roles which by their archetypal nature
bring him closer to an admission of his plight.

Thus, though his identity is precious above all else, Martin
at last succumbs to professional habit and invokes the classical
names that have been implicit in his Promethean setting. He
does so, however, only when his self-created world begins to
crumble, as a means of bracing himself for the final frenzied
effort to survive:

> "I am Atlas. I am Prometheus."
> He felt himself loom gigantic on the rock. His jaws
> clenched, his chin sank. He became a hero for whom the im-
> possible was an achievement. [p. 164]

His self-administered enema becomes a piece of theater, accompanied by background music—"snatches of Tchaikovsky,
Wagner, Holst" (p. 164). Such theatricality emphasizes how
far the imagined scene is removed from both physical reality
and the heroic dimensions of myth.

Here a similarity suggests itself between Martin and Jack
Merridew, another parodic Prometheus, who steals fire (in
the form of spectacles) from Piggy, a parodic Zeus. Piggy and

Pete correspond to modern notions of a supreme being, weakened by rationalism and susceptible to cynical manipulation; but the true God, who comprehends the world's darkness, bides his time until the final reckoning.

As his illusion suffers further breakdowns, Martin changes roles more often, frantically switching back and forth among the Shakespearean, the Miltonic, and the classical. When he decides on madness as an explanation of his inadequacy as a creator, he thinks, "There was still a part that could be played—there was the Bedlamite, Poor Tom" (pp. 177–78). Martin's decision to adopt the disguised Edgar's role from *Lear* is doubly ironic: first, as a tacit admission that his madness is feigned; second, as a parody of Edgar's attempt to escape the injustice of his father. Furthermore, if Martin resembles any character from *Lear*, it is the bastard Edmund, who, like Martin, bears allegiance to a damning creed of egotism and unchecked impulse: "Thou, Nature, art my goddess; to thy law / My services are bound" (1. 2. 1–2). And like Edmund, Martin attempts to influence destiny through other men's wives. In the scene that follows, Martin, confusing his producer with the powerful God he now faces, attempts to sway this Pete-God as he has done in life, through Helen (totemized in a pile of rocks): "I wouldn't ask anyone but you because the rock is fixed and if he'll only let it alone it'll last forever. After all, my sweet, you're his wife" (p. 178). But in this scene—which parodies, too, the Miltonic temptation of Eve—Martin's concept of roles is hopelessly confused. And this Eve refuses to yield, as Helen had refused to intercede with Pete in Martin's efforts to avoid service in the war.

Martin's next choice of parts is Lear himself—"Now I am thin and weak. . . . My eyes are dull stones" (p. 188; *Lear*, 3. 2. 18–19)—but his misquotation merely shows his unsuitability for the role, and the suggestion of weakness cannot be long tolerated by the "centre." So it is back to Prometheus:

"Hoé, Hoé! Thor's lightning challenges me! Flash after flash, rippling spurts of white fire, bolts flung at Prometheus, blinding white, white, white, searing, the aim of the sky at the man on the rock—" (pp. 188–89). And again, to the accompaniment of "storm music," he shouts, "Ajax! Prometheus!" (p. 192).

But the increasing incoherence of his illusion forces him back to the pose of insanity. This allows him to accept as hallucinatory the dialogue with God that follows, during which he acknowledges his attempt to usurp God's role as Creator: "On the sixth day he created God. Therefore I permit you to use nothing but my own vocabulary. In his own image created he Him." But God's voice is relentless, demanding that Martin consider the reality of his death. And when Martin responds, "I will not consider! I have created you and I can create my own heaven," God's reply spells final doom for Chris and his factitious universe: "You have created it" (p. 196).

Abruptly diminished from pretensions, however ironic, to the stature of Milton's Satan, Martin petulantly echoes Adam's "Did I request thee, Maker, from my clay, / To mould me man?" (*Paradise Lost*, 10. 743–44), demanding, "If I ate them [the people he has victimized in life], who gave me a mouth?" And like Milton's God, Golding's refuses to respond, merely saying, "There is no answer in your vocabulary" (p. 197).

Unlike Adam, Martin remains unregenerate, refusing to accept God's will. He returns in parody to the posture of mad Lear:

> *Rage, roar, spout!*
> *Let us have wind, rain, hail, gouts of blood,*
> *Storms and tornadoes . . .*
> . . . .
> *. . . hurricanes and typhoons. . . .* (p. 197; *Lear*, 3. 2. 1–6)

The profoundest irony in this misquotation is that the actual
speech ends:

> . . . And thou, all-shaking thunder,
> Strike flat the thick rotundity o' th' world,
> Crack Nature's moulds, all germens spill
>   at once,
> That make ingrateful man! (*Lear*, 3. 2. 6–9)

And carrying the speech to its conclusion, God strikes the
scenery from Martin's stage, reducing him, after a last, silent,
pseudo-Promethean cry—"I shit on your heaven!" (p. 200)—
to his final primeval role: he becomes a pair of huge lobster
claws, hopelessly clinging to life while God's all-destroying
black lightning advances, "playing over them, prying for a
weakness, wearing them away in a compassion that was timeless and without mercy" (p. 201).

But *Pincher Martin* does not end here. A chapter follows
in which Mr. Campbell, the discoverer of Martin's body, and
Captain Davidson, the naval officer who comes to claim it,
discuss inconclusively the significance of mortality. This chapter, in which Davidson notes that Martin "didn't even have
time to kick off his seaboots"—establishing beyond doubt the
postmortem nature of Martin's ordeal—provoked harsh, or
at least puzzled, response from early reviewers and critics.
Though time and judicious criticism have clarified the issue,
one's immediate reactions to the book are likely to be confused, and the source of confusion is worth examining.

Even a cursory rereading of the novel confronts one with
many clues to Martin's actual situation: his fear of sleep
(pp. 91–92); his sight of a red (hence, boiled) lobster swimming in the sea (p. 167); his realization that guano is insolu-
ble—hence, that rainwater cannot be held in his drinking-
pool by the soluble film of guano he has imagined (p. 174).
And perhaps most glaringly, his recognition of his illusion's

source: "His tongue was remembering. It pried into the gap
between the teeth and re-created the old, aching shape. It
touched the rough edge of the cliff, traced the slope down,
trench after aching trench, down towards the smooth surface
where the Red Lion was, just above the gum—understood
what was so hauntingly familiar and painful about an isolated
and decaying rock in the middle of the sea" (p. 174). One is
himself so concerned with survival, so afraid of death, that he
seizes at first, like Martin, on any explanation that will preserve the protagonist's life—or the *illusion of life*—ignoring
evidence to the contrary. Truth, in short, becomes abhorrent
in comparison to self-deception.

Martin's emulation of heroic roles thus serves to advance
through irony Golding's elaborated restatement of his view of
modern man's use and misuse of creativity. As technology
dominates science, pragmatism dominates modern thought.
Martin's illusion is doomed not merely by its falsehood, but
also because his creation is at second hand, using materials he
values only for utility. The modern mind, Golding seems to
say, has steadily refused to confront the darker side of experience, a side that ancient myth and religion confront squarely.
To fear death so much as to attempt to deny its significance is
to begin a process of delusion that sees a kind of death in
every denial of individual desire.

Many critics persist, however, in seeing Martin as a character who confounds his creator's intentions. Peter Green observes: "Pincher—like Milton's Satan—breaks away from his
creator's original intention. However despicable his character
. . . he nevertheless compels our admiring respect for his
epic, unyielding struggle in the face of overwhelming odds."[12]
Such readings of the novel lend force to Golding's point
about modern man. For, although the word *gimmick* can be
misleading in a discussion of Golding, in *Pincher Martin* his
traps are clearly out for the unwary reader. The desire to see

Martin as a heroic figure confirms Golding's view that we are concerned too much with survival and too little with the ethical problems it may pose.

This reading of the novel is further strengthened by an examination of Chris's saintly friend and rival, Nathaniel Walterson, who succeeds in winning Mary Lovell, a girl for whom Martin feels obsessive lust. Nathaniel, a mystic in the mold of Simon, concerns himself, as Chris does not, with the reality of death. Discussing the "technique of dying into heaven," Nat says, "Take us as we are now and heaven would be sheer negation. Without form and void. You see? A sort of black lightning destroying everything that we call life" (p. 70). And these images remain with Martin, becoming the beginning and end of his struggle on the rock.

Nathaniel is not merely mystic; he is prophet too, for he says to Chris, "—You could say that I know it is important for you personally to understand about heaven—about dying—because in only a few years—" (p. 71). And Chris, horrified at the implication "because in only a few years you will be dead," rejects Nat for a fool and comes to harbor a secret hatred of his friend, especially after Nat wins Mary Lovell. Ironically, Chris's last order from the bridge, seconds before the torpedo strikes, is intended to murder Nat, now his shipmate, by throwing him into the sea from his perch on a rail. The guilt Martin feels cannot be dispelled by his blustering rationalization: "And it was the right bloody order!" (p. 186).[13]

One may compare Nat to Simon in *Lord of the Flies* and to Tuami in *The Inheritors:* in each case Golding points out that the interpreter of truth—whether saint or artist—is often ignored, or misunderstood and maligned, if not actually murdered. Obviously, then, those who aspire to such status must take care in embodying and communicating their visions. Golding seems resolved to make his readers see truth through eyes other than their own—hence his experimentation with limited viewpoints, and especially his controversial endings. His creation of such characters as Simon, Tuami, and Nat shows his conviction that, bleak as man's condition may be, other possibilities exist.

In this respect one must deny, with Golding, Christopher Martin's universality: he represents an extreme position, as does Nat. But Nat's existence illuminates Golding's real point: not a condemnation of modern man, but rather a warning—to the Campbells and the Davidsons—to seek out and accept the truths of life and death, as the only way to avoid the egotistical excess that leads Martin to his tangled web of deceit and annihilation.

Golding builds the phantasmagoric structure of *Pincher Martin* with great skill, creating torturously precise images of a man under severe physical strain, while at the same time clearly recording the inexorable breakdown of a desperate illusion. To accomplish this he weaves together Martin's self-created present and the intrusive scenes of flashback and nightmare, as well as several complex symbolic motifs and a host of literary and mythical or religious allusions. It is by any standard a scintillating performance, made more admirable by the fact that its apparent confusion is underpinned by a rigorously logical foundation.

The flashback scenes, grounded in dialogue that illuminates Martin's character, may be seen as Golding's main concession to critics who assailed his eccentricity. Martin emerges from the contemporary milieu, possessing a profession, a circumstantial past, and an individual psychological makeup. But Golding makes sure that Martin's background and individuality are functional within the larger context of the novel. And though the book is concerned with modern man, the critics have hardly viewed Golding's concession as such.

And the point is debatable. Golding affords only sketchy glimpses of Martin's past, denying, as Kinkead-Weekes and

Gregor observe, "assumptions about 'character' and 'relationships' which we may tend to think of as . . . axiomatic for the novel" (p. 156). Furthermore, the startling conclusion of *Pincher Martin* seems to distinguish the book as an assertion of Golding's earlier methods, rather than as a concession to novelistic conventions. Nonetheless, a subtle shift in the direction of those conventions is apparent.

John Peter, comparing *Pincher Martin* with Golding's first two novels, describes it as "richer because exploratory, a configuration of symbols, rather than an allegory," concluding that "it will bear an intensity of attention that its predecessors could not sustain." Whether or not he might have quarreled with Peter's assessment, Golding described his next project as an attempt to show "the patternlessness of life before we impose our patterns on it."[14] The resulting work was his fourth novel, *Free Fall* (1959), his first full-fledged effort to write a social novel. Thus, one may see *Pincher Martin* as a transitional work, both an end and a beginning; and also, in John Peter's words, "as brilliant a conception as any fable in English prose."[15]

---

1. See Frederick R. Karl, *The Contemporary English Novel* (New York: Farrar, Straus and Cudahy, 1962), 259.

2. See Frank Kermode, "The Meaning of It All," *Books and Bookmen*, 5 (October 1959), 10.

3. Mark Kinkead-Weekes and Ian Gregor, *William Golding: A Critical Study* (London: Faber, 1967), 156.

4. See Karl, *Contemporary English Novel*, 258–59; James Gindin, *Postwar British Fiction: New Accents and Attitudes* (Berkeley: University of California Press, 1962), 201–2.

5. *The Two Deaths of Christopher Martin* (New York: Harcourt, 1957), 7; the title of this first American edition of *Pincher Martin* reflects the early critical confusion concerning Martin's death.

6. Jack I. Biles and Carl R. Kropf, "The Cleft Rock of Conversion: *Robinson Crusoe* and *Pincher Martin*," in "A William Golding Miscellany," *Studies in the Literary Imagination*, 2, no. 2 (October 1969), 27–28.

7. "A William Golding Miscellany," 5–16.

8. Ibid., 14–15.

9. Kermode, "The Meaning of It All," 10.

10. For a discussion of the parallel to the biblical creation see Kinkead-Weekes and Gregor, *William Golding*, 135–53.

11. Cp. *Robinson Crusoe* (New York: Washington Square Press, 1963), 45–46, 57–61.

12. Peter Green, "The World of William Golding," *Transactions and Proceedings of the Royal Society of Literature*, 32 (1963), 50.

13. James R. Baker, in *William Golding: A Critical Study* (New York: St. Martin's, 1965), 45–47, discusses this scene and shows that Martin's later dialogue with God need not be taken literally as evidence of Golding's Christian orthodoxy.

14. John Peter, "The Fables of William Golding," *Kenyon Review*, 19 (Autumn 1959), 591; remark in an unpublished interview with Owen Webster, as quoted by Baker, *William Golding*, 56.

15. "Fables of William Golding," 590.

Jay L. Halio

FREE FALL: GOLDING'S MODERN NOVEL

FREE FALL is a departure from the earlier Golding novels. The others are versions of *fable*, but *Free Fall* is a fiction, despite specific aspects of fable of which it partakes.[1] Owing something to Dante's *Vita Nuova*, the *Künstlerroman* (with comparisons to Joyce's *Portrait* and Lawrence's *Sons and Lovers*), the Gospel story of Christ's temptations, and Camus's *The Fall*, Golding's novel is yet very much its own thing.[2] It is Golding's first attempt to write a "modern" novel. It is a novel of discovery as well as communication, an effort to trace crucial events of Sammy Mountjoy's life to that moment when he lost his freedom. "For once, I was free. I had power to choose," Sammy insists at the outset, and we may take this as a donnée of the novel.[3] "When did I lose my freedom?" becomes a motivating force that propels him and the reader. But we are also propelled by a good deal more.

"How did I lose my freedom?" is a more important question and leads to the rationale Golding adopts for the form of this novel. Beginning to answer his questions, Sammy says: "I must go back and tell the story over. It is a curious story, not so much in the external events which are common enough,

but in the way it presents itself to me, the only teller" (p. 6).
The structure, therefore, is extremely important. Golding
wrote several drafts of the book, and it took longer to write
than his other novels. "It changed a lot," he has said. "I can't
remember how it changed, but it did. It was reorganized, and
things were thrown out and things put in."[4] As intriguing as it
would be to compare various drafts, scholars will have to wait
until they are available. Meanwhile, we have the novel as
published, and we know that *Free Fall* has a studied, deliberate form—a shape whose meaning is part of the meaning of
the novel.

A chronological narrative follows the introductory paragraphs, but after the first three chapters this sequence is interrupted. Other interruptions occur. "For time is not to be
laid out endlessly like a row of bricks," Sammy says. "Time is
two modes. The one is an effortless perception native to us as
water to the mackerel. The other is a memory, a sense of
shuffle fold and coil, of that day nearer than that because
more important . . . and out of the straight line altogether" (p.
6).

This second mode has affinities to Bergsonian duration, of
time felt as *intensive* experience rather than extensive event.
Other relations to Bergsonian concepts, such as the nature of
free will, become clear. For example, *Free Fall* traces the
process of Sammy's ideas and, as language, must resort to the
homogeneous, extensive mode of duration and its concomitant falsifications or distortions. Hence, Sammy's momentous
decision appears ultimately as a finite choice made in space
and time. But the strategy of the novel really points to a *process*, an evaluation. Despite the diagrams of choice that
Sammy lays out, diagrams that directly contrast with Bergson's analysis of free will, the reality appears otherwise.[5] The
matter is complicated by the retrospective search, "for the
psychic state, when it reaches the end of the *progress* which
constitutes its very existence, becomes a *thing*," as Bergson

says (p. 198). Things may then be described, but freedom—
"the relation of the concrete self to the act which it performs"
(p. 219)—is indefinable. Like the taste of potatoes, Sammy
says, free will "cannot be debated but only experienced" (p.
5). To define this experience becomes well-nigh impossible,
but within the recognized limitations and paradoxes of the
endeavor, Golding's achievements are considerable.

Another important principle of composition is selectivity.
"Living is like nothing because it is everything—is too subtle
and copious for unassisted thought. Painting is like a single
attitude, a selected thing" (p. 7). This is at once the strength
and weakness of art and its distinction from nature. Sammy's
story is thus an artificial construct. Its value will be measured
by both what it excludes and what it includes. Its unity is an
abstraction—events chosen and arranged in a meaningful sequence defying the incoherencies of daily living. It is more: it
is an effort to communicate, at least in part, the essence of
Sammy's being: "the unnameable, unfathomable and invisible
darkness that sits at the centre of him, always awake, always
different from what you believe it to be, always thinking and
feeling what you can never know it thinks and feels, that
hopes hopelessly to understand and to be understood" (p. 8).
This perplexity points to the fundamental paradox of Sammy's
enterprise: understanding and communication can never be
complete, but our humanity requires them nevertheless. That
some communication and understanding are possible removes
the endeavor from the realm of the absurd: "I may find the
indications of a pattern that will include me," Sammy remarks, "even if the outer edges tail off into ignorance" (p. 9).[6]

Sammy begins his story with his birth. This bastard son of
a warm, simple woman aptly describes her as "a creature"
who "shared pleasure round like a wet-nurse's teat, absorbed,
gustily laughing and sighing" (p. 15). He never knew his father, but in Ma's stories, his identity ranges from parson to
Prince of Wales. Living with Ma in a slum street in a provin-

cial town, Sammy "crawled and tumbled in the narrow world of Rotten Row, empty as a soap bubble but with a rainbow of colour and excitement" around him (p. 17). Existence was as innocent as it was dirty and free. Defined more in terms of function than in appearance, Ma's importance comes down to this: a *mater magna*, she is "the warm darkness between me and the cold light." Down the passage Sammy makes in time, she looms massive and real. "Beyond her there is nothing, nothing" (p. 15).

Sammy recalls events of this period not as "stretched-out time," but as sharply focused instants, not unlike Words-worth's "spots of time." A quarrel at their bog while playing boats in a gutter; the death of their lodger and Sammy's fren-zied dash to the "Sun" to fetch Ma; the arrest of the twins— these and stories told by Evie, the older girl who accom-panied him to school, stand out in Sammy's effort to find a pattern, though he knows full well "that all patterns have bro-ken one after another, that life is random and evil unpun-ished" (p. 25). Hence he refuses to be "literary," he says, and shape his story to neat but distorting emblems. Open inquiry, searching rather than shaping, characterizes this position. Nevertheless, a few pages later Sammy yields to aphorism. Contemplating the importance of Ma and Evie and his warm life with them, he concludes: "love selflessly and you cannot come to harm" (p. 33). Much of the rest of the novel deals with violation of this precept—or the consequences of love that exploits.

Evie eventually detaches herself from Sammy, and he goes unescorted to school. He recognizes that he became the inhabitant of "two linked worlds"—Rotten Row and school—both of which he enjoyed. (Only later, under the tutelage of his science and religion teachers, does Sammy recognize two other, unlinked worlds and tries to bridge them.) As he moves from childhood into boyhood, the second world expands. As in chapter 1, so in chapter 2—devoted to boyhood experience—two characters emerge from the pictures Sammy draws. The first is Johnny Spragg, an innocent whose love of airplanes is contagious (and for Johnny, in World War II, fatal). Sammy frequently accompanies Johnny to the airfield to watch the old DeHavilands. On one occasion they witness a crash and are chased. But more important is another adventure—sneaking into General Plank's garden on Paradise Hill. Being small boys of romantic imagination, they accept the rumor that the grounds harbor wild animals, a belief that heightens their sense of adventure and adds to Sammy's sense of primordial existence. Most significant is Sammy's vision of the garden just before they depart:

> Before we buried ourselves in undergrowth again, I turned to look back. . . . The moon was flowering. She had a kind of sanctuary of light round her, sapphire. All the garden was black and white. There was one tree between me and the lawns. . . . The trunk was huge and each branch splayed up to a given level; and there, the black leaves floated out like a level of oil on water. . . . Later, I should have called the tree a cedar and passed on, but then, it was an apocalypse. [pp. 45–46]

Does this vision mean a farewell to innocence, to Eden? Not quite, as subsequent chapters show. But the stillness and beauty Sammy finds here in nature will not be glimpsed the same way again. Replacing or surpassing them will be the compelling loveliness of the human form.

Although two paragraphs later Sammy repudiates any real identity with the boy in the garden or in Rotten Row—"he is not I. He is another person"—important connections remain. They are more than the sum of memories the older person carries with him. The apocalyptic vision of the tree connects with the visions Sammy later experiences in the prisoner of war camp after his release from solitary confinement, and more directly with his vision of the tree when, at the end of

the novel, he returns to the general's house, now a mental
hospital, to visit Beatrice, the girl he seduced and abandoned.
But at this early stage, these are not the connections Sammy
seeks; he is looking for "the beginning of responsibility, the
beginning of darkness, the point where I began" (p. 47). And
in the life of the ragged, innocent boy he sees no such beginnings. They are two different persons, he insists.

Philip Arnold, the other boyhood friend, is different from
Johnny. If Johnny is Sammy's good angel, a model of innocence and generosity, Philip is his evil one. One notices the
bilateral nature of Sammy's relationships.[7] This morality-play
aspect of the structure is significant, for a major theme is
Sammy's surrendering his free soul to sin. But Sammy's relationship with Philip is more complex and subtle; moreover, it
exercises another function in providing a negative pull that,
neutralizing Johnny's, keeps Sammy suspended between
forces and in this sense "free."

Nevertheless, Sammy maintains that none of his childhood relationships altered him as Philip did. He does not spell
out how he was changed but shows this in two episodes which
Philip instigates—stealing cigarette cards from smaller boys
and defiling the altar of a church. Although at the end of these
episodes Sammy says neither cost him his freedom nor points
to the beginning of responsibility and darkness, it seems clear
that what changes for Sammy is his experience of exploitation,
which he had gained not by exploiting but by being exploited.
Already at an early age Philip "knows about people"; he knew,
as later Dr. Halde knows (despite the disclaimer in the last
line of the book), how to use people to his own ends while
arranging the reverse impression for his victims. (It is hardly
ironic that afterwards Philip attains a high government position equal in eminence to Sammy's as a painter.) Later, when
Philip reappears as a young man whom Sammy takes to a
Communist party meeting, the same themes emerge: Philip
uses Sammy to gather information he wants—not of politics,

but of the *feeling* of what it's like at the branch meetings—
information that could be valuable in charting his future
career. Embedded in the first long chapter dealing with
Sammy's gradual seduction of Beatrice, his attempts to
"know" her as intimately as possible, this episode is part of
the "shuffle fold and coil" of time rather than the dead row of
bricks, of events that mirror each other affording material
light.

Desecrating the altar puts Sammy in the hospital, the result of a crack behind the ear by the verger. His experience
there is the subject of the brief third chapter. During this
"endless world of the ward"—a world which, like Rotten
Row, now conveys a sense of timelessness—Sammy's mother
dies, and the matron gives him a stamp album to distract him
from grief. The verger comes to visit and ask forgiveness, and
Sammy responds so far as he is able, for he can see little to
forgive. Yet this experience, like the whole experience of the
ward, characterized by compassion, prevents any stain of bit-
terness or guilt. It is not here that Sammy lost his freedom.
His innocence, like his unconsciousness of happiness, remains intact, epitomized by his vision of the little black girl in
the bed opposite his, speaking a language no one could understand, inspiring love from everyone, an image of pure joy that
remains unchanged in his recollection.

Sammy is adopted by Father Watts-Watt and goes to live
at the rectory. A new life begins; the old one ended with the
verger's blow. But he does not proceed directly to describe
life at the rectory; its place in the shuffle fold and coil comes
later (chapter 8). Still later (chapters 11 and 12) come Sammy's
experience at grammar school and the moment, he at last recognizes, when he surrendered his freedom. One reason for
the delay is that Sammy must first recount and reject the
events that would seem to explain his loss of freedom. More
important, he must relive the experiences that give him the
insight to see what he is and what he has done. The episodes

in the grammar school become meaningful not only in retro-
spect, but in a retrospective view that first includes the il-
luminations of Sammy's prison camp experience.[8] Finally,
the structure of climaxes dictates postponement of the most
crucial one to the last, even though in chapter 10 the perceptions that follow Sammy's release from solitary confinement
may provide the true apex. In terms of the stated quest, however, discovery of when and how Sammy lost his freedom is
the logical culmination of events, succeeded only by a de-
nouement.

The next three chapters, then, like the first three, form a
trilogy, this one on the theme of Sammy's seduction and
abandonment of Beatrice. He confesses at once that, as he
prepares to initiate his long seduction of her, he is "not
entirely free. Almost but not quite" (p. 79). Committed to his
course, he presumably has the freedom not to pursue it. (Intention, awareness, and action, as in Christian theology, are
all necessary for sin.)[9] His image is of a nineteen-year-old on a
bike waiting for a light to change so that he may cross a bridge
that leads to the part of London in which Beatrice lives.[10] A
victim of compulsion—and of a maddening jealousy of her
femininity, her education, her religious devotion, her friends,
and everything that may associate with her—Sammy is lost:
he crosses the bridge.

Despite his yearning "not to exploit but protect" (p. 85),
Sammy's involvement with Beatrice is exploitation. Like
Philip's use of Sammy, the exploitation is impelled by a relentless urge to know, to solve the mystery of her being. It is
flanked on one side of his experience by Philip's urge to resolve the mystery of the church through Sammy's desecration
and on the other by Dr. Halde's need to discover Sammy's
suspected secrets. What has happened is that Sammy has lost
the spontaneity of the soap bubble in exchange for this driving necessity to explore the sanctuary of Beatrice's nunlike
soul.[11] For Sammy, Beatrice is "the most mysterious and

beautiful thing in the universe" (p. 84). Like Chillingworth in
The Scarlet Letter, Sammy seeks to penetrate the inmost recesses of her heart. "I want you," he cries out, "I want all of
you . . . I want to be with you and in you and on you and
round you—I want fusion and identity—I want to understand
and be understood—oh God, Beatrice, Beatrice, I love
you—I want to be you!" (p. 105). After four years of this
fever, Sammy succeeds in bringing Beatrice to his bed, be-
lieving he will know her. But he is mistaken. Submissive,
yielding, obedient, she nevertheless is not there, not for him.
Desperately trying to elicit some genuine response, he de-
grades himself in further excesses: "What was to be a triumphant sharing, a fusion, the penetration of a secret, raising of
my life to the enigmatic and holy level of hers became a desperately shoddy and cruel attempt to force a response from
her somehow" (p. 123).

Sammy therefore begins to question the reality of his experiences of Beatrice: Was his agony self-created? Was she
after all what he thought she was? Was her transfigured beauty merely projected by his artist's eye? No; her reality, her
beatitude, is genuine. Even when Sammy tries to paint her
with some of the terror that he feels in response to his own
self-contempt, her picture eludes the "electric light-shades of
Guernica" he has introduced to convey it. Instead, there
emerges one looking "as though she had been blessed." Her
beatitude is real, but its source and significance Sammy cannot comprehend. Thus, after a party meeting (when he meets
Taffy—a dark beauty to contrast with Beatrice's light), he per-
suades himself that he is deluded about Beatrice and, aban-
doning her, marries Taffy. He disclaims responsibility for
these actions because, he says, he had already lost his power
to choose and "cannot be blamed for the mechanical and helpless reaction" of his nature (p. 131). He is vastly different from
carefree Johnny Spragg, whom he recalls vividly for "one perfect and definable instant," soaring up a hill on a motor-bike,

his head turned and one arm around the neck of the girl behind him he is kissing. Once again he will recall Johnny in juxtaposition to a recollection of Beatrice, and his "natural goodness and generosity" will help Sammy remember the light that shone out of her face, the "simple and loving and generous and humble" qualities that link her also with his remembered vision of the hospital ward. But not now, not here. That way of seeing still remains before Sammy.

Sammy credits Dr. Halde, the Gestapo psychologist, with helping him acquire the capacity to see "unusually far through a brick wall," the development of "a new mode of knowing." Chapters 7 to 10, including the intercalated chapter 8 on life at the rectory, trace the process that begins in the interrogation room of the prison camp with Halde's efforts to extract from Sammy the plan for a mass escape. Here, Sammy changes places with Beatrice as the object of mystery, a "mystery in you which is opaque to both of us," Halde says and he becomes the victim on the rack, tortured because of the other's wrong choice, or loss of freedom. Like Beatrice also, the heart of his mystery is an enigma—he both knows and does not know what Halde is after. Unable, therefore, as well as unwilling to reveal what he is not sure he knows, despite threats, pleas, and blandishments, Sammy is thrown blindfolded into a dark, narrow cell. There he is left to the stages of self-torment which Halde knows are inevitable.

But before that experience is examined, Sammy's narrative flashes back to his life with Father Watts-Watt and the question "How did I come to be so frightened of the dark?" For it is the fears that develop within him in his darkened cell that he at first associates with his lonely life at the rectory. But if he suspects that his fear derives from going to bed in a strange room where he is forbidden to turn on the light, or from his painful relationship with Father Watts-Watt, who suffers from persecution mania and repressed homosexual tendencies, he finally concludes he is wrong. The darkness he

fears is of another, interior sort. Events of chapter 8, however, showing the parson's ineffectual, awkward attempts to
know Sammy, serve to mirror Sammy's own attempts to know
Beatrice or Halde's to know Sammy.

In chapter 9 Sammy explores the nature of his dark confinement. He progresses simultaneously up the steps of torment beginning with the discovery of his basic situation and
proceeding to the mysterious substance at the center of his
cramped cell. But during this confinement and torment, or in
the immediate, apocalyptic aftermath, Sammy acquires a new
way of seeing and learns two important truths. The center is
indeed the secret, but it is the central core of his own being
that he discovers—projected in the cell as the torn genitals of
some imagined corpse suspended above him on a ceiling he
cannot reach, but later generalized as the creative tendency
of his own nature to produce "the most loathsome substances
that man knows of" (p. 190). Actually this analysis of his own
interior identity follows and is illuminated by his new perception of the world "in all its glory." He acquires this vision after
his release from the cell when he bursts through the door of
the prison of his self, "a man resurrected" (p. 186).

What he bursts through is as much a door leading out of
the prison of his fleshly pleasures and his perverted egocen-
tricity as it is the door of what we discover to be a broom
closet. His surname points to this: Mountjoy is not only
"Mons Veneris" but also the name of a well-known Irish
prison.[12] The prison, moreover, can only be unlocked by
one's own insight into the nature of the confinement and by
an effort of will. These accomplished, Sammy moves again
into the prisoner-of-war camp, and his vision penetrates
through and beyond the physical substance of all natural objects: "The paper wrappings of use and language dropped
from me. Those crowded shapes extending up into the air and
down into the rich earth, those deeds of far space and deep
earth were aflame at the surface and daunting by right of their

own natures though a day before I should have disguised
them as trees. Beyond them the mountains were not only
clear all through like purple glass, but living. They sang and
were conjubilant. They were not all that sang" (p. 186).

Human figures are similarly transfigured. What has
changed for Sammy is that, to use Bergson's terms, he no
longer perceives things as *objects* but as *processes;* thus, he
accords them a real duration instead of freezing them into the
appearances of ordinary social life. Sammy briefly recovers
his "fundamental self," but paradoxically he can only communicate this to us through words; hence his discourse requires a style that is distinct from usual language if communication is to take place at all.[13]

This new way of seeing himself and the transfigured world
not only brings Sammy new knowledge—particularly of "the
relationship of individual man to individual man" (p. 189)—
and new freedom; it also brings him, and us, back to the original question: When did Sammy change? What separated him
from the small boy trotting alongside Evie and the young man
waiting at the bridge for the light to change? Unable any
longer to take the world for granted, unable also to rest easy
with either intellectual rationalism or religious belief, Sammy
turns now to his schooling at the hands of his two most important teachers to search once more for that moment and
manner of choice that he believes cost him his freedom.

The experience in the prison camp not so much gives as
restores to Sammy a way of seeing he had had as a boy much
drawn to the world of miracle evidenced in scripture and
taught by Miss Pringle. To be more precise, what Sammy
gains is a new awareness of the worlds of rationalism and of
spirit. Between these he had alternatively passed under the
hands of Nick Shales, his science teacher, and Rowena Pringle, but at a decisive moment he chose between them. In a
way, part of the choice was made for him. By nature drawn
more to Miss Pringle and her world than to Nick Shales's cool,

orderly science, Sammy is rebuffed and finally repelled by Miss Pringle's cruelty and brought instead into the orbit of the other through his personal kindliness. But this is hardly a rational, free choice—not the momentous decision he seeks. Rather, it provides the foundation for the decision he makes in adolescence when, driven by sex but also by his awareness of Beatrice's loveliness, he rationalizes his compunctions about good and evil and determines to attain her—making a commitment that costs him not less than everything.

The mounting sense of ambiguity and paradox that pervades these chapters seems deliberate, and it brings us to the heart of the matter. The contradictions inherent in the characterizations of Nick Shales and Rowena Pringle introduce and underscore this theme. Earlier, oppositions appeared to Sammy between Johnny Spragg and Philip Arnold; but now he discovers that they may be embodied in the same person and even in himself: "At the moment I was deciding that right and wrong were nominal and relative, I felt, I saw the beauty of holiness and tasted evil in my mouth like the taste of vomit" (p. 226). Sammy falls, falls freely because it is by his own conscious choice that he makes his commitment. It is the plummet from spontaneity to necessity, from the unselfconscious happiness of a timeless boyhood to the conditioned, determined world of manhood. But this decision also marks the end of his "free fall"; the end that is, until his release from the darkened cell in the prison camp, when once again opposing forces set up a contradictory pull. Sammy's haggard, unshaven fellow prisoners look like his boyishly admired "kings of Egypt," and the drawings he makes of them become the "glory" of his right hand and are likely to remain so.

> What had been important dropped away. What had been ludicrous became common sense. What had had the ugliness of frustration and dirt, I now saw to have a curious reversed beauty—a beauty that could only be seen, out of the corner of the eye, a beauty which often only became apparent when it

was remembered. All these things, of course, were explicable
in two ways; the one explained them away, the other accepted
them as data relevant to the nature of the cosmos. There was
no argument possible between people holding either view. I
knew that, because at different times of my life I had been
either kind in turn. [p. 188]

The contradictions of his experience are heralded here by the
opposing tendencies of Halde and his more compassionate
counterpart, the unnamed commandant. But so it has been
throughout Sammy's experience—the natural goodness and
generosity of a Johnny Spragg balanced by the wicked ego-
centricity of a Philip Arnold; the simple amorality of Ma by
the paranoid intelligence of Father Watts-Watt; the perception of Beatrice's beatitude by the recognition of her vacuity.

Yet where does this leave Sammy, and us? The last two
chapters attempt to resolve enigmas that have occurred and
recurred throughout the novel. By their very nature, Sammy's restored freedom and vision are intermittent, not constant: the practicalities of ordinary social life presumably
make their claim upon him as upon all men.[14] Still oppressed
by guilt and desiring expiation, Sammy brings himself after
the war to visit Beatrice at the mental hospital where she has
been confined since he abandoned her years before. Yet he
finds expiation impossible. "The innocent cannot forgive"
(p. 248; cp. pp. 74–75). Her inmost being never having been
penetrated, Beatrice remains inviolate, and, paradoxically,
Sammy remains guilty. Again, bent on doing good—enlightening one and forgiving the other—Sammy sets out to visit
his spiritual parents, Nick Shales and Rowena Pringle. Both
efforts fail: Nick is dying and does not need Sammy's explanations; Rowena, victorious in total self-deception, has escaped the net of the guilty and is "living only in one world."
She has become another kind of innocent to whom Sammy's
forgiveness is meaningless.

The conclusion is that both worlds—Nick's and Rowena's—are real, and that there is no bridge. Yet in the preceding chapter, after confrontation with Beatrice, Sammy had written: "Cause and effect. The law of succession. Statistical probability. The moral order. Sin and remorse. They are all true. Both worlds exist side by side. They meet in me" (p. 244). The guilty—unlike the innocent or the wicked—must live in both worlds at once, must torture one another "here and now" (p. 115), because of their lost freedom. But that lost freedom is lost freedom only in the theological sense. Golding also shows that Sammy's "free fall" leaves him again suspended between the opposing worlds of his experience, each real, each exercising its appropriate pull, neutralizing gravity.[15] Sammy lives now on "Paradise Hill, ten minutes from the station, thirty seconds from the shops and the local" (p. 5). Paradise Hill is also where Beatrice lives, in the asylum. The contradictions persist. Dr. Enticott cannot assure Sammy whether his affair with Beatrice hurt or helped her: it may have tipped her over into madness; it may have given her an extra year of sanity. The puzzles remain.

Or do they, quite? The final paragraphs, describing Sammy's release from the cell, reveal Golding's predilection—his innate optimism—that I believe inclines the novel toward man's redeeming goodness and compassion.[16] If Halde "does not know about peoples," as the commandant asserts in the last line, it is in the sense that he does not know about the other side of human nature. This side Sammy himself has learned, and he describes it best in a paragraph on the children's ward: "I have searched like all men for a coherent picture of life and the world, but I cannot write the last word on that ward without giving it my adult testimony. The walls were held up by sheer, careful human compassion. I was on the receiving end and I know. When I make my black pictures, when I inspect chaos, I must remember that such places are as real as Belsen. They, too, exist, they are part of this enigma, this living" (p. 77). This enigma, this living.

Drawn between the opposing tendencies in their own natures, men are nevertheless free to choose in which world they will live—free, at any rate, to withstand external forces arrayed against them. This seems to be part of the humanism of Golding's novel.[17] Another part is summed up in Sammy's comment, "People are the walls of our room, not philosophies" (p. 226). Not what Nick and Rowena said, but what they were became most meaningful to their pupils. Ella Sands makes a similar point at the end of Angus Wilson's novel *Hemlock and After*, when she tries to assess the value of her late husband's life: "Doing doesn't last, even if one knows what one's doing, which one usually doesn't. But Bernard *was* something to people—lots of people—me, for example—and that has its effect in the end, I think." Bernard Sands died torn of the tensions set up by the opposing tendencies of his all too human nature. Sammy survives; or is his survival a living death leaving him still divided, still falling freely between the poles of his being and experience? Having chosen once and, as it were, having recanted, is he nevertheless condemned to this limbo of confessed but unforgiven guilt?

According to Kinkead-Weekes and Gregor, the answer is yes, because Sammy fails to develop the kind of double vision that is required to see truly: he remains, at the end, fluctuating within a "pattern of mutually exclusive modes" that lack necessary juxtaposition.[18] I believe that the book gives plenty of evidence to the contrary, such as the passage about the children's ward. But looking at the situation from another perspective, we can see the point differently. Sammy's two selves—the innocent boy trotting alongside Evie and the guilty seducer of Beatrice—are hardly the two selves that Bergson describes as the "fundamental" (or free) self and its spatial or social representation; but Golding is concerned intimately with both kinds of freedom, both sets of selves. Hence one of Sammy's selves, the self that is married to Taffy and lives on Paradise Hill, his "social" self, is opposed to his other self, the self that, "violently searching," plumbs the utmost depths of consciousness and experience and recovers, during moments of intense vision, his freedom. The following from the conclusion of *Time and Free Will* may serve, not only to sum up this dimension of the problem, but to explain, also, Sammy's preoccupation with time and its relation to his pressing questions:

> There are finally two different selves, one of which is, as it were, the external projection of the other, its spatial and, so to speak, social representation. We reach the former by deep introspection, which leads us to grasp our inner states as living things, constantly *becoming*, as states not amenable to measure, which permeate one another and of which the succession in duration has nothing in common with juxtaposition in homogeneous space. But the moments at which we thus grasp ourselves are rare, and that is just why we are rarely free. The greater part of the time we live outside ourselves, hardly perceiving anything of ourselves but our own ghost, a colourless shadow which pure duration projects into homogeneous space. Hence our life unfolds in space rather than in time; we live for the external world rather than for ourselves; we speak rather than think; we "are acted" rather than act ourselves. To act freely is to recover possession of oneself, and to get back into pure duration. [pp. 231–32]

Sammy does succeed in getting back into "pure duration," perhaps more often than most men. But even the artist cannot live long at this point of intense awareness. Hence he is "self-condemned" in this sense, also. But his achievements in art—his portraits of Beatrice and of the haggard "kings of Egypt," for example—are earnest, like Golding's novel, of bridges that can be built between material reality and imagination. They are as important in their way as are the pillars of human compassion that serve to hold up the walls wherein we live.

---

1. Frank Kermode, "The Meaning of It All," *Books and Bookmen*, 5 (October 1959), 9–10; cp. Jack I. Biles, *Talk: Conversations with William Golding* (New York: Harcourt, 1970), 78.

2. See Arnold Johnston, "The Novels of William Golding" (Ph.D. diss., University of Delaware, 1970), 103–4, 120, and passim; Bernard S. Oldsey and Stanley Weintraub, *The Art of William Golding* (New York: Harcourt, 1965), 101–2.

3. *Free Fall* (New York: Harcourt, 1962), 5.

4. Biles, *Talk*, 63.

5. Henri Bergson, *Time and Free Will*, trans. F. L. Pogson (1910; reprint ed., New York: Harper, 1960), 165 ff.

6. Cp. Bergson, *Time and Free Will*, 133–34: "Now, if some bold novelist, tearing aside the cleverly woven curtain of our conventional ego, shows us under this appearance of logic a fundamental absurdity . . . we commend him for having known us better than we knew ourselves. This is not the case, however, and the very fact that he spreads out our feeling in a homogeneous time, and expresses its elements by words, shows that he in his turn is only offering us its shadow: but he has arranged this shadow in such a way as to make us suspect the extraordinary and illogical nature of the object which projects it; he has made us reflect by giving outward expression to something of that contradiction, that interpenetration, which is the very essence of the elements expressed. Encouraged by him, we have put aside for an instant the veil which we interposed between our consciousness and ourselves. He has brought us back into our own presence."

7. Cp. Bernard F. Dick, *William Golding*, Twayne's English Authors Series, no. 57 (New York: Twayne, 1967), 69.

8. Cp. Mark Kinkead-Weekes and Ian Gregor, *William Golding: A Critical Study* (London: Faber, 1967), 187: "The peculiar chronology of *Free Fall* is not willfully obscure, but logical. Insight into the beginning can only *follow* insight into the nature of what is begun." These critics note also "a new quality of explicit analysis" governing Sammy's recollections after the emergence from his cell.

9. Cp. Bergson, *Time and Free Will*, 172. "In short, we are free when our acts spring from our whole personality, when they express it, when they have that indefinable resemblance to it which one sometimes finds between the artist and his work." See the rest of this important passage.

10. For the allusions here and elsewhere to Dante, see Kinkead-Weekes and Gregor, *William Golding*, 174–77.

11. See Bergson on spontaneity and necessity, *Time and Free Will*, 215–21.

12. Ted E. Boyle, "The Denial of the Spirit: An Explication of William Golding's *Free Fall*," *Wascana Review*, 1 (1966), 6, identifies the Irish prison but otherwise interprets the significance. Cp. Kinkead-Weekes and Gregor, *William Golding*, 184–86.

13. See Bergson, *Time and Free Will*, 128 ff., for an excellent analysis of the function of language or social symbols, which hide us from our true selves, and of the dilemma the novelist faces who tries to reveal our true selves to us (see note 6, above). This is exactly Sammy's, or Golding's, dilemma, as noted at the outset. On the "fundamental self," see ibid., 231–32 (quoted below).

14. Ibid., 130: "our outer and, so to speak, social life is more practically important to us than are inner and individual existence."

15. Cp. Golding in Biles, *Talk*, 81–82: "The particular poignancy, as I see it, of what I may call the model intellectual of the twentieth century—which is what we most of us are, unless we have committed ourselves to something; in which case, we're lucky—the poignancy of the model intellectual is that he is literally in this state of free fall. . . . It is where your gravity has *gone*. . . . Do you see what I mean? Where for hundreds of thousands of years men have known where they were, now they don't know where they are any longer. . . . [This] is an attempt to put the other version, the two contrasting views of life, neither of which really makes sense because the other exists. Either, on its own, makes sense, but when you've got them both there—and this *is* the situation—neither one taken alone does."

16. Biles, *Talk*, 105.

17. Cp. Boyle, "Denial," 10.

18. Kinkead-Weekes and Gregor, *William Golding*, 198. See also Howard S. Babb, *The Novels of William Golding* (Columbus: Ohio State University Press, 1970), 127–30.

E. C. Bufkin

THE SPIRE: THE IMAGE
OF THE BOOK

*So far from losing ourselves in the world of the novel, we must
hold it away from us, see it all in detachment, and use the
whole of it to make the image we seek, the book itself.*
—Percy Lubbock, *The Craft of Fiction*

THE SPIRE is a subtle, paradoxical exploration of the
theme of pride. In essence a variant of the myth of Babel, the
novel may be viewed as a structure combining two traditional
narrative patterns: the Gothic tragedy of pyramidal rise-and-
fall and its reverse, the Christian comedy of sin and redemption. Both are moralistic, and both move toward suffering and
death. While events in *The Spire* progress chronologically, its
real structure—that image of the book itself which Lubbock
would have us seek—is thematically controlled by rising and
falling lines.[1]

The novel belongs to Jocelin, dean of the Cathedral
Church of the Virgin Mary at Salisbury, who intends to glorify
that house by building on it a four-hundred-foot spire. He
received a vision of the spire (he says) from God, and that
makes the building of it an "overriding necessity."[2] "The
children of men," Jocelin explains, "require a thing to look at"

(p. 120). The center of action is the narrow world of Jocelin's mind, to which the narration is severely limited. This restricted point of view is appropriate to the theme of pride. It places the reader in the area where the real action—the internal conflict of the emotions of passion and reason, of faith and doubt—occurs; and the reader, participating in that drama, is pressed into identification with Jocelin. The advantage gained is the immediacy and intensity of "felt life," the signature of the Golding novel.

This point of view isolates Jocelin, placing him in the position of the tragic figure whose pride has separated him from other men. At the same time it places him in the position of a sinner, whose atonement and redemption are a matter of the individual soul and mind—a personal not a public responsibility. "We are each responsible for our own salvation," says Jocelin (p. 86). Related to this technical separation is an important motif, the contrast between inward and outward; yet, as the structure will clarify, the inward and the outward are equivalents which come together for Jocelin in the last minutes of his life when he, as well as the reader, breaks free of the confines of mind.

The Spire is composed of three phases of four chapters each, corresponding to the three phases of Gothic tragedy— rise, apex, fall. The opening paragraph establishes the theme of pride: "He [Jocelin] was laughing, chin up, and shaking his head. God the Father was exploding in his face with a glory of sunlight through painted glass, a glory that moved with his movements to consume and exalt Abraham and Isaac and then God again. The tears of laughter in his eyes made additional spokes and wheels and rainbows" (p. 7). Jocelin is already well into the first of the three pyramidal phases, the ascendance. His physical stance and his insensibility to the emblematic, admonitory implications of the illuminated window are overt manifestations of pride. His first statement, "I've waited half my life for this day!" (p. 7), gives evidence of his long-held ambition. Pride and ambition together constitute the ground from which tragedy will grow like "a plant with strange flowers and fruit, complex, twining, engulfing, destroying, strangling" (p. 194).

Jocelin's hubris soon becomes apparent. His first prayer, self-congratulatory like his confessions, shows him blindly pharisaic: "*Lord; I thank Thee that Thou has kept me humble!*" (p. 22). His rank as a great man is due to his high position in the Church as well as to his heroic stature. Tall and gaunt, he is linked with the original builders of the cathedral, "the giants who had been on the earth in those days" (p. 188). He is represented moreover as resembling an eagle, the bird of pride and, because of its great powers of vision, the emblem of Saint John the Divine. Seeing in the air a "great bird" and "remembering Saint John," Jocelin asserts, "It is an eagle." It is not; but when corrected, the priest insists, "Well. As far as I am concerned it is an eagle" (p. 107).

Jocelin also associates himself with John; he is as proud and ignorant as two deacons believe him: "He thinks he is a saint!" (p. 13). Jocelin establishes the identification on the evidence of the vision he has had of the spire, which represents the Throne of God on a cathedral, itself the earthly City of God. To Jocelin the cathedral is "a stone bible" which his spire will complete as "the apocalypse in stone." Correspondences between priests and saint are easily perceived; noting them himself, Jocelin rises by analogy. But ironically his mind is closed to Old Testament prophecy: "Though thou exalt thyself as the eagle, and though thou set thy nest among the stars, thence will I bring thee down, saith the Lord" (Obadiah, 4). The entire organization of the first half of the novel documents this subjective humor of pride: Jocelin sees only what it pleases him to see.

His self-centeredness is exerted in his display of pride of possession: "My place, my house, my people" (p. 8). His constant unawareness of his own faults but not those of others is relentlessly underscored by Golding's irony. In one scene Jocelin chides Pangall: "Didn't you say once that this [church] is your house? There was sinful pride in that" (p. 61). And of course the vision belongs to Jocelin too, uniquely, and it is through the reckless exertion of his will that he intends to realize that vision in wood, stone, and metal. Any situation or person that threatens the construction excites his irritation and impatience, and anger comes more and more to replace the joy of the opening chapters. By an imperceptible transition Jocelin's will becomes God's will, and in an interview with his master builder, Roger Mason, to whom Jocelin stands in opposition since he sees him as having neither vision nor faith, he uses the two wills as one: "You'll see how I shall thrust you upward by my will," he tells Roger. "It's God's will in this business" (p. 40).

Jocelin tolerates no obstruction; no alteration, no compromise. By the power of will he hardens his heart; he uses other people as instruments. Roger Mason is to Jocelin but his tool, his "slave for the work." Father Adam he calls Father Anonymous; Father Anselm he patronizes; the Lady Alison, his aunt, he rejects, though he accepts her money. As pride continues to possess him, Jocelin ignores the adulterous relationship of Roger Mason and Goody Pangall, "my dear daughter-in-God," because he knows that, so involved, the master builder will not desert the work on the spire: "She will keep him here" (p. 64).

Jocelin's initial folly has been to disregard the opinion of the Chapter, the members of which do not unanimously support the erection of the spire; and it is this act that marks the dean's rise to autonomy and the beginning of his alienation. In the plotting of his own tragedy he sets himself squarely against his fellowmen.

He compounds this error by setting himself against both architectural concepts and nature herself. As Roger makes plain, the cathedral lacks foundation for the soaring structure

Jocelin demands; therefore, to build it is to act irrationally. "The solid earth," warns Roger, "argues against us" (p. 85). The paradox is impressive: God's vision to Jocelin goes counter to God's cosmic order as exhibited in nature.

The same point of proud defiance of the divine is made in architectural terms. The proportions of Gothic architecture being commensurable with the proportions of the human body, a cathedral is an image of the crucified Christ, as a model of Jocelin's cathedral shows. It is "like a man lying on his back. The nave was his legs placed together, the transepts on either side were his arms outspread. The choir was his body; and the Lady Chapel . . . was his head. And now also, springing, projecting, bursting, erupting from the heart of the building, there was its crown and majesty, the new spire" (p. 8). By erecting so tall a spire, Jocelin violates principles of proportional design and destroys the traditional analogy between building and man. The magnitude and size of Jocelin's spire thus make manifest—in glass, iron, stone—his own pride (and—as has been made clear by novelist and commentators alike—his suppressed sexuality, the mixture in himself "of dear love and prurience" [p. 127]). And the size is something more: being a violation of natural, divine, and aesthetic order, it is a harbinger of disorder.

In several instances Golding identifies Jocelin with the cathedral: it is not only Jocelin's house, it is Jocelin. Thus the inside drama of his mind is objectified in the outside drama of the spire. In his vainglory Jocelin has appropriated the church; he even builds himself into the spire by having four images of his head carved in stone for the sides of the tower. When people look at the spire, they will see not divine order, as is proper, but Jocelin's vision. Thus the dean's pride has placed him in competition with God, though ironically, as his monomania approaches madness, he fancies "a race between me and the Devil" (p. 160) and fastens the spire to the sky with a Holy Nail to prevent Satan from knocking it down.

In chapter 5 Jocelin reaches the pinnacle of tragic experience, a point almost exactly at the middle of the narrative. The spire is slowly going up like "a miracle" and Jocelin mounts it dizzily to the top, up where he can be "free of all the confusion" below (p. 104). He stands erect, with the "same appalled delight . . . a small boy feels when first he climbs too high in a forbidden tree" (p. 101), and looks "out into the world" (p. 105). The following pages are a brilliant evocation of a sense of triumph: "His joy beat at him like wings. I would like the spire to be a thousand feet high, he thought, and then I should be able to oversee the whole country" (p. 106). Egocentrically, he understands "how the tower was laying a hand on the whole landscape, altering it, dominating it, enforcing a pattern that reached wherever the tower could be seen. . . . Presently, with this great finger sticking up, the City would lie like the hub at the centre of a predestined wheel" (pp. 107–8).

Read within the framework of medieval *contemptus mundi*, this episode reveals Jocelin's peril. The wheel—that instrument on which proud men are carried from high to low, from felicity to misery—has an ominous connotation, as it had in the first paragraph. The very world Jocelin surveys is subject to the law of mutability and to chance. His vision of the spire in diagram—"the invisible geometric lines that sketched themselves . . . above the battlements of the crossways, up there, where a bird wheeled, and drew to a point, four hundred feet up in the sky" (p. 35)—and the spire itself are configurations of the pyramid-shaped Gothic tragedy of fortune. Unlike Roger Mason, who suffers from acrophobia, pride-blinkered Jocelin dreads to go down, for he enjoys the heights, like Milton's Satan, for whom "highest is best." The dean thinks, "Here is my place"; but he must go down, "since no man can live his life with eagles" (p. 110).

Jocelin's tragic disintegration begins in chapter 6 with a hallucinatory vision of the tower's fall, a vision that portends his own decline. After the vision fades he is "sick with falling through the air" (p. 119), a phrase that signifies because it suggests Lucifer's archetypal descent. Whereas events have previously challenged Jocelin, they now resist him. The exercise of pride has resulted in general disorder summed up in the phantasm of toppling he has just undergone. Church services have been disrupted, causing resentment among both clergy and laity. The church has been defiled by workmen— "Murderers, cutthroats, rowdies, brawlers, rapers, notorious fornicators, sodomites, atheists" (p. 167). Adultery has been committed and in effect condoned. Accidental deaths have occurred, and murder. Pangall vanishes, sacrificially slain by druidic heathens. After being delivered of a dead child, Goody dies. Roger takes to drink, attempts suicide, and, left blind and dumb, must be tended by his barren wife, Rachel, herself tainted with guilt of Goody's death.

As Leighton Hodson has observed of *The Spire*, "the pattern whereby Jocelin has been in the ascendant, moving people around as objects in a game," is now reversed, and the dean, in the descendant, becomes "just as much an object to be manipulated as anyone else." [3] The reversals are of two kinds. Some are retributive, the consequences of Jocelin's pride-flawed character: the interrogation and dismissal by the Visitor and his commission, the vindictive and uncharitable charges by Anselm, the assault by the rabble in the City. The others, however, are workings of chance and come upon Jocelin as blows of fortune. One example is that the four apparently solid pillars supporting the spire are actually filled with rubble. Two of these blows of fortune contribute particularly to the dean's decline. They are the revelation of the Lady Alison (she, not God, chose Jocelin for the Church), which strikes at him spiritually, and the irruption of the disease that destroys him physically.

But before his death Jocelin will fall utterly, completing

the pyramidal course of his tragedy and the shape of the novel. Now suffering in soul and mind as well as in body, he goes to confront Roger. Thrown out of the house and reviled by the besotted builder, Jocelin is attacked by an angry mob and pursued like an animal, as was Pangall. "My children! My children!" the afflicted priest says in an effort to quell the people, but they pounce on him and strip off his clothes. When they see his disease-devoured back they desist. In this ignominious fall through folly, Jocelin's proud remark—"the children of men require a thing to look at"—echoes with infernal irony. Reenacting Lucifer's fate, Jocelin staggers naked "into the gutter and out again; though once he fell in it" (p. 216). With death to come, the tragic pattern is now complete.

The Spire is thus a pyramidally structured narrative, taking its protagonist to the heights of ambition and then to the depths: to tower at midpoint, gutter at the end. But to demonstrate so much is to discover only half of the book itself. Unlike Golding's other novel of pride and fall, *Pincher Martin*, this one involves two, contrary movements. The dominant lines in *Pincher Martin* are downward, but in *The Spire* the lines move upward as well. For, in distinction to Christopher Martin, Jocelin learns the technique of dying into heaven. The Gothic tragedy in *The Spire* is juxtaposed to the Christian comedy of redemption; and, with their lines overlapping, pride gives way to humility, autonomy to dependence, resistance to acceptance.

The Christian pattern structures the novel just as the Gothic does. A spire, we learn, "goes down as far as it goes up" (p. 43); and this architectural requirement is a corollary of a point of Christian doctrine which is a sort of paradox according to Saint Augustine. There is, he says, "a kind of lowliness which in some wonderful way causes the heart to be lifted up, and there is a loftiness which makes the heart sink lower."[4]

Hence, the higher Jocelin lifts himself up, the lower he falls; and the fall of the exalted self leads to the rise of the humble. This paradox is the central matter of *The Spire*, observed and analyzed but not resolved. It is, divinely, a mystery. And no man knows more than Jocelin learns: *"There is no innocent work. God knows where God may be"* (p. 222).

Jocelin's spiritual descent and his ambitious ascent have a common point of departure and are coterminous. The pit at the crossways of the church, "the heart of the building," is an outward analogue to the man's inward rottenness; as the spire rises, the pit deepens. Leighton Hodson has stated: "In this climactic experience of his life the erection of the spire upwards counterpoints Jocelin's obligation to descend into himself and learn the truth about himself that he has conveniently buried there in the dark cellarage of his mind."[5] The middle chapters of the novel (5 through 8) contain the reversal of movement. The spiritual ascent—that is, graphically but paradoxically, the *descent*—begins in chapter 8, and the language, both in matter and in ambiance, signals an approach to climax:

> It was a beginning, not an end. The lines of the tower drew together downwards now, so that the whole thing was not massively based, but an arrow shot into the earth, with up here, an ungainly butt. The perceptible swaying was no longer soulclutching . . . but there was in the rhythmic heaviness and lightness a kind of drain, not so much on the muscles as on the spirit. Jocelin learnt how the strain built up, so that after a time you would find you had held your breath, and clutched at something with frozen violence. Then you would let this breath out in a gasp, and be easy for a while. [pp. 147–48]

The switch in movement is effected—with Jocelin again atop the tower—by means of a single symbol, a sheet of metal. This object can, like a looking-glass, serve the vanity of pride—or it can aid the quest for truth: for Jocelin it becomes, in the tradition of *de casibus* tragedy, a cautionary mirror for high magistrates of the church. Just before sunset, the workmen having left, Jocelin senses that he is not alone in the spire:

> Someone else was facing him. This creature was framed by the metal sheet that stood against the sky. . . . when he lifted his hand, the figure raised one too. So he crawled across the boards on hands and knees and the figure crawled towards him. He knelt and peered in at the wild halo of hair, the skinny arms and legs that stuck out of a girt and dirty robe. He peered in closer and closer until his breath dimmed his own image and he had to smear it off with his sleeve. After that he knelt and peered for a long time. He examined his eyes. . . . He examined the nose like a beak and now nearly as sharp, the deep grooves in the face, the gleam of teeth.
> The kneeling image cleared his head. Well Jocelin, he said soundlessly to the kneeling image; Well Jocelin, this is where we have come. [pp. 154–55]

The shock is an enlightenment—and a contrast to the window of sacrifice, depicting Abraham and Isaac, of whose meaning Jocelin was oblivious. Now, as night falls, he will see more than his own reflection, in yet another contrast—that with the earlier scene of his first panoramic view from the spire:

> He saw a fire on the rim and guessed it was a haystack burning; but as he moved round the rim of the cone, he saw more and more fires round the rim of the world. Then a terrible dread fell on him for he knew these were the fires of Midsummer Night, lighted by the devilworshippers out on the hills. . . . he remembered his crew of good men, and he knew . . . where they were gone. . . .
> "It's another lesson. The lesson for this height. Who could have foreseen that this was part of the scheme? Who could

know that at this height the thing I thought of as a stone diagram of prayer would lift up a cross and fight eye to eye with
the fires of the Devil?" [pp. 155–56]

And now the peripeteia:

He wept bitterly without knowing what he wept for unless it
was the sins of the world. . . .
   Slowly his mind came back to its own life. If David could
not build the temple because he had blood on his hands, what
is to be said of us, and of me? [p. 156]

Henceforth the imitation will be of Christ, not of Lucifer.

In addition to this moment of self-revelation, another factor in Jocelin's regeneration is the consumption of the spine
from which he has suffered since the beginning of the novel,
though in his egotism he originally supposed the fire at his
back to be a guardian angel warming and sustaining him. Saint
Augustine tells us that pain of body is suffering of soul arising
from the body; and, following him, C. S. Lewis has termed
pride "spiritual cancer" and identified the effect of suffering as
redemptive because of its tendency to reduce the rebel will.[6]
In Jocelin's case the parallel between *spine* and *spire* (as
Kinkead-Weekes and Gregor have pointed out) is pertinent:
caught between the external conflict of erecting his spire and
the internal agony, mental as well as physical, caused by disease of his spine, Jocelin reacts with a genuine humility, as
well as with a recognition of its source: "Pain did it, pain did
it, pain did it" (p. 139).

If pride is a fall upward, then humility is a rise downward;
and Jocelin now sets out on the paradoxical course of redemption by lowering himself. Contrite, he seeks counsel and comfort from Father Adam—"Help me!" he cries in his suffering
(p. 196); he seeks forgiveness from Father Anselm—"Forgive
me for being what I am" (p. 203); he faces Roger Mason in a
confessional spirit—"Now I've come in pain and shame, to ask

you to forgive me" (p. 211). Jocelin's figures of speech betoken the calamitous consequences of pride, perceivable because of his new awareness of himself and his detachment from things of this world. No longer is the spire a crown; it is a "colossal spike." And he himself is a compendium of heresies, a fool, "a building with a vast cellarage where the rats live" (p. 210). Pain and suffering have stripped away pretense and deception, just as the crowd strips away his clothes; and Jocelin submits to truth: "I thought I was doing a great work; and all I was doing was bringing ruin and breeding hate" (p. 209).

Pride has led to love of self; humility will lead to love of others. By following this new pattern, Jocelin frees himself by turning from inside to outside. He sees exploitation of others as sinful because it is exploitation of God ("I traded a stone hammer for four people" [p. 222]), and he now seeks wholeness through human compassion and communion ("To love all men with a holy love" [p. 209]). "If I could go back," Jocelin reflects, "I would take God as lying between people and to be found there" (p. 220).

Golding has never been more the skillful craftsman than in *The Spire*. In chapters 10 through 12 he plays the patterns of Gothic tragedy and Christian comedy off against each other like fugal themes, and fits beginnings and endings together harmoniously. Jocelin's career began when the Lady Alison persuaded her royal lover to favor her nephew and extracted his promise, "We shall drop a plum in his mouth" (p. 184); it ends, in the last sentence, when Father Adam lays "the Host on the dead man's tongue." The plum precipitated the fall; the Host concludes the redemption.

Only in chapter 10 do we learn directly and completely about Jocelin's vision, as Father Adam reads aloud from the book in which Jocelin wrote it down. Then almost immediately following, in chapter 11, Jocelin has another vision, this time of an apple tree:

A scent struck him. . . . He twisted his neck and looked up
sideways. There was a cloud of angels flashing in the sunlight,
. . . uttering this sweet scent for joy of the light and the air.
They brought with them a scatter of clear leaves, and among
the leaves a long, black springing thing. His head swam . . .
and suddenly he understood there was more to the appletree
than one branch. It was there beyond the wall, . . . laying hold
of the earth and the air, a fountain, a marvel, an appletree; and
this made him weep in a childish way so that he could not tell
whether he was glad or sorry. Then, where the yard of the
deanery came to the river and trees lay over the sliding water,
he saw all the blue of the sky condensed to a winged sapphire,
that flashed once.
    He cried out.
    "Come back!"
    But the bird was gone, an arrow shot once. It will never
come back, he thought, not if I sat here all day. [pp. 204–5]

The final chapter brings together the visions of spire and
apple tree; brings outside inside; and recapitulates the first
paragraph by means of window, light, and images of faith,
sacrifice, suffering, sin, death, life. For the first and last time
Jocelin, dying, sees the completed spire through "the window, bright and open"—the very window whose confinement, we recall, "sometimes gave what he saw from it a kind
of extra definition and importance, like a picture in a frame"
(p. 66):

Something divided [the window]. Round the division was the
blue of the sky. The division was still and silent, but rushing
upward to some point at the sky's end, and with a silent cry. It
was slim as a girl, translucent. It had grown from some seed of
rosecoloured substance that glittered like a waterfall, an upward waterfall. The substance was one thing, that broke all the
way to infinity in cascades of exultation that nothing could
trammel.
    The panic beat and swept in, struck the window into

patches that danced before either eye; but not the panic nor the blindness could diminish the terror of it and the astonishment.

"Now—I know nothing at all." . . .

In the tide, flying like a bluebird, struggling, shouting, screaming to leave behind the words of magic and incomprehension—

It's like the appletree! [p. 223]

This setting is, wonderfully, paradisal in detail and in implication of past and future, lost and regained. Jocelin reminds us of another dean, hymning to God in his sickness:

> We thinke that *Paradise* and *Calvarie*,
>   *Christs* Crosse and *Adams* tree, stood in one place;
> Looke Lord, and finde both *Adams* met in me;
>   As the first *Adams* sweat surrounds my face,
>   May the last *Adams* blood my soule embrace.

It all ends with a Babelic confusion of tongue: "Father Adam, leaning down [over Jocelin], could hear nothing. But he saw a tremor of the lips that might be interpreted as a cry of: *God! God! God!*" (p. 223). Jocelin's composite vision and Donne's "text" and "sermon" proclaim, in a mixture of "terror and joy" the same paradox: "that he may raise the Lord throws down."

Thus the experiences, meanings, implications, connotations come together: the substance is one thing. Jocelin sees a spire, which is an apple tree, which is a cross; and they merge into a sublime unity. And the reader, too, sees the spire, which is a diagram, which is lines rising and falling while paradoxically falling and rising. He sees, that is, the pyramidal shape of *The Spire*, the image of the book itself.

---

1. Since I am mainly concerned with theme and what Percy Lubbock in *The Craft of Fiction* (New York: Scribners, 1921) calls "form, design, composition" (p. 9)—"the book, the thing [the author] made, [which] lies im-

prisoned in the volume" (p. 5)—I have dealt with other aspects of *The Spire* only insofar as they are pertinent. More comprehensive discussions of the novel are numerous; the best are those by Mark Kinkead-Weekes and Ian Gregor, *William Golding: A Critical Study* (London: Faber, 1967), 203–35; James G. Livingston, *William Golding's The Spire* (New York: Seabury Press, 1967); Leighton Hodson, *Golding* (Edinburgh: Oliver & Boyd, 1969), 88–99; David Skilton, "Golding's *The Spire*," *Studies in the Literary Imagination*, 2 (October 1969), 45–56.

2. *The Spire* (London: Faber, 1964), 168.

3. Hodson, *Golding*, 93.

4. *City of God*, 14:13.

5. Hodson, *Golding*, 88–89.

6. *Mere Christianity* (New York: Macmillan, 1960), 97; *The Problem of Pain* (New York: Macmillan, 1962), 112.

Richard S. Cammarota

THE SPIRE: A SYMBOLIC ANALYSIS

IN *The Spire* Golding traces Dean Jocelin's attempt to fill in with a stone spire the diagram of prayer he saw in a vision. Jocelin is obsessed with the task, but when the spire is completed, the lives of those around it lie destroyed. The moral thesis is, however, more complex. Jocelin is not only unaware of another side of man's nature, but also convinced that the spire compensates for anything harmful which might occur: "Let it be so. Cost what you like."[1] His slow recognition of his dual nature and the destruction his undertaking has caused culminates in a form of the Golding moral vision unsurpassed in the earlier novels. In Jocelin we see the vision developing. The result is doubly effective. Far more than an experience of man's dual nature, it is the realization that life is complex, embracing light and darkness, beauty and ugliness, good and evil, and that all these influence man at once.

The creation of such a vision depends not so much on the accuracy of narrative as on the variety and scope of symbol. Certainly dependence on symbolic suggestion is dangerous for an author who wishes to create a precise vision. But the symbolic suggestions lead, for the most part, to the concluding vision; yet they are varied enough to allow freedom from rigid interpretation. David Skilton feels that imagery "plays a key role in the presentation of the subject matter through Jocelin's refracting consciousness, because, in this narrative technique, the imagery is his, and not used by a narrator to express . . . states of mind and perceptions."[2] Told in the third person, yet expressing the inner thoughts of its protagonist, shaped by imagery which is Jocelin's yet also universal, the moral vision is as dichotomous as what it expresses.

Symbolism in so thematically compact a structure as the fable has more than merely overt significance.[3] While the latitude of suggestion is restricted to the moral view, the metaphorical devices are more than simple signs. As Northrop Frye puts it, "a poet's intention is centripetally directed. It is directed towards putting words together, not towards aligning words with meanings."[4] Golding's symbols work with the moral significance of the fable, but they also work independently to create a wider range of suggestion. All symbolic interpretation is directed toward the action and development of theme, but suggestions and meanings the author may not have thought of apply as well, contributing to the impact and success of the total structure. Rather than destroying the tight fiber, symbolism embellishes the thesis and major themes.

The images and symbols of *The Spire* parallel the fundamental moral thesis. An image pattern parallels the exposure of the base side of man's nature and its entangled effect of that on the whole man. Within this pattern are allusions to pagan elements, water and cellar symbols, and images of trees, webs, nets, tents, and Goody's hair. Characteristic of the loftier, spiritual side of man's nature are images of birds and angels, and symbols of fire, light, and the great spire. Many images from each group suggest both aspects of man's nature. The spire, light, fire, birds, trees, the cathedral-as-body simile, the cathedral-as-ship simile, and the gargoyles develop opposite and contradictory suggestions which act on their new narrative environment. Discussing each image or symbol separately, I shall stop short of its appearance in the climactic visions of apple tree, kingfisher, and spire. At the conclusion I shall discuss all the imagery as it appears in these contexts.

The atmosphere in and around Jocelin's cathedral is a combination of spirituality and paganism. Allusions to pagan elements create a tension which helps force the climax of Jocelin's revelation. Looking at the incongruous barricade of wood and canvas in the nave, Jocelin begins an important image pattern: "I could think this was some sort of pagan temple; and those two men . . . the priests of some outlandish rite—Forgive me" (p. 10). The master builder's men commit murder, a fact he is willing to overlook because of their aid in the construction of the spire. They later murder Pangall in a pagan ritual of propitiation. Considering the pit, Jocelin thinks the material on the bottom "Doomsday coming up," and then speculates that it is "the living, pagan earth, unbound at last and waking" (p. 80). As the base side of his nature creeps surfaceward, Jocelin looks out from atop the unfinished tower at the rounded downlands: "They were soft and warm and smooth as a young body" (p. 106).

The Edenic snake image becomes a device in the pagan pattern. Two heraldic beasts on the floor tile have "snakey necks entwined" (p. 63); seeing them as he watches the attraction between Roger and Goody manifest itself, Jocelin recognizes sexual connotations. In the tower-top survey, Jocelin sees the three rivers, "leagues of water that snaked towards the cathedral" (p. 106). Even the long rope hanging down the center of the tower well "lay on the pavement like a dead snake" (p. 142). The devils outside the cathedral beat at Jocelin "with scaly wings" (p. 175); later, like the rope, Jocelin's body "threw itself round the crossways like a broken snake" (p. 188); and finally, Rachel, bending over the broken dean, has "hair fallen in snakes that brushed over him" (p. 219). Though not a major image, snakes contribute to the sense of corruption and entanglement.

A group of references to pagan superstition surround Pangall. The workers ridicule the poor, misshapen man and make him a general mascot. He asks the dean why he has been made their fool and even accuses Jocelin of the same insult. Roger's explanation is "It's our way of keeping off bad luck" (p. 42). Pangall's role as fool functions in the same way as the chant the men break into as they fill the pit. Also connected to this pattern is Jocelin's description of Rachel's taunting with the story of her coital laughter: "She stripped the business of living down to where horror and farce took over; particoloured Zany in red and yellow, striking out in the torture chamber with his pig's bladder on a stick" (pp. 59–60). Significantly, the Zany is the character in old comedies who mimicked the clown; also important is that this Zany is particolored red and yellow, colors Golding has used to suggest decay and corruption.

In one of the richest image patterns, trees and plants have a central role in The Spire. The tree images appear early and recur frequently: "There were shafts and trunks of sunlight overhead" (p. 25); the ladders around the pillar made it look "like a firtree with the branches cut back" (p. 53); the ropes hanging in the crossways made it look as if "the building . . . had begun to grow some sort of gigantic moss" (p. 53). Even the tower breaks "into a grove of pinnacles" (p. 123), and Jocelin embraces the dumb sculptor, "clinging as to a pillar or a tree" (p. 96). These images create a sense of the Edenic tree and complement the sensuous suggestions of the pagan allusions.

The mistletoe twig and the burgeoning plant develop aspects of this image pattern and characterize the growing corruptive power of Jocelin's obsession. The mistletoe twig is an image uniting trees, Pangall's death—thus paganism—and the spire itself. After the riot at the crossways when Pangall is buried, Jocelin notices something quite disconcerting: "Among the rubbish at the bottom of the pillar he saw there was a twig lying across his shoe, with a rotting berry that clung obscenely to the leather" (p. 95). The sight immediately generates a "vision of the spire warping and branching and sprouting; and the terror of that had him on his feet" (p. 95). Much critical work has been done on this image. Babb finds that "mistletoe has a rich range of implications: it is sacred, protects one against witchcraft, promotes fertility, and is associated with sacrificial killing."[5] Crompton finds significance for this image in the Balder legend of Norse mythology.[6] Interesting as these views are, they do not emphasize that the word *obscene* connects the image with Jocelin's emerging repressed base nature. Jocelin cannot yet see this. Thinking only of the spire, he reasons that "the twig may have come from the scaffolding, which perhaps does not need to be seasoned" (p. 96).

Shortly twig, tree, and plant begin to coalesce. Knowing he will not help Goody, Jocelin likens his will to a plant: "I am like a flower that is bearing fruit. There is a preoccupation about the flower as the fruit swells and the petals wither; a preoccupation about the whole plant, leaves dropping, everything dying but the swelling fruit" (p. 97). This passage seems to indicate a paradise not perfect but infected with the presence of fallen man. Further Edenic suggestions occur in references to the first tree. High atop the incomplete tower, Jocelin "felt the same appalled delight as a small boy feels when first he climbs too high in a forbidden tree" (p. 101). The spire's treelike characteristics are emphasized as Jocelin watches the game below and realizes "that the tower was swaying under him like a tall tree" (p. 133).

The most important aspect of this pattern is the plant image. Uniting twig and unseasoned wood, it begins with Jocelin's realization of Pangall's fate. Looking at the fires dotting the horizon, Jocelin grasps, as Kinkead-Weekes and Gregor put it, "what must have happened to Pangall—the signifi-cance of the rotting mistletoe berry."[7] Trying to explain the berry's role in his new awareness, Jocelin talks in terms of a plant: "I had a vision you see, a clear and explicit vision. . . . then the complications began. A single green shoot at first, then clinging tendrils, then branches, then at last a riotous confusion" (p. 168). Here is the master image of entangle-ment. As in the other novels, it suggests the complexity and confusion of the actions of fallen men.

The climax of the tree-mistletoe-plant pattern comes as the dean lies wasted, with Father Adam reading from Jocelin's notebook: "No. Growth of a plant with strange flowers and fruit, complex, twining, engulfing, destroying, strangling" (p. 194). Immediately Jocelin sees the foliage, flowers, and overripe fruit: "There was no tracing its complications back to the root, no disentangling the anguished faces that cried out from among it" (p. 194). There is a striking similarity between this and the passage about the flower and fruit on a dying plant. A few lines later there is-terror in Father Adam's voice "as if he had glimpsed the plant and felt the swift touch of a tendril on his cheek" (p. 195). The tendril reminds us of Pincher Martin's upside-down apple tree and the black light-ning. Glimpsing for a moment the roots of his own base nature, Jocelin justifies his actions: "Only something so deep, it must lie close to the root of the plant, made him cry out to the stone rib and the delicate anxious face. 'My spire pierced every stage, from the bottom to the top!' " (pp. 197–98). The cul-minating image of this pattern is the apple tree, and its role as one of the last three visions is paramount.

Connected to these images of entanglement and trees is Goody's hair. The image begins in Jocelin's dream as Satan rises "out of the west, clad in nothing but blazing red hair" (p. 65). This masturbatory fantasy, eliciting suggestions of redness, creates a subconscious meaning for the hair no amount of denial can erase. Goody's hair is in his mind when this dream occurs: "It hung down; on this side splayed over her breast in a tattered cloud of red; on that, in a tangled plait which doubled on itself, and draggled with green ribbon half-undone" (p. 90). *Green* and *tangled* connect the hair with the plant imagery and develop suggestions of man's base nature. Again Jocelin sees a fall and tangle of red hair on green cloth, and cannot re-create the simple face behind it. Goody is an anonymous creature with red hair: "It was as if the red hair, sprung so unexpectedly from the decent covering of the wimple, had wounded all that time before, or erased it" (p. 91). The red hair irks him (p. 99), discomforts him, and he feels like a child that seeks comfort from its mother.

The blazing red hair begins to dominate his mind: the scaffolding "was now grouped round the tower top like a head of unruly hair" (p. 124); even when he looks up at the tower for help, "a fall of red, knotted hair blazed there so that he would cower away from it" (p. 127). In the scene outside Pangall's cottage red hair is everywhere: Rachel beats Roger with a broom, "a whisp of red hair caught in her fingers" (p. 135); Goody, inside alone, has her head "dropped, in a cascade of red, torn hair" (p. 136); and when Jocelin prays for her, "the hair and the blood blinded the eyes of his mind" (pp. 136–37). In addition to its connection with fire, the hair is often described in terms of water. The most significant occurrence of the image comes when Jocelin sees the children (devils) playing outside, and one in particular, with "hands behind her back, red hair straggled this way and that" (p. 178). This child is Goody re-created: he cannot see the child's face, but she hums from an empty mouth, which only the dumb sculptor and Goody do. At the end Jocelin knows that his subconscious mind knew about Pangall's impotence: "It was her hair, I think. I used to see it, blowing red about a thin, pale face" (p. 213). On his deathbed the image concludes as he sees a "tangle of hair, blazing among the stars. . . . 'Berenice' " (p. 221). Father Adam asks if he means Saint Berenice, but he means the constellation of hair in the heavens: "Berenice dedicated her hair, her 'crowning glory,' to sexual love, and erected it to the stars."[8]

Among these suggestions of entanglement and confusion is a similarity with the creepers and weed-tails of the first two novels. Also similar is the pattern of images which includes threads, ropes, collars, mazes, and tents. The relationship between Jocelin and Anselm had been "a rope binding them heart to heart," the thread was "thick and long," and Anselm obeys the dean's orders "because of the frayed thread that bound them" (p. 35). For Roger and Rachel, the relationship is not so willing; it is one of Keeper and Kept: "He saw the iron collar round Roger Mason's neck, and could follow the slack chain back from it to her right hand" (p. 139). For Jocelin, as he hears the coital moan from the swallow's nest, the metaphor of traps and nets is cogent: "It was the moan of some trapped animal, a roedeer, perhaps, past the time of kicking in the snare and now become nothing but helpless misery" (p. 125). And Roger chooses a rope in his attempted suicide.

The most important image in this group is the invisible tent: "He saw they were in some sort of tent that shut them off from all other people" (p. 57). Jocelin once sees Roger "half-turned from the ladder, drawn by invisible rope towards the woman crouched by the wall. It was Goody . . . feeling the ropes pull" (p. 63). Even Roger uses the trap metaphor when Jocelin tells him to "break the web": "It's only gossamer, after all. Who ever would have thought it!" (p. 86). After the rioting workers chase Pangall, Jocelin thinks Goody "has broken out of the tent, and those men saw her half naked, her hair fallen" (p. 92). Connected with hair, the image is also connected with sexuality. Indeed, Jocelin tells Roger to "build quickly—quickly! Before you consent to the major evil and the net never break—" (p. 122). As recognition comes to Jocelin, he admits to God that he saw the tent, yet consented. Like many of the images connected to the base side of man's nature, this one is also associated with the other side: it isn't Jocelin's net. "It's His. We can neither of us avoid this work" (p. 120). Ultimately, the metaphor extends to everything; even the enclosure in the tower's steel skin is a "tent-like space" (p. 153).

Similarly, as Jocelin's spine decays, a tightening cable comes around his chest. After Goody's death, Jocelin feels her presence through the "golden maze in the close and the church and the market" her feet made (p. 143); the men keep their "eyes averted from ground level where the golden maze of her feet was spread below" them (p. 144); even Jocelin can think, work, "if he could avoid the golden maze" (p. 146). Goody is indeed, Jocelin tells the Visitor, "woven into it everywhere" (p. 166). Finally he admits that the vision of the spire is supreme: "And woven through it, a golden thread—No. Growth of a plant with strange flowers and fruit" (p. 194). Vast, ambiguous, this pattern of webs, tents, and entanglement is at the core of the novel, expressing the repercussive complications of Jocelin's great diagram of prayer.

Initiated as Christopher Martin's, the cellar becomes a powerful symbol in *The Spire*, beginning as the pit at the crossways. Jocelin calls it "a grave for some notable" (p. 13), and "A pit to catch a dean" (p. 39). The irony is obvious. Not only is Pangall the notable whose grave the pit becomes, but the pit—emblematic of Jocelin's own "cellarage"—does catch the dean. The pit reveals that the cathedral rests atop a huge underground marshland. It has literally no foundation. Oddly enough, Rachel explains: "Didn't expect their foundations to be dug up before Doomsday and why not, after all they must have been under contract like my man here—" (p. 42). Roper, among other critics, tells us that traditionally the pit under the spire is the pit of Hell.[9] Many things suggest this; yet its primary suggestions are more physical. For example, as Jocelin smells the pit, he recoils. He also remembers, ironically, that "Here, where the pit stinks, I received what I received, all those years ago" (p. 53). The pit is at the spot where Jocelin received his vision. It seems logical to say that "in terms of the physical analogy, it would represent the bowels, the center of corruption and the darkness of man's heart." [10]

The cellar suggests that part of man's mind which he refuses to admit exists. Jocelin notices the big boys who were "heavy eyed from nightmares of noseless men who floated beneath the pavements, their flat faces pressed against a heavy lid" (p. 54). More than physical analogy, the pit, for Baker, "signifies, rather, that human pride wishes to deny any connection with the death, decay, and corruption apparent in all nature." [11] Before long we see this in Jocelin: "Then an anger rose out of some pit inside Jocelin" (p. 58). When the rains stop, the waters sink in the pit, and Jocelin thinks: "Doomsday coming up; or the roof of hell down there. Perhaps the damned stirring, or the noseless men turning over and thrusting up; or the living, pagan earth, unbound at last and waking, Dia Mater" (p. 80).

The climax of the pit imagery comes as the workmen torment Pangall. Jocelin watches involuntarily: "He glimpsed the hole that still gaped in the pavement; and saw between the legs that it was not entirely plugged yet" (p. 89). He watches as the weight of brown bodies presses Pangall down; he sees Goody, her hair down, her dress ripped, looking "towards Roger on this side of the pit, his arms spread from his side in anguish and appeal" (p. 90). Pangall is thus murdered, his body buried in the pit along with Jocelin's stone heads. Later, as he looks out over the countryside, Jocelin realizes "The earth is a huddle of noseless men grinning upward, there are gallows everywhere, the blood of childbirth never ceases to flow, nor sweat in the furrow, the brothels are down there and drunk men lie in the gutter" (pp. 106–7). After he realizes who the workmen really are, Jocelin repeats a doubly ironic phrase: "a grave made ready for some notable" (p. 156). Ultimately, amid the growing suggestiveness of the symbol, recognition becomes conscious: "And I must have known about him before, you see, down in the vaults, the cellarage of my mind" (p. 166). The knowledge is, of course, of Pangall's impotence and Goody's potential use as an incentive for his master builder. When Jocelin visits Roger, the master builder tells him that he stinks like a corpse, and once again Jocelin tries to explain about his "cellarage where the rats live" (p. 210). Having seen but not understood the visions of apple tree and kingfisher, Jocelin asks, "What's a man's mind Roger? Is it the whole building, cellarage and all?" (p. 213). Finally, in his deathbed vision, Jocelin sees the noseless men return, this time as "people naked, creatures of light brown parchment, which bound in their pipes or struts" (p. 222).

In *The Spire* water becomes a dominant symbolic device. The novel has a great deal of water: the three cascades "joined by leagues of water that snaked towards the cathedral" (p. 106); the surrounding marshland, adding ironic support to the spire; and the rain. Amid the bursting sunlight of the beginning we know it is spring, for the floods are rising and prevent further digging; the spring rains are close behind. The cathedral itself "was slimy with water streaming down over moss and lichen and flaking stones" (p. 51). Water invades the pit, the cathedral, and the greasy streets. More horribly, the water, "with guessed-at stealth, had invaded the graves of the great on either side of the choir" (p. 53). Foreshadowing what will happen morally and spiritually, the central portion of the novel, filled with lust, murder, and sin, is also filled with water. Outside the gutter at the foot of the cathedral, "the earth had swollen with water and pushed up the coarse grass, so that the stone seemed to dint the earth and the main impression was not now one of God's glory, but of the weight of man's building" (p. 67). In a novel which dwells on the weight of things, this image is significant. When the rain stops, the threat of its return is always present. In the harrowing scene in which Jocelin drives in the Holy Nail, the rain "cascaded down the front from a dozen gullies, spouted from stone mouths, and washed in a constant sheet over the gravel before the steps" (p. 170). Literally the rain hampers the progress of the spire; figuratively it does more.

In the joyous beginning of the novel, Jocelin is full of emotions expressed in terms of water: "A tide of emotion swept Jocelin up" (p. 47); he is "buoyed up by his joy" (p. 48); "The tides of unspeakable feeling seemed to engulf Jocelin" (p. 62); and, as Jocelin thanks God for sending His angel, "there was no angel; only the tides of feeling, swirling, pricking, burning" (pp. 62–63). The tides of feeling suggest more than sexuality; they imply a rising of man's essential wickedness which, including sex, contains all unspiritual drives. Trying to grasp what is wrong after Goody's death, Jocelin "would be aware of a feeling rising in him, coming up towards the chest like a level of dark water" (p. 138). The images of tide and pit are now associated with the cable, which also tightens. The tides swallow him up and thus connect with the minor image pattern of mouths.[12] Even the Visitor's commission bows "like the crest of a wave" (p. 163). Associated with the dark side of man's nature, the subconsciousness takes over as the waters of sleep rise. Jocelin sees Father Adam's shaking as if connected "to an infinite sea of grief which sent out an arm to fill him and overflowed liberally at his eyes" (p. 197). Both literal and metaphorical floating suggest that the cathedral, the spire, Jocelin, and all connected with the construction are adrift on a strange sea of revelation. Jocelin asks Roger to believe "the building floats" (p. 38); the noseless men float beneath the pavement. More significantly, the four pillars at the crossways float. Jocelin concentrates on the model of the spire "to right the swimming world" (p. 104); there are days when "the fog drowned even the tower" (p. 112); the workers labor at ground level on bad days and "would work as at the bottom of the sea, in sheds and arbours" (p. 113); Jocelin's thoughts and images float through his mind; and dying, like Pincher Martin, "He floated above the unction which had relevance to nothing but the leaden body" (p. 219).

While the sea is general, more specific images of wickedness engulf the builders. In Jocelin's masturbatory dream, the dean-cathedral "writhed on the marsh in the warm water, and cried out loud" (p. 65). Apparently suggestive of sexuality, warm and hot water also seem associated with fear and Jocelin's spinal disease, "a weight of hot water seemed to run from his neck into the back of his head" (p. 78). As he describes the churning in the pit, he calls it "the darkness under the earth, turning, seething, coming to the boil" (p. 79). While rain sets the perspective for the water symbol, the images of water— floods, tides, wells, and seas—suggest that condition of man which prevents his being the supreme visionary, that basic animality which links him to the earth.[13]

Each of these symbols and images is based on suggestions of man's base nature. Yet many exhibit suggestions of the other side as well. Similarly, enveloped as they are in the total moral vision, the following images and symbols, which begin as part of the spiritual side, also suggest the base side. Aside from the spire, light is the first symbol: "God the Father was exploding in his face with a glory of sunlight through painted glass" (p. 7). The light here "piled into the open square of the cloisters" (p. 8). "It smashed through the rows of windows in the south aisle, so that they exploded with colour, it slanted before him from right to left in an exact formation" (pp. 9–10). The sunlight is bright and heavy; yet its solidity comes from fine dust which "gave these rods and trunks of light the importance of a dimension. He blinked at them again, seeing, near at hand, how the individual grains of dust turned over each other . . . like mayfly in a breath of wind" (p. 10). The novel opens, then, not with sunlight but with sunlight and dust. Kinkead-Weekes and Gregor conclude, "The novel will turn out to be about seeing in a very literal sense, seeing neither sun nor dust but 'sundust.' "[14] This tension between sun and dust—whole, bright light and divided light—and light and darkness is to be the symbolic model of the tension between the dichotomous aspects of the thesis. To Jocelin, however, "The dust danced in the sun" (p. 14).

Throughout chapter 1, in the blindness of his vision, Jocelin walks amid sunlight and dust. As he prays, "Joy fell on the words like sunlight" (p. 21); there is the "spark and shatter of the sun" (p. 22); there are "shafts and trunks of sunlight" (p. 25). His aunt writes asking for a burial spot "where the sun comes in" (p. 28). As chapter 2 opens, "The dust was thicker than ever, like yellow smoke" (p. 30); Father Anselm complains about it and blames the workmen for dirtying the air "with dust and stink." The sunlight surprises Jocelin and irritates him (p. 45); yet the bishop's letter is held up "so that the sunlight fell on it" (p. 47). With the rains comes a loss of direction of light to show north and south, the crossways become dark, and the darkness becomes figuratively moral: "A dark night had not descended on the cathedral, but a midday without sun and therefore blasphemously without hope" (p. 54). A new terror settles on the old men: "Day and night acts of worship went on in the stink and halfdark, where the candles illuminated nothing but close haloes of vapour; and the voices rose . . . in fear of darkness and a universe without hope" (p. 55). The light symbol develops hope, faith, and aspiration; through its absence, it suggests desperation and hopelessness. The "quiet light" of the altar now becomes "out of reach, . . . a divided thing, a light in each eye" (p. 62). With Easter returns "a confusion of light, honey-bars from the windows, phantom lights that swam through his head" (p. 69). The spring mud dries and dust returns; "Sunshafts were bright with it, monuments held it in little films and screes" (p. 72).

With the metal sheet set up to illuminate the pit, light

takes another turn. The sun is trapped by the sheet "and hurled straight down the pit" (p. 78). With the singing of the pillars come wheels and flashes of light; light "seemed all run into dazzles and haloes that lay round every object" (p. 88); and the noises of Pangall's murder "were as confused as the lights that swirled in his head" (p. 89). Jocelin thinks it all a nightmare, "since things happened and stuck in the eye as if seen by flashes of lightning" (p. 89). Light has progressed from bright, dust-laden sunlight to the darkness of the rains and divided lights to brilliant wheels and haloes that surround the novel's nadir. As he climbs the tower, the light dazzles Jocelin; even the tower's arches draw the light together "so that all their transparencies would seem part of one thing, a single deed" (pp. 103–4). The similarity between the image and the central moral vision is apparent, but Jocelin is unable to capture the single vision. The tower's lengthening shadow develops "a kind of quivering indecisiveness about the end of it" (p. 130). Light in the second half of the novel loses brilliance, becomes gray; even the "inside of the cone was darkening as the skin drew together" (p. 150).

In the last part of the work, light takes on radical characteristics. The saints "jumped and rattled in the windows" (p. 169), the sky becomes high and light, and Jocelin, on his deathbed, watches the lightning illumine his spire: "He knew that the bulk in the middle of the light was the tower but could not tell exactly how it was shaped" (pp. 172–73). Indecisiveness, blurred shapes, and haloed sight indicate not only Jocelin's physical degeneration but also man's weak moral vision. And things that happen in a flash of lightning take on magnified importance. Pangall's murder and the tower here are heightened, focused instants of insight. Jocelin's attempt to plant the Nail finds the lights not only outside but "swimming inside his eyes" (p. 175); when he descends, he can hardly see for "the glossy lights that danced round him" (p. 176). The candles in the hall are like "the glossy patches that sometimes swam before his eyes" (p. 180). The candles suggest the distance that grows between the pure light of spiritual vision and the ability to see that light.

With Pangall's story of his great-great-grandfather's saving the cathedral from fire, the major image pattern of fire begins. The symbol is associated with many things and is a measurement of intensity. The joy that falls on the dean's words ignites them: "They took fire" (p. 21). Roger's quarrels with Rachel were "like flares, blown out presently by some wind" (p. 43); he bursts into "raging flames of temper" (p. 113). The tower's steel band is fired and streams of sparks fall. The most significant of the literal fires are those of the devil worshipers. Reminding him of the obscene berry, these fires bring a new awareness: "The story, with disjunct sentences, burned before his mind; and at the crossways, the replaced paving stones were hot to his feet with all the fires of hell" (p. 157). Fire indicates the searing intensity of passion and faith, spirituality and paganism. In its use as an image of Jocelin's determination, fire exhibits its fullest development. His will is referred to as burning fiercely, a "refiner's fire," a "blazing certainty." Consonant with orthodox symbolism, the use of fire to suggest strength, determination, and durability is appropriate if not a bit ironic in view of the impurities associated with Jocelin's will. There is a great fire of love between the dean and Roger, and Jocelin promises more money "among the flames of love" (p. 152). The tower, in Jocelin's notebook, grows until "at the utmost tip it burst into a living fire. . . . the thing I had felt as a flame of fire" (p. 191). The phrase is similar to Sammy Mountjoy's "flake of fire." Seeing its destructive capabilities as well, Jocelin recognizes the dichotomous characteristic of the image.[15]

Paralleling this fire imagery is the angel at Jocelin's back. Narratively deprived of modern medical terminology, we learn rather late that Jocelin's angel is an advanced case of infectious disease. To us and Jocelin, the warmth at his back is his guardian angel. The angel comes persistently, always warming, comforting. At times of noticeable trial, as when the tides of sexual feeling arise, "there was no angel" (p. 62). Soon both angel and devil begin to visit; the warmth of the angel's comfort becomes too much and bends his back; finally, the angel changes into angel-devil: "Then his angel put away the two wings from the cloven hoof and struck him from arse to the head with a whitehot flail" (p. 188). As he lies dying, Jocelin is comforted by Father Adam, "but the terror of the angel's approach was on him" (p. 197). In a subtle progression from comforting, warming angel to tormenting devil to the terrible dark angel, the image conveys both physical and spiritual degeneration by the forces which generate the spire itself.

An image illustrating the difference between illusion and reality of spiritual vision, birds play an important role in the symbolic structure. Swallows and their nests appear regularly. Pangall's cottage leans against the cathedral "like the accretions under the eaves of an ancient house," where swallows have nested (p. 17). More significantly, Jocelin watches the dumb artist's palm "sweep through the air in a swallow flight" and guesses he means an eagle: "You are thinking of the Holy Spirit?" (p. 24). Doped by his vision, Jocelin guesses above the mark. The aspect of swallows most used in the development of the image is, however, their renowned building ability.[16] The scaffolding in the tower "climbed up inside, so that to look up from the crossways was like looking up a chimney where very methodical birds had been building" (p. 72). On a day when no one is working in the cathedral, Jocelin looks up and sees "that all nests were bare of birds in the chimney" (p. 76). The tower is called "the square chimney with its geometrical birds," "the birdhaunted tower top," and its hut, "a swallow's nest." Jocelin looks at the stone head and

again misinterprets: "Nose, like an eagle's beak" (p. 23).
Eagles, too, play a central part in this pattern, forming one
boundary of the image. At the incomplete spire's top, "A
great bird floated up there on spread wings, and he said
aloud, remembering Saint John: 'It is an eagle' " (p. 107). He
refers to one of the four beasts round the throne of God which
John says was "like a flying eagle." [17] To Jocelin, the bird represents freedom from the entangling ground-level existence,
the Holy Spirit: "free in a world of branches" (p. 102). As
he grows to recognize the unnaturalness for man of such a
height, Jocelin descends, "since no man can live his life with
eagles" (p. 110). In one picture of the dean, Alison, his aunt,
calls him "a great bird hunched in the rain" (p. 184); Jocelin
remembers that long ago "the eagle stooped on me by the
sea" (p. 195); and Anselm saw young Jocelin as "flying like a
great bird" (p. 201).

The bird providing the other boundary of the image is
the raven or crow. As Jocelin looks from the tower, "a raven
slipped past his face, slanting on the wind with a harsh expos-
tulation at the people lifted so boldly into its kingdom" (p.
105). The raven's squawk is "sane and daylight and matter-of-
fact" (p. 133). The raven is anything but an image of prayer
and inspiration. It is, although Jocelin insists not, a sane,
matter-of-fact black bird. This tendency to put reality and illusion into perspective persists in the bird imagery, especially
in metaphor. Jocelin walks in the beginning with joy like
wings. Yet this simile changes in two subsequent appearances, paralleling the vision's change from spiritual, inspirational vision to tangled contradiction. As the faithful fall
around him, "he understood how the wings of his joy were
clipped close" (p. 49), and later, Jocelin's joy "beat at him like
wings" (p. 106). The metaphor concludes, without joy, in the
devils who beat at the dean "with scaly wings" (p. 175). As the
final, plangent storm assails the tower, Jocelin hears "thin
screams, bird noises" (p. 173). [18] Whether they are the sounds

of stone crashing or devils beating the windows does not matter; the image of eaglelike, inspirational vision is destroyed.

The gargoyles and the stone heads bear comparison with the bird image. Just a lump of stone at the beginning, the heads take shape with the spire. As Jocelin studies one of them, he thinks: "Nose, like an eagle's beak" (p. 23). As in the eagle, Jocelin sees in the stone head his own spirit, which follows the sacred vision: "Rushing on with the angels, the infinite speed that is stillness, hair blown, torn back, straightened with the wind of the spirit" (p. 24). Once again the reference is to that idea of spatial-temporal, split-second perception which now includes mayfly, lightning, and angels and will culminate in the apple tree and the kingfisher. To be placed halfway up the spire, these heads are made of timeless stone and are to Jocelin images of his pride in his vision. Yet they remain gargoyles and succeed a history of grotesque, misshapen ugliness. They erupt as the rainy season arrives, uttering "water as if they were yet another penalty of damnation" (p. 51). Jocelin thinks they seem "burst out of the stone like boils or pimples, purging the body of sickness, ensuring by their self-damnation, the purity of the whole"; like the ravens, they yell "soundless blasphemies and derisions into the wind, yet made no more noise than death in another country" (p. 67). In a strange way, as the gargoyles are ugliness and blasphemy designed to purify and save the whole, so are Jocelin's heads used to fill the stinking pit and save the cathedral. The new stone heads reflect a changed Jocelin. They are soon raised up the spire where they lie "shouting silently and exulting in the height of heaven and the brightness" (p. 104). In the climactic scene for this image, Jocelin stares into the steel sheet: "He examined his eyes, deep in sockets over which the skin was dragged—dragged too over the cheekbones, then sucked in. He examined the nose like a beak" (p. 155). What the visionary saw in himself as Holy Spirit, eagle, angel of God's will, has become the voracious hunter and deformed gargoyle that the dumb artist saw all along. As Jocelin later tells Roger: "Clean water through the mouth of a dead dog" (p. 210).

The spire itself represents what Frye has called a heraldic symbol. In its position as the central symbol of the work, it touches every other device. Skilton has described it: "The central symbol of the book is the spire itself, which has an obvious and explicit dual significance as on the one hand the completion of the 'diagram of prayer,' crowning it and aspiring heavenwards; and on the other hand a phallus."[19] The representation of the church as a man lying on his back establishes the phallic aspect: "And now also, springing, projecting, bursting, erupting from the heart of the building, there was its crown and majesty, the new spire" (p. 8). Jocelin is also the spiritual surgeon who lays his hand on the very body of his church. The model is caressed and cradled "as a mother might examine her baby" (pp. 55–56), and in Jocelin's nightmare, the people "knew the church had no spire nor could have any" (pp. 64–65). Golding is fully aware of his craft here, of the universal character of phallic symbolism. This occurrence not only implies impotence, but Jocelin's forced impotence in the face of increasing sexual awareness. The workmen, aware of Pangall's impotence, taunt the servant, "one of the army dancing towards him, the spire projecting obscenely between his legs" (p. 105). As prayer and phallus, the spire unites aspiring man and instinctual man, heaven and earth, spiritual and primitive impulse; it thus becomes one more powerful symbol of that complex, tangled condition of man which is at the heart of Golding's moral thesis.

The spire is many things. It is a "great finger sticking up" (p. 108); it is "an ungainly, crumbling thing" (p. 193); it is "the stone hammer" (p. 204); and for Roger it is "me old cock!" (p. 208). But more interestingly, through a series of similes and metaphors it becomes a mast and the church a ship. Jocelin almost takes the "solid" light to be real "and so believe that my stone ship lay aground on her side. . . ." (p. 10); he knows the people regard the church as "the security of the stone ship, the security of her crew" (p. 11); the church is the only good thing, "the ark, the refuge, a ship to contain all these people and now fitted with a mast" (p. 107). The construction is described as an impossible task, "to build a ship on dry land" (p. 121). Realizing that Roger has begun to drink, "Jocelin had a moment of panic, like a passenger in a ship with a drunken master" (p. 143). The August gales set the spire swaying like a mast, the cable for the octagons is "strong enough to hold a ship," and the dean, in his passion to implant the Nail, is "like a man climbing a mast at sea." This church-as-ship simile serves to isolate the action and intensify the drama which erupts within it.

In the last three visions Golding brings all the imagery of the novel to a climax. Crippled by the emptiness of his spine, denied forgiveness by Anselm, watching his diagram of prayer sway dangerously and threaten to fall, the visionary wanders out into the churchyard and sees the apple tree: "There was a cloud of angels flashing in the sunlight, they were pink and gold and white. . . . They brought with them a scatter of clear leaves, and among the leaves a long, black springing thing. . . . It was there beyond the wall, bursting up with cloud and scatter, laying hold of the earth and the air, a fountain, a marvel, an appletree" (pp. 204–5). Once again we find the familiar dichotomous image. The tree is a fountain but, most important, it lays hold of the earth and the air at one time. Like the spire, like man, it is embedded in the fertile earth yet reaches heavenward. It is a picture in space: unified, whole, a contradiction, a painting.

Next, as Kinkead-Weekes and Gregor point out, comes a similar analogy in time: "Then . . . over the sliding water, he saw all the blue of the sky condensed to a winged sapphire, that flashed once. He cried out. 'Come back!' But the bird was gone, an arrow shot once" (p. 205). Uniting sliding water, which suggests the subconsciousness and consequently man's base nature, and the sky and arrow, the image recalls the mayfly and raven in Jocelin's lecture about time and life (pp. 116–17).[20] Looking at his feet Jocelin thinks he must look like an old crow, and the eagle/kingfisher and swallow/raven contrast is renewed. Irony persists as he remembers he came looking for "many reasons and they're all mixed up." That is the point of these two emblematic visions: things *are* all mixed up; man is neither branch nor root, kingfisher nor crow, but both, inextricably bound together.

The apple tree and kingfisher visions appear before Jocelin asks for Roger's forgiveness, and their significance only affects him later. When Jocelin finally shames himself before Roger, and is subsequently mobbed outside, he is cleansed long enough so that the final vision on the last page has for him true significance: "There were two eyes looking at him through the panic. . . . The two eyes slid together" (pp. 222–23). The degeneration from brilliant sunlight, to a midday without sun, to the divided altar lights is reversed as the lights of the window slid together. He looks at the window: "Something divided it. . . . The division was still and silent. . . . It was slim as a girl, translucent. It had grown from some seed of rosecoloured substance that glittered like a waterfall, an upward waterfall. The substance was one thing, that broke all the way to infinity in cascades of exultation" (p. 223). The girllike slimness and the seed suggest association with the entanglement images.[21] It is also a waterfall, which links it with the kingfisher and makes it a point of knowledge, as the waterfall is in *The Inheritors*. Like the sight of Pangall's murder and the spire through lightning flashes earlier, "wild flashes of thought split the darkness. Our very stones cry out" (p. 223).[22] Uniting flashes of knowledge and vision with the sense of infinity, the image creates an atmosphere for the final, terrible moral analogy:

What is terror and joy, how should they be mixed, why are they the same, the flashing, the flying through the panicshot darkness like a bluebird over water?

"A gesture of assent—"

In the tide, flying like a bluebird, struggling, shouting, screaming to leave behind the words of magic and incomprehension—

It's like the appletree! [p. 223]

The basis of the novel, the moral vision, of life itself, is at the heart of these three visions. The flashing, the flying through "panicshot darkness" suggests light, birds, joy, and the spirit. As Jocelin is unable to look upward at all times, so this spire-vision, "struggling, shouting, screaming to leave behind the words of magic and incomprehension," cannot separate itself from its planted origin. No man can live with the eagles—for long. *"It's like the appletree!"* is, of course, the shibboleth. "It" can mean virtually anything, and that's the point. "It" is man, life, spiritual vision, total existence, and all of these at the same time. The phrase becomes, like the novel and the moral vision, a tautology, providing all questions with all answers. None of Golding's other protagonists has perceived such universality in his search for the answer.

In *The Spire* Golding achieved the most successful expression of his moral vision. Like the vision itself, *The Spire* includes all the novels which precede it and requires all of them for its complete effect. The incredible clarity and, at the same time, ambiguity of the vision is the result of a complex, interacting series of image and symbol patterns which not only develop their own suggestions, and develop suggestions in others they contact, but push the tangled unity of symbolic meaning to the three symbolically dense visions of the conclusion. The result is a precisely constructed novel which, in its simultaneous expression of dichotomous premises, is almost a mythic, archetypal expression of the moral thesis. Only by bringing to the final three groupings the key images and symbols does this tangled wealth of meaning become clear, through vision, not logic.

---

1. William Golding, *The Spire* (London: Faber, 1964), 35. Further references are to this edition.

2. David Skilton, "Golding's *The Spire*," *Studies in the Literary Imagination*, 2 (October 1969), 53.

3. William Golding, "Fable," *The Hot Gates* (London: Faber, 1965), 85.

4. Northrop Frye, *Anatomy of Criticism: Four Essays* (Princeton, N.J.: Princeton University Press, 1957), 86.

5. Howard S. Babb, *The Novels of William Golding* (Columbus: Ohio State University Press, 1970), 154.

6. D. W. Crompton, "The Spire," *Critical Quarterly*, 9 (Spring 1967), 77.

7. Mark Kinkead-Weekes and Ian Gregor, *William Golding: A Critical Study* (London: Faber, 1967), 219.

8. Ibid., 230.

9. Derek Roper, "Allegory and Novel in Golding's *The Spire*," *Wisconsin Studies in Contemporary Literature*, 8 (Winter 1967), 22.

10. Crompton, 72.

11. James R. Baker, *William Golding: A Critical Study* (New York: St. Martin's, 1965), 85 n.

12. The image of the mouth, suggesting acquisition and consumption, has a lively history in the novel. Besides the concentration on the stone head's mouth, there is Jocelin's "dark corner" forcing "his mouth to utter words that had no logical meaning" (p. 75); the wind holds the dean in its "mouth" (p. 174); Rachel talks "as if the furious womb had acquired a tongue" (p. 59). The pit "swallowed" Rachel's words (p. 44) and Jocelin's laughing is "sucked" up by the tower (p. 94). Finally, the dumb man, the little devil, and Goody all hum from an "empty mouth" (pp. 12, 159, 178, 210).

13. Also important are the animal similes: the dumb sculptor smiles "doglike" (p. 12), has eager "doglike eyes" (pp. 23, 24), looks at Jocelin like "a good dog" (p. 99), is a "good dog" (p. 104); even Anselm is "like a dog" (p. 200), and to Roger Jocelin calls himself a "dead dog" (p. 210). Roger looks "like a bull" (p. 39), climbs the spire "like a bear" (p. 94) and, weighted by the erupting forces, scrambles "like a crab" (p. 151). Thoughts leap into Jocelin's mind "like a live thing" (p. 63), and he regards Roger as "the animal" (p. 86). The sum impression of these devices is of instinctualism, helplessness in the face of the basic, physical drives of the human, and finally subjugation.

14. Kinkead-Weekes and Gregor, *William Golding*, 204.

15. There are also in this pattern "a flash of fire through his head" (pp. 76, 84, 86) and the entire body on fire (p. 85).

16. *The Bestiary: A Book of Beasts*, trans. and ed. T. H. White (New York: Putnam's 1960), 147–48.

17. Revelation 4.7. Note that Saint John's "four beasts" had "each of them six wings about him; and they were full of eyes within" (4.8), similar to Jocelin's angel, who comes "unseen with six wings and stood to warm his back" (p. 132).

18. The motif of sound and song is a small but effective one. The workmen lend an agglomeration of sounds (pp. 9, 68, 89); Jocelin's artist hums (p. 12); the dean thinks the "thin sound of mattins" is the model's breathing (p. 13); and the choir makes the same sound as the workers (p. 26). The pillars' singing is the most obvious incidence (pp. 80, 143). There is also the raven's "squawk" (p. 133), the "bird noises" (p. 173), the song around the Holy Nail (p. 161), and, ultimately, at the nadir, "the noise of all the devils out of hell" (p. 175) and the slavering sounds of the mob (p. 215).

19. Skilton, "Golding's *The Spire*," 53–54.

20. The image of the arrow, like that of birds, is persistent and contradictory: there is the "arrow of love" (p. 8), the thought as a "thrust of a spear" (p. 63), the beams "like arrows" (p. 71), and the spire itself, "an arrow shot into the earth, with up here, an ungainly butt" (p. 147). There are also the pillars, "four needles stuck in the earth" (p. 148), themselves ironically symbolic.

21. The word *spire* comes from the Middle English *spir(e)*, which means "a slender stalk." For an examination of the plant image, see Jeanne Delbaere-Garant, "The Evil Plant in William Golding's *The Spire*."

22. Stones are a favorite metaphor, in most cases connected with words: Anselm's words are "pebbles" (p. 49); the church is "the bible in stone" (p. 51); and the Visitor's question about the mistletoe berry is "hard and sharp as the edge of stone" (p. 167).

David Skilton

THE PYRAMID AND COMIC
SOCIAL FICTION

In BEING A FUNNY BOOK with serious things to say,
The Pyramid belongs to an important tradition of comic social
fiction, as the evocation of the spirit of Anthony Trollope is
intended to make clear. But far from sharing in the sentiment
and nostalgia which the twentieth century has read into Trollope, Golding's comic masterpiece is filled with laughter
caused by discomforting awareness of the limitations and ab-
surdities of life. The writing is witty, as the tradition demands, but the author risks destroying the delicate web of
English social comedy by a number of astonishingly heavy
jokes, which turn out to be part of a calculated shock he is
administering to the form in order to brace it once more with
a satisfying rigor of thought. In all his novels Golding em-
bodies unresolvable complexities of existence in stories which
are among the most mythopoeic of the century. In *The
Pyramid* the complexities are there again, and this time Golding makes the difficult reconciliations of the comic fiction of
English society with sharp, penetrating criticism, and of
finely discriminating social perceptions with the downright
dirty joke. It is remarkable that he could take a tradition so

well established and use it for his own ends without falling victim to the nostalgia, sentimentality, and intellectual softness that bedevil it, and instead, by playing on its conventions, produce a thoroughly antinostalgic and biting work.

In part *The Pyramid* is about the narrator, Oliver, growing up, and consists of three stories, interlocking in a complicated pattern.[1] The first section concerns Oliver's sexual initiation with Evie Babbacombe in "the erotic woods."[2] In the second, he overcomes his calf love for Imogen Grantley and brushes with transvestite homosexuality, which he does not understand. The final part is devoted to the longer process by which he emancipates himself from other crippling elements in his upbringing, especially a guilt-complex and the crushing influence of his music teacher, Miss Dawlish. This process is not completed until he is in his forties, a prosperous family man, but still needing to be protected from the world by "the security of leather and steel and glass" of his car (p. 159).

The story of Oliver's early life is not merely related against a social background; a social field of force impinges on his every thought and deed. The problem of the individual's relation to society has always been a fruitful area of investigation for the novelist, and the doubts raised about the possibilities of free action connect with the concerns of Golding's other novels. *The Pyramid* in fact occupies an intersection of the interests of the earlier Golding with the great Victorians. Oliver is seen not as an individual simply acting with regard to those around him, but as one whose being is to an alarming degree determined by external pressures.

In the first place, the social distance between himself, the dispenser's son, and Evie, the town crier's daughter, is the key to his dealings with her and is expressed at the beginning by an elegantly simple "of course we had never spoken. Never met. Obviously. . . ." (p. 13). By virtue of her low status, Evie seems to Oliver to have an understanding and experience of the world which he lacks. He belongs to that

insecure section of the lower middle class that is more deprived, in a social sense, than anyone else in Stilbourne. Just
as obviously, the doctor's son, Bobby Ewan, who wanted to
make Olly his slave when they were toddlers (p. 23), is so-
cially out of Olly's range—the gulf exaggerated by Bobby's
"Duke of Wellington's profile" (p. 57). Oliver can overcome
Ewan's boarding-school superiority, but only by dirty fighting
or low cunning, without regard for gentlemanly conventions—that is, by the sheer efficiency which later makes him
successful in chemical-warfare research. Bobby Ewan, whose
instinct for self-preservation is less dominant than Oliver's,
enters the Royal Air Force as a fighter pilot.

Because of his insecure position Oliver has to assert himself and grasp at all the advantages he can with all his intellectual and sexual vigor. Yet as a successful man over forty-five,
he remains bitter at the way the doctor's family patronized
him: "And ruefully I remember how the Ewans always gave
me a present at Christmas. They also vibrated in time to the
crystal pyramid" (p. 178). The social order controls everyone,
and from the beginning Oliver, maimed by convention, is
aware that his personal freedom is circumscribed.

The social workings of *The Pyramid* are more complicated
than this, but to the alert reader the nuances are explained in
the narrative. As so often in novels in which social relations
play a large part, the novelist convinces us of the coherence of
what he presents not by referring us outside his novel to some
external truth, but by incorporating into his novel the rules by
which his fictional society operates. In *The Pyramid* these
rules are those obtaining in the world in which the contemporary reader lives, and the novel is in this sense realistic. The
English reader feels a pleasure of recognition, but everything
the reader needs to know is in the text, and one of Oliver's
functions is to interpret otherwise cryptic social information.

To point up the Stilbourne hierarchy, there is emphasis on
army ranks: Sergeant Babbacombe, Sergeant Major O'Dono-

van, and Captain Wilmot. The whole question of Oliver's exact social level as the dispenser's son can be condensed into a hilarious dispute as to how he should be addressed when he plays the palace guard in *King of Hearts*. His mother will not have him called "Sergeant," which would put him on a level with the Babbacombes, while "Colonel" is too lofty. This dispute rages around a silent Oliver, and the final compromise of "Captain"—reached without his consent—is an analogy of Oliver's whole social history.

In the third section, another sort of comedy is developed around the Stilbourne activity of watching neighbors and intuiting intimate details about their lives from their smallest movements. Life in Oliver's world is experienced at one remove from reality. Like other women of Stilbourne, Oliver's mother plays this game with consummate skill, not concealing her scorn for her menfolk when they fail to follow her logic. She has a social radar of her own and can use young Olly as "a kind of interplanetary probe" (p. 177)—an inanimate tool to exploit without regard to his feelings about "the unforeseeable perils of interplanetary travel" (p. 180), much as he will later exploit others. Incidentally, his mother is a great comic character, with her preternaturally acute perceptions and a style of delivery which defies mundane logic much as Mrs. Nickleby's does.

Nothing said so far indicates that *The Pyramid* is more than good social comedy, with an eye to the psychological development of its protagonist. But this is a partial interpretation. What disturbs the mode of the novel is a series of dirty jokes almost too crude for the more subdued comedy in which they are set. One can instance Olly's father's preference for "a *good grind*" on his violin (p. 140) or the nickname *Kummer* that Bounce uses for Oliver—eventually revealing the sexual significance of the name when she asks if he is looking for a girl in the woods. Jokes of this nature manifest the unstable aspects of the fictional world, which tends to erupt pe-

riodically into farcical hilarity with disturbing implications.
For example, there is the way Bounce's car moves off almost
under its own volition while Bobby Ewan and Evie are having
sex in it, as a parallel to the way Henry Williams and his machines take over Stilbourne and, by implication, the world.

Again, Oliver's embarrassment at having to take his hal-
berd through the auditorium during *King of Hearts* exemplifies man's inability to organize a secure existence in the face
of the anarchy that threatens him. Olly, unable to get his
weapon "up the back passage" and advised to "enter from in
front," cries out a despairing, "But they'll see me!" (p. 152).
This moment in the second section of the novel, paralleling
Oliver's exposure to his father's binoculars while having intercourse with Evie in the first part, is one of the shattering
experiences that disturb the placid, flat "coloured picture of
Stilbourne" and show the impossibility of security in the
world. The three story-segments are punctuated by such
traumatic moments, most of them involving the nakedness
and exposure of Oliver or those around him. In these moments the harshness of life is laid bare, and the surface of
social comedy is ripped open to reveal the alarming disorder
that reigns underneath. Like the weals on Evie's backside
from Captain Wilmot's beatings, these moments of violent
awareness impress themselves on Oliver as though they were
marks on the cosmos, radically contradicting the fundamental
myths of Stilbourne society. Is not Miss Dawlish happy only
when she goes out into the street without her clothes on?

Avril Henry has drawn up an impressive catalog of the
varieties of sexual activity described or hinted at in *The
Pyramid*, including incest, flagellation, and transvestism.[3]
But the shocks the author administers in the traumatic flashes
are not on the level of newspaper scandal, from which Stilbourne gets its "shocked purging" (p. 114). Such revelations
in *The News of the World* ultimately reinforce the status quo,
but *The Pyramid* makes the reader aware of the deforming

pressures of its fictional society. *The Pyramid* is necessarily unnostalgic, since life in Oliver's world cannot be imagined as ever being other than hard, dangerous, and destructive. When in the third part the narrator recounts his return to Stilbourne to confront his childhood and youth, nostalgia is inappropriate after the pain of the first two sections. The perfectly controlled relationship between Oliver as narrator and Oliver as a child can be compared to Dickens's mastery in *Great Expectations*, which is understood through the attitude of Mr. Pirrip, the middle-aged narrator, to the young Pip. A fitting contrast is provided by the opposition set up by George Orwell in Bowling's return to Lower Binfield in *Coming Up for Air*—although Orwell's simpler nostalgic formula is justified by his polemic ends. The narrator's final awareness in *The Pyramid* has nothing to do with sentimental attachment to the past but is an understanding of self, when at last he recognizes his own moral physiognomy in the face of Henry Williams, the archexploiter and evil genius of materialism.

The traumatic flashes in *The Pyramid* register themselves on the narrator's mind in much the same way as do Jocelin's in *The Spire*. It is this kind of indelible picture which Jocelin sees of the men having Pangall at the broom's end, while Goody Pangall, her dress torn, clutches the pillar behind her: the sight "was printed on his eye for ever. Whenever there should be darkness and no thought, the picture would come back."[4] A comparable picture for Oliver is Evie's face with its depth of hurt, "make-up struck on a dead, white face," as she asks for tenderness and he responds with a Rabelaisian gesture. Such pictures "burn themselves into the eye and can be examined ever after in minute detail" (p. 89). Oliver explains the process when he describes a very early memory of Mr. Dawlish smashing the Poor Man's phonograph:

Now you may wonder how, at the age of three, I knew these people, their names and provenance; but a child's retina is

such a perfect recording machine that given the impulse of
interest or excitement it takes an indelible snapshot. . . . I saw
them numberless times later and compared them with the
snapshot that lay in my head, and indeed, still lies there. I take
the snapshot from whatever drawer it lies in and sort my im-
pressions into two piles—one of primary, ignorant perceptions; the other a gradual sophistication which tells me the
horseshoe was cooling, my own white shoes made of kid, and
Mr. Dawlish a thwarted man. [pp. 164–65]

Nearly always in Golding we are presented with raw, uncom-
prehended experience, and the central movement in all his
novels is from ignorant perceptions, through increasingly
complex awareness, to understanding. The moments of perception are eddies set up in the flux of experience by hard
obstacles which obtrude from below and belie the orderly
flow of daily life.

The three story-segments interlock chronologically and
are not defined principally in terms of the protagonist's psychological development. The long outer sections examine an
ideal by which men might seem to seek to live—love in the
first part and devotion to art (music in this case) in the last—
and each demolishes a proposition or motto related to the apparent ideal. In the first, the "Amor vincit omnia" of Chau-
cer's Prioress is debased through Olly's crude translation,
"Love beats everything" (p. 37), which shows its ironic significance when the weals from Captain Wilmot's beating are
revealed on Evie's backside. "Heaven is music," which Henry
Williams inscribes on Bounce's monument, forms the ironic
motto of the last part. It is discredited by the misery of
Bounce's life, by the physical torture of the infant Oliver
when he is twisted into the position necessary for violin-
playing, and by the recurrent crack of Mr. Dawlish's ruler
across his daughter's knuckles. Oliver comes to realize that
real music is elsewhere, so that hopeless exclusion is added to
his other frustrations.

The short middle section, or scherzo, concerns the Stilbourne Operatic Society, whose initials are a cry for salvation that will never come. This part contains the major themes of the outer movements in hilarious compression. It could be called a burlesque of them were they not already presented in comedy that frequently bursts into farce. This middle section is not just a bridging passage, but an epitome of the rest of the novel—a small pyramid that forms the top of the large pyramid, part of the whole yet geometrically similar to it, completing it at a still higher level of high comedy.

The English comic social novel does not often discredit society so radically. There is usually a level at which the vision of the novel ceases to be out of accord with the ideals of society as constituted at present or at some future date, or as it may be supposed to have been in the past. Yet from *The Pyramid* it would be hard to extract a model of a satisfactory social system, past, present, or future.

Golding based some of his earlier fiction on the demolition of certain propositions about human nature and life. In *Lord of the Flies*, he announces his intention of discrediting the pious optimism of *The Coral Island* and to this end appropriates the names of Ballantyne's characters for ironic effect, while underlining his message by reference to the title of the South Sea idyll near the beginning. At the end, the naval officer's "Jolly good show. Like the Coral Island" is a savage twist in the tail. *The Coral Island* provides a kind of false standard against which Golding's modern fable is played, and the allusions to Ballantyne open up a path into the heart of the book. *The Pyramid*, too, has a set of negative allusions, as well as its three ironic mottoes, being full of glances at Trollope's *Chronicles of Barsetshire*. It may help interpretation of the relation of *The Pyramid* to comic social fiction to establish what part these Trollopian references play.

Although the name Stilbourne is not taken from Trollope's Barsetshire, Golding places it in the vicinity of Barchester,

between that city and Omnium. (The latter name, so suitable
for Golding's purposes, is taken from a Trollopian duke.) Although Barchester is mentioned fairly frequently, this does
not seem important at first, and none of the action takes place
there. Golding would not be the first novelist to rifle the
Chronicles for a ready-made setting, furnished with a full set
of associations and complete in all its geographical detail, but
he is not really concerned with the county Trollope created.
Instead, he builds up the topology of Stilbourne with meticulous care.

The Trollopian allusions, then, are not individually useful
borrowings. But taken together, they provide a standard to
which all of Stilbourne life is referred, and the effect is central
to the scheme of *The Pyramid*. We tend to regard Barsetshire
as an archetype of Victorian England; by showing what it has
become over the years, Golding uses the contrast to emphasize the twentieth-century quality of his account of English
life. *The Pyramid* was published in 1967, exactly one hundred
years after *The Last Chronicle of Barset*, and the changes
from Trollope's time to Golding's are seen in such minor
shocks as buses plying to and from Barchester, and the
motorway which runs through Barsetshire, while satellites are
passing over Trollope's county and scanning it. Faced with
such large-scale change, the reader is unlikely to assume that
English country life is one unchanging idyll.

In less obvious form the allusions extend much further.
Imogen Grantley, vain and empty and so much out of Olly's
reach, is grandniece of a dean of Barchester, and a transformation of the proud, frigid Griselda Grantley, the archdeacon's
daughter and the old bishop's granddaughter, who marries
into the aristocracy. Mr. De Tracy comes from the metrop-
olis and has different standards from those of the inhabitants
of Barsetshire, rather like the de Courcys in, say, *Doctor
Thorne*, while Mr. Harvey, the incumbent of Bumstead

Episcopi and double-bass player for the Stilbourne Operatic Society, is a transmogrification of Septimus Harding, the warden of Hiram's Hospital and father-in-law to the Rector of Plumstead Episcopi.

These references are not cheap jokes; together they form an ironic comment on the world of Stilbourne. One almost suspects a suppressed Trollope-trollop pun underlying the first section of the novel, for the crude sexuality of modern Barsetshire translates Plumstead into Bumstead Episcopi. But the irony has another edge and reminds us that facile nostalgia for Trollope's world does not correspond to Victorian social realities or to the truth about Trollope's novels. Mr. Harvey is buried under a load of hay, but his innocent prototype is crushed by political forces; Plumstead Episcopi displays a gross lack of spirituality, and the name as clearly indicates the misapplication of church funds as Bumstead does the abuse of the body. A widespread, false, and cozy view of Trollope is the standard of reference behind *The Pyramid*, where the source of ironic contrast depends upon something essentially false—a nostalgia for a world that never existed.

The most significant mention of Barchester comes just before Olly has intercourse with Evie for the last time, while his father watches them. Olly emerges from the woods on his way to meet her: "It was said you could see the very tip of Barchester Spire from the crest of Pentry Hill and I circled the whole thing, before I climbed to the top. But there was a blue distance where Barchester and its spire might be" (pp. 97–98). Turning from the prospect that is reputed in Stilbourne myth to contain the cathedral but does not, he catches sight of Evie waiting for him, a tiny white speck in view of Stilbourne and the whole country round about. A spiritual focus is lacking in Olly's world, but a sexual one is easy to find. Similarly, the main social institution of Trollope's Barsetshire, the Church of England, and Barchester Cathedral, with its sym-

bolic spire, are actually out of sight. And the different grades
of clergy in Trollope are replaced by the almost spurious army
ranks of *The Pyramid*.

This scene may contain a covert reference to Golding's
The Spire; there, the spire is all-important and plays a part
the eponym of *The Pyramid* certainly does not. In the earlier
book, the spire is the central, focal symbol, providing the
chief organizing principle and physically structuring the fictional world as well. The title has a direct relevance to that
novel at all levels, but the relation between the body of *The
Pyramid* and its title is not explicit but of problematic, allusive complexity. Avril Henry has investigated the possible
meanings of the title and linked them to the complex time-
structure of the novel. She concludes: "The Pyramid refers to
monument, metronome and crystal, all linked by similar
shape and by their relation to Time whether gesturing against
it, imposing it or simply enjoying it. Between them the three
carry a wide range of connotations: social and religious op-
pressiveness and aspiration, ancient traditions and crippling
conventions, regulating and destructive discipline, communication and detection."[5] The pyramid of the title has no exact
physical representative in the fictional world of Stilbourne, no
obvious symbolic significance, and no clear role in the social
structure. If the pyramid is Bounce's monument, or her
metronome, it is only inexactly so. If it refers to the crystals
used in time-keeping devices and in radar, this relation with
the imagery of the novel is by no means realized *in* the novel,
and the reference is, to say the least, oblique. Any
significance which operates through the single mention of
Henry Williams's possible Egyptian holiday or through the
epigraph from the *Instructions of Ptah-hotep* is equally indi-
rect. To take it as the social pyramid, on the other hand, is to
respond accurately to a resonance in the title which har-
monizes with the rest of the work; but this depends on a significance which has to be imported by the reader himself.

So this wonderfully complex novel is not epitomized by its title. At some depth, such a complex of connotations as those listed by Avril Henry may well have a formative role in the book, but *The Pyramid* is significantly unlike *The Spire* in that it is not a working out of the meaning of its own title. The title stands at a remove from the body of the novel, vibrating sympathetically in response to the several aspects of it that Avril Henry enumerates. Novel and title are not to be united by a simple parallelism but stand in a complex, suggestive relationship that opens up as many questions as it solves. Things are not straightforward in Golding's fictional world.

---

1. For a valuable examination of this and various other aspects of *The Pyramid*, see Avril Henry, "William Golding: *The Pyramid*," *Southern Review: An Australian Journal of Literary Studies*, 3 (1968), 5–31.

2. *The Pyramid* (London: Faber, 1967), 46.

3. Henry, "*The Pyramid*," 5–31.

4. *The Spire* (London: Faber, 1964), 90.

5. Henry, "*The Pyramid*," 5–31.

Leighton Hodson

THE SCORPION GOD: CLARITY, TECHNIQUE, AND COMMUNICATION

IF THERE IS a short formula to define the art of Golding it must surely be "Nothing twice." Herein lies the explanation for the range of content he has encompassed since *Lord of the Flies* and especially the unique form he has found for each work. The complexity of each book often demands the greatest concentration from the reader and pushes him out of the role of passive consumer into that of active interpreter. This is reflected in a statement Golding made in 1959:

> It seems to me that there's really very little point in writing a novel unless you do something that either you suspected you couldn't do, or which you are pretty certain that nobody else has tried before. I don't think there's any point in writing two books that are like each other, and if I thought that *The Inheritors* as a book rose out of another book which provided me with a kind of technical background, then I wouldn't have written it. . . . I see, or I bring myself to see, a certain set of circumstances in a particular way. If it is in the way everybody else sees them, then there is no point in writing a book. If it seems to differ from the accepted point of view, there is a

point in writing the book because it . . . could be a contribution to other people's view of reality.[1]

The challenge implied here for the creator and the desired impact of his work as stimulus to the reader's thinking and aesthetic pleasure reflect attitudes fundamental to Golding and consistent with his approach in *The Scorpion God: Three Short Novels*.

This is not the first occasion on which he has presented a triple bill. *The Pyramid* was arranged as three separate works connected by the development of a single character. Reconsidering for a moment the problem in interpreting *The Pyramid* will prove helpful in the reading of *The Scorpion God*. Although parts of *The Pyramid* were published as separate stories before the book appeared, their full meaning became apparent only when they were placed in sequence. Something of the same effect arises in *The Scorpion God*, since the third part, *Envoy Extraordinary*, has been published separately. On the question of unity of structure *The Pyramid* nonplussed reviewers, who could see no unity in it and little justification for its title. Critical opinion dismissed its third part as not leaving "any lasting impression."[2] The justification of the enigma of the title, it seems to me, lies in the invitation Golding offers to the reader to reorganize his understanding of reality as he reads, so as to make a parallel between himself and the main character, Oliver.

The occasioning of heart-searching parallels between characters or situations in the novels and in the reader's life is the hallmark of Golding's writing. The now famous difficulty and austerity of his style stem from the desire to force the reader not only to feel differently but also to end up thinking differently and judging himself and others anew.

One is forced to read not only between the lines of *The Pyramid* but also between the stories, as it were, and make connections by theme and character. Golding is inviting us to read the whole book as Oliver's progress. The pyramid could then evoke the idea of evolution in character and become in fact the pyramid of experience. It is rewarding for the reader to make a spiritual journey that corresponds to Oliver's progress so as to achieve through him a maturity of understanding. As Oliver—ascending the pyramid of experience—learns to know himself better, so can the reader, not by simple identification but by imaginative participation. For all the pessimism in the stories, indeed in the whole of Golding's writing, the end result is therapeutic in that the author suggests a good to which the reader, through literature, may aspire, inasmuch as the greatest good any man may attain is to know himself.

The common procedure that underlies the style of any Golding work is the use of a given form to provoke the reader into hermeneutics, into interpreting and examining the situations of the novels so that he makes a correlation between his aesthetic experience and some aspect of life. Golding is never far from wishing to make his readers self-critical. The apparent "elsewhere" of the settings for *Lord of the Flies*, *Pincher Martin*, and *The Spire* is a device to evoke universals applicable to any reader in any part of current society. The culmination of a Golding novel, the outcome of his style and justification for his virtuosity, is the reader's self-awareness.

The strength of *The Pyramid* is that its inner unity evokes in poetic fashion the process of living itself. The author projects the necessity for maturity and the ideal of emerging emotionally uncrippled at the end of the day by contrasting Oliver with Evie, De Tracy, and Bounce. This he does by forcing the reader to make connections; the author avoids spelling out his possible meanings. Experiencing the three stories of *The Pyramid* is really a process of hard imaginative work.

In *The Scorpion God* we see this procedure carried to a new limit. Golding presents in the first two stories taxing but contrasted works and completes the trilogy with a piece that is lighter, though not included for entertainment value only. The book comprises three exercises for the reader's imagination and three different stimuli to the reader's modes of thinking.

By the time he wrote *The Pyramid*, Golding was saying that the reader must be his own interpreter. *The Scorpion God* fits into the author's development startlingly; in its challenge to the reader's feelings and ideas it keeps Golding in the front line of writers. He has always considered art as having the social obligation to communicate: "Art that doesn't communicate is useless. . . . you may create it, but it remains useless if it doesn't communicate."[3] As for the medium of language, he believes the writer may use a difficult style if it is the result of what he wants to say. Likewise, oblique narration is preferable to flat statement so as to make the reader work hard; the writer may also fool the reader if he is justified in making a strong communication and if he can make the reader think, " 'My God, that is what happened! He never said so, but that's what happened,' this is ten times more powerful a communication than the direct saying of 'Then he went and then he did.' "[4] Certainly, in the first two stories of *The Scorpion God* Golding presents his work so densely that almost the first reaction of the reader is that here is a challenge in interpretation greater than in *The Pyramid*.

In *The Scorpion God* one is reminded of Flaubert's *Trois Contes* and the endless search by commentators to explain the work's unity. In *The Scorpion God* there is no general title to help, and the subtitle is a plain *Three Short Novels*, no more help than Flaubert's title. Yet it would be misleading to discuss the work as three stories conveniently published together. They present three variations on the theme of literature as didactic and participative. In the first two, *The Scorpion God* and *Clonk Clonk*, the detail is so dense that the reader not only has to work but has at times to sweat his way through. The entertainment is intellectual and austere; only in the third story, *Envoy Extraordinary*, can he relax. One bond common to all three is the didactic purpose that emerges once the reader's imagination has been stimulated and has been made to participate. As always with Golding the final page suggests the problems for consideration. Through the title work of *The Scorpion God* we come to meditate on the lonely figure of the Liar, who in the final moments is shown isolated from the bonds of religion and challenged by new possibilities. What is man to do when God is dead? The challenge faces not only this lonely outsider but also our own century. In *Clonk Clonk* we have again to await the end before we are prompted to see, beyond the integration of the primitive hunter Chimp with the tribal mother Palm, the poetic suggestion that sexual union is a constructive equilibrium and not a divided state. By setting his story at the dawn of human history, Golding invites the reader to see himself at his most primitive. The choice of this earliest phase of the human story calls forth a correlative in the sophisticated reader; he is stimulated to think about himself, or about human nature in general, in its simplest, crudest state. Here he will see what human nature is at its most basic—a set of divisive urges. In the story the hunters point up our aggressive drive and the female characters exude a constructive, all-embracing warmth. By the union of Chimp and Palm we are invited to think on the therapeutic integration that awaits humanity if it will see its nature for what it is in its separate urges and attempt to transcend them by blending them together creatively.

While the first two stories invite the sophisticated reader to think about himself in simple terms, first as a religious animal, then as a social animal, the third story in its lighter vein brings the reader up to date with the technological miracle-worker who may be too clever for the good of his own species. Again it is the ending that prompts thought. Phanocles is packed off with his explosives and printing to China, where these technologies remained in cold storage for centuries.

The book builds up a formidable unity as commentary on our times; if the first two stories touch on man's basic urges, the last is an ironic comment on man the clever monkey. There is therefore a unity of theme here, although not easily seen at first glance. One may take the book as a sequence of meditations on human thinking: the unsatisfactoriness of religion as a force outside man, the obligation man has to see himself as a social animal where active and passive urges are balanced, and finally the potential dangers of the meddling intellect. No direct answers are provided except the most valid of all, which is the necessity of facing the problems, of coming close to them through literature, through imagination. This is as far as the artist can take us. He makes his statement about the human predicament by inviting that therapeutic participation in the problem which art alone can provide. This seems to me to be Golding's special quality. *The Scorpion God* carries the stringency of Golding's style-vision to extremes.

The Scorpion God is a brief novel yet not small in scale; on the contrary the effect is grand, though there is no denying a tightness in expression that applies equally to description, dialogue, and sequence of events. The intensity of the opening description is not only economical but serves also to establish the attitude of deep concentration the reader must sustain.

We come rapidly to the opening riverside scene, a place of heat and stillness and bright oppressive color. There is a running figure with crowds watching. By his crook and flail we sense that we are in ancient Egypt, in some small locality ruled by a headman and a god-king. The running figure is hailed as God Great House and is performing a ritual that proves his power to bring fertility by making the river rise, but he trips and falls. He is accompanied by the Liar, whose role it is to tell over and over his lies about places far away where water goes solid and where the land is surrounded by water that is salt. Great House must atone for his fall by drinking poison so that he may enter the eternal Now and make the river rise. It rises and goes on rising. His mummified body is given special burial where it will watch over the river for eternity. The Liar is made to witness this final assertion of life-death but refuses to accompany the god-king into the beyond. He astounds the priests by asserting that he will reject eternal god status and be satisfied with his human span. He is cast into a pit.

The river, however, does not cease to rise, and the danger the little valley faces must stem from the god's anger. An explanation is offered by the god's daughter, the princess. She confesses to the headman her secret love for the Liar and is shocked to think she has shattered the laws of nature. But the headman concludes that the anger of the god turns on the fact that the Liar is still alive in the pit, having refused to accompany him into death. The headman attempts to bribe the Liar to die and be mummified in splendor. The Liar revolts against this suggestion. He offers himself to the princess and is prepared to play the part of Great House in a bid to take power. In the skirmish that follows he is driven out into the flood but manages to escape to a ridge of higher land. In the final scene the wounded headman realizes the force of this outsider, who sees through godhead and will take over the role of god for political power. A new order is proposed, and the princess, suggesting they may survive after all, prepares to open negotiations with a new master.

New ways of conducting life—this is the revelation made by the Liar. He is saying there is a world beyond the flooding river, and this makes the headman bleed within as if scorpion-bitten. The final picture of the Liar-Outsider trying to escape gives the impression of bitter revelation—a new truth that means the end of an old order. What is proposed may be full of dangerous ambitions; a political set-up is possibly only slightly fairer than a theocratic one. It might be less perverse, but it is not necessarily less cruel. What is certain is that religion has failed and the Liar's proposed power politics is to get its day. The future of the little valley is assured, perhaps at the cost of conflict. Though theocratic power has been shown to fail, we know there is no certainty that a politico-religious one will not corrupt. The reader may cast his mind back to *Lord of the Flies:* Golding has said, "The politician is likely to be a Jack and at best a Ralph—never a Simon."[5] However, a tragic outcome is avoided and replaced by a qualified hope—a solution to the princess's private problems but also a hint of problems to come. The headman might well say of the new world opened by the Liar, "This blessing left a scorpion's tail behind."

The origins of this story must lie in Golding's preoccupation with ancient Egypt, "the Egypt of mystery, of the pyramids and the valley of the Kings," as he points out in his essay "Egypt from My Inside." He concludes, "I am, in fact, an Ancient Egyptian, with all their unreason, spiritual pragmatism and capacity for ambiguous belief." Even if the Egyptians were really life-loving, the image we have of them is of their preoccupation with life-in-death and death-in-life: "Whatever the Egyptians intended, they brought life and death together in the most tangible way possible."[6] Here is a suggestion of the fundamental theme of *The Scorpion God;* it is as if the author is in the minds of God Great House and the Liar simultaneously. The story evokes the disturbing ambiguity the modern reader finds in the fact that religion may be accepted and rejected at the same time. The Liar sees the way religion puts the question of life or death since he is going to be put to the test and made to give up his life for a religious idea. He suggests the commonsense view that no religion can be right to ask a man for his life. He is existentialist and not essentialist. The Liar has resilience, life force, that makes him

reject the passivity of the people in the valley and calls forth
the potential political pragmatist. This is one way of surviving;
yet the story ends on a questioning dissonance. The resolving
chord is never played, except in the way that will best please
each reader, by his inward ear.

By this metaphor we can approach the manner of Golding's presentation in *The Scorpion God*. Here more than
anywhere else Golding relies on minimal suggestion, the
slightest detail to stir an inner music in the reader. The full
melodies are never written out. With this economy of expression, the reader is left to fill in the gaps, much as the listener
must do for Webern's music. There is, of course, a price to be
paid. Lushness, fullness (but flabbiness too) will disappear,
and lightness, dryness will take their places, along with
obscurities that may drive the reader away. These qualities
have appeared in previous works of Golding's; some readers
have not forgiven him the hard work needed for an understanding of *Free Fall* and *The Spire*. Should not the teller of
the tale direct sufficient light into the appropriate place? The
fear that the explicit will destroy atmosphere and poetic structure lies behind this technique of withholding the light. At
important places in *The Scorpion God* Golding's obscurity affects the thematic strength of the tale. As the Liar is taken to
the burial chamber, he is recalcitrant enough to shout, "I
don't want to live." This is too puzzling at first reading; the
reader expects him to say "die." We then see how the others
accept their poisoned drink and follow their god-king while
the Liar shouts "The awful thing, the dirty thing, the thing
that broke up the world"; that is, he wants to keep the life he
has. In hindsight we realize that the first "I don't want to live"
is used ironically but also with unwarranted obscurity, to
mean "I don't want to be made to live the life of eternal companion in death of God Great House." Obscurity weakens
theme and characterization. Above all we should be made
aware of the Liar's clear thinking, since this would establish

better the new attitude he presents as the outsider from the big world in the petty surroundings of a death-oriented society. There are of course compensations. The reader is stimulated. The deliberately fashioned style used for descriptions is punctuated in dialogue passages by down-to-earth phrases which make the reader participate in the story not only on the poetic level but also on the level of social behavior so that the protagonists are humanized for him. We can thus shift from the legendary setting into the perplexed minds of the characters as they (and we too) are faced with the conflict between old religious and new socio-religious possibilities. The method gives opportunity for comic observations so that the tone of the story is not unremittingly somber. Here, for instance, the princess is formally receiving the people with her brother, a ten-year-old with whom she is officially and incestuously involved, but with little sexual satisfaction:

> His nurses helped him on to the dais and he stood there, blinking. Pretty Flower leaned, undulating. Her smile became one of love and she touched his cheek in an exquisitely feminine gesture with the back of her hand. She murmured down to him.
> "You've been crying, you little runt."[p. 17]

In the closing stages of the story Golding's allusive and elliptical style-vision pays off. The finale changes the reader's perspective, and instead of observing a ritual from the outside we seem to be standing with the princess contemplating the meaning of life the outsider has brought. In the final picture of these two figures, facing each other but widely separated, Golding manages to end on a questioning tone. Not only the girl but the reader, too, is awakened to new possibilities, to a change of emphasis that places existence before essence. The human psyche must accept the process of evolution, just as the valley of the god-king must eventually relate itself to a reality beyond itself. This evolution is exhibited also in the new sexual awareness of the princess. The myth of incestuous procreation for the sake of the continuity and fertility of the valley dies with the god-king. It is shaken off by the princess as personality flowers and she accepts exogamous union with the outsider. As with *The Pyramid*—though perhaps only after deeper reflection—this tight little tale begins to expand poetically in the reader's consciousness to evoke the processes of change, development, evolution.

Thoughts of a new order come to mind with *Clonk Clonk*. The neat contrast that Golding makes here with the first tale gives satisfaction to the reader. Where the first ends questioningly with no certainty of happiness, in *Clonk Clonk* Golding moves to an affirmative ending.

The setting is a primitive paradise. There are grasslands for hunting, rocky outcrops and hot springs for settlement, where life can be lived in simple nudity. Chimp emerges from the male world of hunters and is integrated with the women through Palm, a great mother or senior tribal midwife. Palm feels time passing and wants a man to replace her lost mate. Her role of midwife does not completely satisfy her; she expresses the overflow of her emotions towards the girl Minnow in an innocent, homosexual way.

The hunters also express their emotions towards each other in a narcissistic, homosexual way like children in a game—fractious, then kissing and hugging by turns. Chimp is something of an outsider because of his limp, a weak ankle that goes "clonk" with pain. Isolated from his fellows he longs for maternal comfort. He returns to the settlement to find the women wildly drunk by the light of the full moon. He is chased and sexually initiated by a horde of them. Palm takes Chimp to her hut and installs him as lover, mate, and chief. Chimp's loneliness parallels Palm's need for a man. As he finds comfort in her, tribe-namer and mother-figure, so she finds sexual fulfillment in him.

The basic structure again makes us wait for the last pages before we perceive meaning in the puzzling relationships. We then see how the work has evoked a definition of sexual differences as sensed by an unsophisticated primitive mentality. The principal quality that the story projects is the way the participants (they cannot really be called characters) have to grope for meanings amid the natural phenomena surrounding them. Life is parceled off into hunting (done by the males) and birth mysteries and liquor brewing (done by the females).

Stylistically Golding's method is once more both to suggest the poetry of archetypal myth and to launch the idea that the reader is observing and feeling the very emergence and growth of the self. Chimp and Palm move towards enlightenment as a result of their sexual attraction. Chimp's little defect—his weak ankle which would have merited his being drowned at birth if it had been discovered—makes him ridiculous among his fellow leopard men, but it also isolates him from them so that he stumbles upon Palm and is taken over by her. The weak is made strong by the compassionate understanding and enlightened self-interest of Palm.

Both *Clonk Clonk* and *The Scorpion God* depend stylistically on a mixture of tightly expressed poetic writing and little touches of sly humor that succeed in altering the scale of the writing. The tale of Chimp and Palm manages to work both as poetic evocation of primitive instincts and as comedy. This suggests a pathetic or funny human side to what would otherwise be remote.

Whatever settings Golding chooses, one is reminded that he always writes about a present. As he has said, "The past is not another country, it's joined directly to us."[7] *The Inheritors* is really about human nature as we know it and not a historical novel; in *Lord of the Flies* the island is not distant but wherever we set up social relationships. In *The Scorpion God* and *Clonk Clonk* what Golding evokes is the human scale of his subjects, not their mythic grandeur or isolation. Just as

we place ourselves with the princess at the end of *The Scorpion God*, so at the end of *Clonk Clonk* we share Chimp's
relief when integrated into the mixed community of male and
female. We are aware throughout of a feeling of incompleteness in the lives of Chimp and Palm. The ending is a happy
one in that for Palm worry is dissolved in the hope of procreation.

With the last of the tales, *Envoy Extraordinary*, Golding
can adopt a more openly witty style though he still holds out
an invitation to criticize. The reader is prodded into thinking
about the dilemmas of technology. The story can be compared with the stage version, *The Brass Butterfly*, in which
Golding stresses the role of Phanocles as a potential danger to
society: "He is indeed, a force of nature. . . . There is no
stopping him; for this is our tragic condition. We must invent
and change, we must control and let loose; if we stop, we shall
die out like the dinosaurs."[8]

Golding's inventor arrives with his toys at the court of the
emperor. He is not expecting to meet a man with disdain for
progress. Only the pressure cooker finds favor; the second
invention, explosives, looks, and is proved to be, dangerous;
and the third, printing, will, it seems to the emperor, breed
too many words. Phanocles, gunpowder, and printing are dis-
patched to China.

Though Golding humorously packs off these potential
dangers, we are left to guess that they will return one day.
The emperor's haughty but laudable desire to keep the
pressure cooker suggests only a partial answer. Something
similar is to be found in "The Rewards of Industry" by Richard Garnett, and possibly Golding had this in mind.[9] Garnett's story is lighter. In it three Chinese brothers in search of
their fortunes reveal to the western world the craft of printing, the use of gunpowder, and the pleasures of chess. The
bringer of printing finds that the caliph of Alexandria does not

want books to rival the Koran; the bringer of explosives is imprisoned for setting fire to Constantinople; but the bringer of chess is rewarded with riches. The third brother concludes: "A little thing which the world is willing to receive is better than a great thing which it hath not yet learned to value aright. For the world is a big child and chooses amusement before instruction."

What makes Golding's story memorable is that the problems, though touched on lightly, are linked to the theme of progress. Golding provokes the reader into thinking about the ironic connections between increase in technological know-how and diminution in quality of life. For all its lightweight form, *Envoy Extraordinary* reflects the disturbing thought we find elsewhere in Golding's work: energy is loaded with the danger of exploitation, and this is the source of evil. Golding's version is less whimsical than Garnett's and reflects the serious opinion that acts of creation carry no guarantee of positive worth but may lead to destruction.

The three short works of *The Scorpion God* confirm that Golding is concerned with diagnosis of the human condition. This does not preclude humor, but it does assert a serious purpose: "the novelist does not limit himself to reporting the facts, but diagnoses them, and his vocation has the same value as that of the doctor."[10]

As for method, in the first two stories Golding seems to have moved towards a highly wrought spareness of expression. Such a feature, present also in earlier works, is here carried very far and may, by risking obscurity, seem to clash with the ideal of clarity inherent in the notion of diagnosis. The writer is saved by the imaginative concentration he demands of the reader and by the way he attends to particulars, leaving generalities and messages to look after themselves— or to be sought out by the reader-interpreter. These three

stories are not dry, literary *exercices de style*. In nothing that
Golding has written are art and life separate entities; there is
nowhere any dilettantism. In the last analysis Golding has the
poetic power to drive the reader back to human roots. This is
what fascinates the reader and disturbs him, drawing him at
the same time into therapeutic participation. The claim made
for Golding and his criticism of life is the same as that made
for Dickens: "The really great novelist can't but find himself
making an evaluative inquiry into the civilisation in which he
finds himself—which he more and more finds himself in and
of."[11]

---

1. Frank Kermode, "The Meaning of It All," *Books and Bookmen*, 5
(October 1969), 10.

2. Bernard F. Dick, *William Golding* (New York: Twayne, 1967), 92.

3. Jack I. Biles, *Talk: Conversations with William Golding* (New York:
Harcourt, 1970), 65.

4. Ibid., 67.

5. Ibid., 49.

6. *The Hot Gates* (London: Faber, 1965), 71, 82, 81.

7. Alex Hamilton, "First Lord of the Novel," *Manchester Arts Guardian*, 20 December 1971, 8.

8. Introduction to *The Brass Butterfly* (London: Faber School Editions,
1964), 4.

9. See Peter Green, "The World of William Golding," *Review of English Literature*, 1(1960), 68.

10. Golding's contribution to "The Condition of the Novel," Conference of European Writers, Leningrad, 1963, in *New Left Review*,
January–February 1965, 35.

11. F. R. and Q. D. Leavis, *Dickens the Novelist* (London: Chatto and
Windus, 1970), 216–17.

Maurice L. McCullen

LORD OF THE FLIES: THE
CRITICAL QUEST

"MANY PEOPLE . . . profess to be admirers of
William Golding," cautioned Anthony Burgess during the
peak of Golding's popularity, "but they read only *Lord of the
Flies*."[1] It was true. Golding's international reputation was
based on his first novel, his subsequent work having been
met, on the whole, by incomprehension verging on hostility.

But it is true no longer; the "Golding vogue" is over.
James Baker wrote its obituary in 1970. Although Golding
finely dramatized anxieties common to a postwar world, said
Baker, the popularity of his most "relevant fable" is declining,
and his later books "have not caught on."[2]

If by the decline of the Golding vogue we mean something like the descent of *Lord of the Flies* from its peak of
popularity, the growing public silence of its author, and the
neglect of the media, the Golding vogue is indeed over. This
is not to say, of course, that the novel has been neglected by
academic critics. Academic interest seems fitting in that the
novel was "Lord of the Campus" (*Time*'s phrase) before it
made Golding the vogue. To invoke a professorial cliché, we
have come full circle.

In the silence created by the passing of the vogue, it is time to survey the critical reception of Golding's most popular novel. With the hindsight of two decades the quest for understanding, for the best critical approaches and perspectives, has an interest all its own.

From the first tentative reviews and notices in 1954, reaction centered on Golding's view of man's nature. His interpretation, embodied in primitive boys, was so finely attuned to contemporary sensibility that early reviewers were suspicious of it. Sensitive perhaps to the affective fallacy, several did not like the story, suspecting that a complex matter had been oversimplified. Walter Allen found the theme of "regression from choir school to Mau Mau" so allegorically overloaded that meaning was inhibited; "it is, however skillfully told, only a rather unpleasant and too-easily affecting story." Later, in *The Modern Novel*, Allen records the same impression. He praises the power, but he doesn't like the works: "Powerful as they are, Golding's novels seem to me to have the weakness normal to and perhaps inevitable in allegorical fiction."[3] Louis Halle compared *Lord of the Flies* invidiously with *A High Wind in Jamaica*. Hughes had inverted the Victorian picture of children, but his world was still "a world for God's pity"; Golding turns that picture inside out and in so doing loses all humanity. Halle finds the novel theme-ridden and overacademic: "One is left asking: what was the point?"[4]

Most early reviewers ranked the novel higher. Douglas Hewitt, though finding in Golding "a tendency to be too explicit," felt that weaknesses were apparent only "on reflection when the book is subjected to the most exacting scrutiny." He found the story "completely convincing and often very frightening."[5]

The mythic dimension was noted from the start. In the *Times Literary Supplement* the reviewer commented: "Perhaps this [his plot summary] makes *Lord of the Flies* sound too much like a variation on a Frazerian theme. It is that, incidentally; but taken purely as a story it is beautifully constructed and worked out, with the various children just sufficiently individuated and with tension built up steadily to the climax."[6] This reviewer thought the novel a fantasy, a classification soon to change to allegory.

Other critical terms, such as fable, soon to be standard in *Lord of the Flies* criticism, were also present from the outset. As the earliest critics reflected, their sense of the surprising resonance produced by Golding's deceptively simple narrative began to sharpen. Two commentators in the 1950s, John Peter and Ralph Freedman, recognized Golding as a major talent and offered insights into his work.[7] Peter's essay defines the term *fable* and calls Golding the best fabulist among current British writers. "Already," writes Peter, "working in a recalcitrant mode he seems to me to have done more for the modern British novel than any of the recent novelists who have emerged. More, it may be, than all of them."

Peter's essay has been called "the first serious essay on Golding published in America," and it did influence criticism—most obviously by the use of the term *fable*."[8] Freedman's essay ranks lower, but it too was an important step toward the Golding vogue.[9] Like Peter, Freedman assumes that Golding is a major writer; and he outlines philosophical and religious approaches which later critics worked out more fully. Both of these essays suggest the complexity of *Lord of the Flies* and point ahead to the wide cultural application of future criticism.

Two other early critics deserve mention: Phillip Drew and Millar MacLure.[10] Drew's "Second Reading," with *The Coral Island* in the background, examines the illustrative elements in Golding's microcosm, but it was already out of date. MacLure, responding wittily to an "astonishingly wrongheaded" review of *Pincher Martin*, asserts that Golding shall not at the same time be misunderstood *and* ignored. He deals with the first three novels somewhat unevenly; but he calls *Lord of the*

Flies "in its kind a masterpiece" and suggests approaches to the book's "nicely articulated but very complex design."

The critic who best spans the fifties is Frank Kermode, "perhaps Golding's most influential champion," and one of his earliest. Kermode's writings appeared from 1958 to 1972 and include the transcript of a BBC interview in 1959.[11] He called attention to the work, explained it, provided sources and analogues, and brought into the open the matter of intention.

In the 1960s Golding scholarship exploded. After four novels Golding was a writer of stature. Criticism adjusted to him with the survey-review article, quarterly style. The survey-review tended to establish a religious or cultural perspective and to survey Golding's work chronologically in terms of it. Some later critics took a superior line with these surveys; but despite a tendency toward thinness and generalization, the essays added to scholarly knowledge and kept the dialogue open. Was Golding religious or atheistic? Conservative or liberal? Were his novels great art or explicit allegory? Opinions varied, but, in general, critics found *Lord of the Flies* Golding's best novel.

The elasticity of the survey-review is illustrated in an essay by Peter Green, read before the Royal Society of Literature and printed in its *Transactions and Proceedings* and in *Review of English Literature*.[12] Green redid the essay in expanded form in 1963; and this version was printed in the *Source Book*. In both versions Green discusses Golding as a religious novelist: "The whole moral framework of his novels is conceived in terms of traditional Christian symbolism." In his summary note he says that Golding "remains the most powerful writer, the most original, the most profoundly imaginative, to have turned his hand to fiction in this country since the war; and if he never wrote another word his place in English letters would be secure."

C. B. Cox, in the summer of 1960, agreed.[13] Cox focused

on Golding's first novel and recorded his belief that it "is probably the most important novel to be published in this country in the 1950s." Accepting a fatalistic reading of the allegory, Cox still felt that the affective quality of the book stemmed from "Golding's faith that every detail of human life has a religious significance."

The same year James Gindin picked up Golding's word *gimmick* and proceeded to haunt him with it. "In each novel the final 'gimmick' provides a twist that . . . palliates the force and unity of the original metaphor."[14] Gindin's essay served to focus attention on the ends of the novels and was a mark to shoot at until it became discredited. His dissatisfaction was as nothing, however, compared to that of Martin Green, who saw Golding as a primitive romantic encamped opposite (and below) C. P. Snow.[15]

Sam Hynes's treatment balanced Martin Green's ill-natured assessment.[16] Hynes discusses Golding as a major religious writer whose depth of concern and ingenuity in adapting allegory (a traditional form for religious utterance) distinguish him from his contemporaries.

Another 1960 essay, by Millar MacLure, Bernard F. Dick calls "strangely neglected."[17] Dealing with allegory, and with the thesis that "the art of this century is haunted by the ghost of innocence," MacLure tests three allegories of innocence to find "we long for innocence but our guilt is inevitable."

Two essays in 1961 are in different ways notable. Margaret Walters's article on two fabulists is weighted on the side of Golding.[18] Picking up where John Peter left off, she attempts to pin down the slippery term *fable:* "Fable is obviously akin to allegory. . . . In the latter, however, the cross-reference between literal narrative and a body of abstractions is usually specific, sustained at length, and rather arbitrary. And while . . . most fables use some allegorical correspondences . . . the more important fact to notice is the way the fabulist always

tries to make his dramatic situation serve as an *analogy* of the
world at large. A fable really offers its individual story as . . . a
metaphor."

This essay in definition took an important step. Fifteen
years later, despite some differences of opinion, most critics
accepted Golding as a fabulist. There was, however, no bolder
attempt than Professor Walters's to pinpoint elements of
formal pattern—even in weightier studies such as Robert
Scholes's *The Fabulators*.

In a controversial article devoted to psychological criticism, Claire Rosenfield argues that Golding "consciously
dramatizes Freudian theory."[19] Her essay set off minor
shock-waves. Disagreement came from Golding himself, who
cheerfully admitted he has read "absolutely no Freud." The
next year rejoinder came from William Wasserstrom, using
Rosenfield's own method. In her reply to Wasserstrom, she
attempted to defend herself.[20] In 1961 Kermode also provided a survey review; E. D. Pendry, one of lesser caliber;
and Carl Niemeyer, looking back to an earlier Kermode
notice, discussed *Lord of the Flies* in the light of Ballantyne's
book.[21]

In 1962 the bibliography began to bulge and titles pro-
claimed the novel's ascendancy ("Lord of the Campus," and
"Lord of the Agonies"). *Time* reported that the paperback
edition had sold more than 65,000 copies (in less than three
years) and that, at least at Columbia University, Golding was
outselling Salinger. During the year there were short notices
by Lionel Trilling, Edmund Fuller, and Douglas M. Davis.[22]
Frederick R. Karl questioned Golding's artistry, and Steven
Marcus praised it.[23] In addition there were laudatory survey-
criticisms by H. M. Williams and by Frank MacShane, and
Paulette Michel-Michot compared the novel with *Robinson
Crusoe*.[24]

Two other critics, Juliet Mitchell and John Wain, probed
Golding's art for weaknesses which have been difficult for

later critics to overlook. Juliet Mitchell deals harshly with Golding's later novels, and even *Lord of the Flies* is subject to grave reservations: "It reveals a basic thematic weakness." Golding's microcosmic world, for Mitchell, is a mirage. Instead of analyzing the problem he sets forth—the origin of corruption—he presents a spurious complexity. Golding arranges his boys to fit the opposition of good and evil, but no resolution is possible because the reference point is really adult society. Thus, "many of his techniques can be reduced to a series of tricks, to a linguistic hypnosis, a vagueness, that achieves its effects simply through rhythms. The meaning rests in a series of empty verbal oppositions.[25] Golding's art has been denigrated as a conjuring trick. From Walter Allen forward, this "too easily affecting" fable has bothered critics.

John Wain ranks Golding highly, depicting him as a philosophical novelist who presents an epic world for "a bedrock exploration of human nature." Wain finds Golding's picture of human nature painful, but powerful and credible. "Golding's Book of Genesis" is his best novel; but the novels to *Free Fall* are "colossal sculptures in metaphor," the work of a major talent. His chief adverse criticism is that Golding's "narrative method [is] too involved; or to use a blunter word, too tricky." But Wain's complaint goes beyond Golding to the contemporary novel in general.[26]

In 1963 Nelson published his *Source Book*, which became a valuable aid for scholars as well as for the undergraduates it was intended to help. Bernard F. Dick's 1967 bibliographic annotation on the *Source Book* and on the Baker and Ziegler's casebook edition of 1964 still seems valid: "All articles in the above books are relevant." The "Related Readings" section of the *Source Book* underscores the close relationship of *Lord of the Flies* to modern thought.

The novel's profound impact, especially in the United States, was revealed in 1963 when the "Lord of the Campus" aroused the American Catholic Church. In a January issue of

America, Fathers Francis E. Kearns and John M. Egan attacked the book on religious grounds.[27] Father Kearns was distressed that *Lord of the Flies* was supplanting *Catcher in the Rye*. In his view Salinger's novel represents humane liberalism, but Golding's "represents that depravity which is inevitable in mankind and which makes futile all human attempts to justice or order." In portraying evil as a dynamic force centered in man himself, *Lord of the Flies* stands close to Calvinism.

Father Egan followed, regretting "Golding's View of Man," particularly because of the novel's influence upon undergraduates. Definitely a non-Christian allegory in Father Egan's view, "this artistic vision, typical of modern art, induces a sense of despair and even hatred of what is human."

While Egan and Kearns conveyed their distress over Golding's picture of evil, Brother Luke M. Grande discussed the appeal of the novel in *Commonweal*, another Catholic weekly.[28]

> In a world that tends to equate evil with unfavorable environment, Golding sees instead man's inner responsibility for choosing between good and evil. . . . [He] projects the timeless predicament of man who, despite his moral weakness, struggles to attain heroic ideals. . . .
> Golding has struck the note to which the strings of the twentieth-century youth are attuned. A student in his teens or twenties has not known at first-hand the horrors of war, but he has seen international hatred and the unbridled tyranny. . . . He has seen a loss of values and of faith. . . . In sum, . . . the frightening possibilities of his own nature. [pp. 458–59]

For Grande, response to Golding's appeal is anything but surprising. This belief had been stated before Grande—most concisely in 1962 by Edmund Fuller.[29]

Later, Kearns and Grande exchanged views in *Commonweal*.[30] In a somewhat pretentious piece Kearns traced

"Brother Luke's misreading of the novel" to "his enthusiasm for Golding's symbolic technique," which for Kearns obscures the story. With heavy irony he accused "Brother Luke" of equating student enthusiasm with a reassertion of "moral responsibility" and sneers at such foolishness. Grande in reply recognized Kearns's "game of picking through the pile for convenient either/or evidence," but refused to be provoked. The novel was written by neither a "happy primitivist" nor a Calvinistic pessimist. "*I* see it," he concluded, "as a persistence of the perennial humanist vision in the twentieth century." In an article written for the *Source Book*, Kearns tried once more to score off Brother Luke.

Father Thomas M. Coskren, in a footnote to this contretemps, recorded his belief that Golding is no Calvinist.[31] Golding, Coskren finds, is teaching hard truths through the medium of fable.

Bernard S. Oldsey and Stanley Weintraub assert that by 1963 critical attention to the novel "has proven various, specialized and spotty."[32] They address themselves first to lineage and genre. *Lord of the Flies'* main forebear, they believe, is *Gulliver's Travels.* As for genre, although they use the words *fabulous, fablelike,* and *fabulist,* the term *fable* makes them uncomfortable. *"The essence of Golding's art resides exactly within the area of overlap"* between the realms of fiction and allegory. Despite their certainty about the essence of Golding's art, the exactitude is more felt than proved. Thereafter, the article deals with what the characters *are* (rather than what they mean) and argues winningly against the application to the novel of strict definitions and neat categories. The intent of the article, seemingly, was to move *Lord of the Flies* scholarship onto center; and that was the effect.

Joseph J. Irwin provides a survey-criticism from the Protestant viewpoint. Golding writes so well, Irwin thinks, that the reader feels his meaning perhaps even better than he knows it—a high accomplishment for the author. And Gold-

ing's thesis is always much the same: man's difficulties stem
not from his intellect but from his nature. But Walter Sullivan
asserts, "The stuff of William Golding's fiction does not seem
promising."[33] For Sullivan, *Free Fall* is Golding's best; he
dismisses *Lord of the Flies*.

In 1964 the casebook edition appeared, as did the first
doctoral dissertation, and the Golding vogue reached high
school classrooms. In addition to some material collected in
the *Source Book*, the casebook edition includes an introduction by Gregor and Kinkead-Weekes, selections from the
Kermode and Keating interviews, a new article by Donald R.
Spangler (on Simon), E. M. Forster's introduction to the
novel, part of a letter from Golding's brother, and a brief
checklist of scholarly publications. Ernest C. Bufkin's dissertation deals with Golding's first four novels as Quest literature. Oliver Warner describes similarities between *Lord of
the Flies* and Marryat's *Little Savage*. And James R. Baker
objects to the religious orientation of *Lord of the Flies* criticism, asserting that the novel should be seen in terms of an
Apollonian/Dionysian polarity.[34]

Other criticisms appearing in 1964 were written by Robert
J. White and R. C. Townsend.[35] White's article examines
classicist Golding's novel in the light of Platonic thought.
Golding, he believes, places his characters between *nomos*
and *physis*, Apollo and Dionysus; but, though critics are
aware of the images for the savage world, images for the world
of the soul are not clear. Thus, beginning with the Greek
word for butterfly, *psyche*, White demonstrates the centrality
of butterfly imagery in the novel. His resolution of tension
between concepts of soul and savagery provides insight into
Golding's treatment of evil.

Townsend's denigration of *Lord of the Flies* suggests Walter Allen, whose key phrase, "too easily affecting," recurs.
Townsend feels that Golding is "exploiting the thousands of
students who are committed to the book," and he reacts

against the affective power of the novel. In a decade marked by negativism, this novel seduces youth into pessimism. The art of the sixties was indeed strongly marked by visions of apocalypse, and Townsend was irked that a delicate subject was manipulated by Golding and that Golding's work then became "required reading" for thousands of students. In illustration of the book's thinness Townsend compares the endings of *Lord of the Flies* and *A High Wind in Jamaica*.[36]

Townsend disagrees with Golding's thesis. He also disagrees with Golding's "luring his reader up a path which leads only to an acceptance of his thesis." The entrapment is accomplished by a graduated series of logical jumps which Golding makes *for* the reader. Townsend also thinks the fable oversimplified.

The status of *Lord of the Flies* in the high schools was commented upon by two critics in the *English Journal* for November 1964. Gladys Veidemanis asserted that its success was "no passing fad." Agreeing with Granville Hicks (in a review of *The Spire*) that the popularity of *Lord of the Flies* stems as much from its artistic excellence as from its faddishness, she states that student empathy is valid and that for "its appeal, compactness, stylistic brilliance, and pertinent themes," *Lord of the Flies* deserves a permanent place in the curriculum. In the same issue Richard Lederer plays down the popular appeal and says the novel's influence is overrated.[37]

Along similar lines, Kenneth Watson describes the technique which gives the novel its power (that "claustrophobic effect"), recording a nearly universal classroom experience: "The clearest tribute I know to the power and realism of *Lord of the Flies* is the shock of its impact on even non-literary students, precisely because it is not 'literary' but unfalteringly tough-minded." His thesis, that *Lord of the Flies* is not essentially religious, is well argued.[38]

Philippa Moody's fifty-three pages of commonsense com-

mentary on *Lord of the Flies* is one of the bright spots of
Golding criticism, introducing the reader not only to Golding's first novel but to further perspectives on the contemporary novel. She gives the reader a way of looking at the work
and a sense of what the characters, scenes, and concepts
really are.[39]

Kenneth Watson's 1964 critique is an early example of
reaction against allegorical readings, and his thesis is rein-
forced by Samuel Hynes in one of three critical works that
appeared the next year. Reconsidering *Lord of the Flies*,
Hynes argues that it is a moral work, "embodying a conception of human depravity which is compatible with, but not
limited to, the Christian doctrine of Original Sin."[40] In format Hynes's monograph is typical of earlier studies. It begins
with a notice of Golding's popularity and originality. Hynes
also considers the terms *myth* and *fable*. He then discusses
the works; *Lord of the Flies* gets most attention, of course.

The two book-length studies of 1965 use the same format
but provide more thoughtful conclusions. Oldsey and Weintraub reprinted their analysis from *College English*.[41] To
complete this chapter, they appended a discussion of the
puzzling quality of Golding's fiction. They see Golding's
method as both original and derivative. This does not run
counter to the claims for originality made in their introduction
because the paradox involved is inherent in their description of the writer as a "literary counter-puncher." In the
context of literary history, Golding is in the purest sense a
"reactionary"—hence, the great importance of *The Coral Island* to an understanding of *Lord of the Flies*. Ballantyne's
book is not just a source or analogue, but the basis of the
counterpunch.

The other book-length study of 1965 is that of James R.
Baker.[42] He works in three directions, showing (1) that Gold-
ing's imagination has been most strongly influenced by the
Greeks, especially Euripides; (2) (in agreement with Steven

Marcus) that Golding is "more precocious than out of date"; and (3) that Golding employs language more closely associated with poetry than with prose.

George C. Herndl's little-known essay compares *Lord of the Flies* with *Catcher in the Rye*, providing an afterword to the arguments of the Catholic critics.[43] As Herndl interprets the allegorical dimension, the important implication is not that man is depraved. Rather, the novel is "an implicit tribute to the humanizing power of social institutions." Herndl bases his argument broadly in the classical and Christian traditions.

In other 1965 publications Howard S. Babb examined passages from four novels, and W. Eugene Davis and T. Hampton pointed out Golding's "optical delusion": Piggy's glasses could *not* light fires. Irving Malin tried to respond to the novels by viewing Golding as a poet of "elemental nature." In addition, E. C. Bufkin analyzed the novel in a *Georgia Review* article.[44] He found traditional elements underlying Golding's technique: classical irony, Miltonic imagery, imagistic motif incorporating other image systems (cosmic symbols, order and reason symbols, animal images, play images), and Jungian types. In his dissertation Bufkin had typed the novel as a quest for order; here he restates his idea that Golding's technique serves to distinguish between opposed concepts of order and disorder.

Two essays published in 1966 examine weaknesses at the center of the novel. For Harry H. Taylor the gimmick at the heart of the novel "exists in the odd, quirkish marriage of symbols between Simon, the mystic, and the 'beast,' the dead airman."[45] Taylor assumes that the "Simon-Piggy Figure" should be viewed as the "dual man" or "dual hero." The *Doppelgänger* has been the subject of renewed interest in recent years, but application to Golding's novel is questionable. Taylor sees Golding's commitment to Simon as an emotional one, which the logic of the novel belies; Simon's inability to communicate proves his incompleteness. It is Piggy, Taylor argues, who "is the real central figure in the book because, despite his limiting blindness, it is his universe not Simon's, and nothing which happens to Piggy or to the symbols around him violates Golding's central symbol of the dead airman."

The other censorial essay, by J. D. O'Hara, is tendentious in a different way.[46] Missing the point that the setting of *Lord of the Flies* is very carefully selected, O'Hara finds it dull, lacking in possibilities for entertainment; he asserts that the subject of the novel "is irrelevant" because academic—"man cannot be cut off completely from his past." O'Hara cannot willingly suspend his disbelief when he sees Golding's children making mistakes and committing cruelties that he would not. Golding's utopia falls apart not because of "man's essential illness" but because of the weakness and ignorance of children.

While Taylor and O'Hara found weaknesses, other critics explored resonance and relevance. Robert C. Gordon dealt briefly with Golding's debt to classical sources, showing that the author draws both image and episode from Homer and Euripides (his note an amplification of White's earlier statement). Suzanne Gulbin found similar situations and symbols in *Lord of the Flies* and *Animal Farm*. Fernando Díaz-Plaja examined the shipwreck motif in *Lord of the Flies* and in Juan Goytisolo's *Duelo in Paraiso*. Hélène Cixous-Berger discussed the novel as an allegory of evil, and Alan M. Cohn found a possible error in a Golding allusion. Charles Mitchell aligned Golding with modern thought in the light of Erich Fromm's *Escape from Freedom*.[47]

Although *Lord of the Flies* received critical attention in 1967, it ran second to *The Spire*. Bernard F. Dick's study in Twayne English Author Series is balanced and judicious.[48] Dick organizes his discussion around a structural principle he calls "polarity of moral tension"—the rational opposed to the irrational. The various methods and levels of articulating this polarity, he believes, give the novel resonance. Dick deals with symbol, irony, and Dionysian/Apollonian dichotomy.

A better book, perhaps because not confined to series format, is by Mark Kinkead-Weekes and Ian Gregor.[49] They argued earlier that fable and fiction occur simultaneously, though fable dominates. In their later study they are concerned to demonstrate Golding's sensitivity and the growth in his artistry. In opposition to Dick, Kinkead-Weekes and Gregor try to show that it is not *Lord of the Flies* that is oversimplified but rather criticism of it. Critics have claimed both too much and too little for Golding's novel. To substantiate what is praiseworthy, they proceed with an "elucidatory" method, a chapter-by-chapter reading, impressionistic in tone, which attempts to retain all of the novel's power and at the same time open it for analysis. Here Golding's technique is described as "revelatory . . . the uncovering of an unsuspected depth to something we have already accepted" (p. 48). By subtle transpositions and repetitions each narrative and symbolic step is linked to the last so that as the pressure of narrative increases, tension results from patterned continuity. Although they do not rate the novel Golding's best, they rate it very high. *Lord of the Flies* is for them a complex work.

Their book is not a favorite with all Golding scholars, and Baker was furious with it. Affronted both individually and nationally (Kinkead-Weekes and Gregor used Baker's title without mentioning him—or, for that matter, *any* American scholar), he sadly arraigned their defensiveness, insularity, and lack of originality.[50] Still it is a good book, and the chapter on *Lord of the Flies* is one of the best.

A slighter work is Paul Elmen's booklet in the Contemporary Writers in Christian Perspective series.[51] Elmen touches upon old issues—fable, the theme of the fall or the death of innocence, political allegory, Freudian insights—on the way to a general statement about Golding's religious stance. Golding sees evil within man, but he does not see that evil is also outside of man, omnipresent and multiform, and that man is forever too weak to combat it.

In a shorter study, Sister M. Amanda Ely compared the worlds of adult authority in *Lord of the Flies*, *Catcher in the Rye*, and *A Separate Peace*. Bruce A. Rosenberg studied the fire imagery and suggested that rather than a pig's head, fire is the central symbol.[52] He sees two kinds of fire at every level of the book: sacred and profane. Although fire symbolism provides straightforward structural and thematic underpinning, Golding sometimes twists his symbol—specific fires may be (ironically) sacred and profane at the same time—thus adding complexity.

Nineteen sixty-eight brought an even greater critical potpourri. In short notices J. C. A. Gaskin commented upon Beelzebub, and Robin Lee compared novel and movie, deciding that the meaning tended to disappear in the film. Evon Nossen traced Golding's "Beast-Man" theme through the novels to show that his view of man is one of guarded optimism.[53] Writers have traditionally resorted to beast analogies to explain man's actions; Golding shows selfishness, greed, fear, hate, blood-lust, and other unsavory emotions in animal terms. Taking a contrary view, Sanford Sternlicht compared *Lord of the Flies* and *The Inheritors* to show that the real song of innocence is the latter. In *Lord of the Flies*, the boys are not innocents, they are the "new people." "Lok died humbly aeons ago," and innocence with him. Henri A. Talon found the novel equally pessimistic; for him, Golding's ironic fable holds out no hope. James W. Nichols treats Golding's irony as satire and finds his concern for the human situation less pessimistic.[54] Golding, thinks Nichols, especially with *The Coral Island* in the background, satirizes theories of the perfectibility of man.

The most interesting essay published in 1968 is by Jack I. Biles.[55] Its genesis was a conversation with Golding in which

Biles was taken aback by Golding's rigid view of Piggy. Golding thought of Piggy as the embodiment of the scientist and imagined him rambling around the island in a laboratory coat, "probably writing papers about this, that, or t'other, and ending up at Los Alamos." Biles, unable to budge Golding, winds up saying, "I'm not quite ready to settle for this."[56]

And he didn't settle for it. In the October 1968 issue of *Studies in the Literary Imagination*, Biles wrote Piggy's apologia—at length. His starting point is that in the criticism there is not much discussion of character. Individual characters—one thinks immediately of Simon—have received some attention; but, surprisingly, almost no attention has been paid to characters as dramatic representations of human beings. E. M. Forster is almost alone in his consideration of the boys as *boys*. Characterization has become a moot concept in the twentieth century (see Ortega y Gassett). The point has been made more than once that the twentieth-century novel is marked by abstraction and depersonalization; but this matter had not surfaced, except in passing, in Golding criticism.

Central as the humanist viewpoint is to modern literature, it is of particular relevance in a consideration of Golding. And it is made more interesting and more difficult by the author's pronouncements on his own work. Biles, with particular reference to Piggy, puts the matter into context: "Some would argue that the lack of critical attention to his people is ultimately Golding's own fault, because he has failed sufficiently to characterize. Golding would not totally reject such a judgment. He says he is more an 'ideas-man' than a 'character-man' " (p. 83).

Thus, Biles finds that "By virtue of the number and diversity of his qualities, Piggy is the best characterization in *Lord of the Flies*" (p. 104). Of the four major characters, Piggy is the roundest: he "is a multifaceted figure, with much color and vividness—a study in contrasts, with various contradictory traits which tend to round out the characterization

and enhance his believability" (p. 87). One is inclined to agree
that Piggy is indeed the "round" character who evaded Golding's intentions for him.

In 1969 Leighton Hodson published a book on Golding in
the Writers and Critics series. He notes the metaphoric complexity and importance of darkness in Golding's work. His
chapter on *Lord of the Flies* is titled "The Metaphor of Darkness"; but in mid-career he pauses to argue with Golding's
critics and abandons his thesis. His argument becomes a
statement of the familiar idea that the novel is not to be
forced. Hodson is critical of those who do not "allow the text
to speak for itself" and thus disagrees with those (like Claire
Rosenfield) who read the novel in the light of a single critical approach. Although he sees Golding's work as weighty
enough to be called philosophical or religious, his defense of
what one could call open reading prevents his doing much
except reacting against earlier critics. Hodson's book is stimu-
lating; however, the Writers and Their Work pamphlet by
Clive Pemberton is the reverse, the weakest example of survey criticism so often applied to contemporary writers.[57]

Neville Braybrook covers two aspects of Golding's fiction
in *Lord of the Flies* and *Pincher Martin*.[58] A one-sentence
synopsis states that "mythic and allegorical meanings are seen
to be more complex than the relatively simple interpretations
critics have offered." Braybrook affirms that the novel is too
many-sided to allow narrow classifications. Nothing new is put
forward here, and there is no attempt to relate *Lord of the
Flies* to *Pincher Martin*.

George Thomson dealt with polarities of grace and pride
to show that Golding writes within orthodox Christian tradition. Matej Mužina expressed the view that Golding is an
existentialist who places man in contingent situations in order
to test religious and scientific orthodoxies. Britta Broberg, uti-
lizing much of the available scholarship, examines connections between *Lord of the Flies* and *The Inheritors*. She

notices certain formal resemblances in construction and articulation of theme.[59]

Three essays in 1969 issues of the *English Journal* were devoted to *Lord of the Flies*. Jerome Martin's article, designed for the secondary school teacher, is a hunt for symbols.[60] The article is set up as a classroom exercise, though it puts a powerful novel to strange uses. As Martin says: "It's all great fun, but your students are sure to get the point [none stated]. Or maybe both you and your students might find it all fits. Who knows?"

Richard Lederer and Paul Hamilton Beattie provoke classroom experience of a higher order.[61] They "recommend the study of *African Genesis* and *Lord of the Flies* in succession so that the student can see how the philosophical naturalist and the novelist can interpret the same intriguing questions about human nature and the environment."

Leon Levitt liked the book but disliked the way in which it is generally taught.[62] Instead of making a case for Golding's own "programme" (the "attempt to trace the defects of society back to the defects of human nature"), *Lord of the Flies* confirms the contrary: the evil lies in Western culture. Levitt's attempt to align Golding with modern social analysts who wish to bring change by manipulating society is provocative; but because of his rhetoric and a lack of evidence, it is not convincing.

Two book-length contributions in 1970 were by Howard S. Babb and Jack I. Biles. Babb's book is a critical study that builds upon his two earlier essays.[63] He concludes that although Golding is deficient in creation of character, he is a major novelist, with closer affinities to Thomas Hardy than to Richard Hughes. Babb wants to "bring out the narrative structure" of the novel, then to examine the characters, and finally to isolate a particular scene in order to suggest how the novel is realized in its language.

Golding's narrative method, writes Babb, is based upon

"the recurrence of some event, situation, or fact in slightly varying form, the variations so managed that the sequence generates an ever-increasing emotional intensity" (p. 12). The plot is linear, but the novel is composed of parallel sequences, all of which move in one direction. Such structuring "helps to explain . . . the effects of clarity and simplicity that the narrative produces on a first reading" (p. 15), and it certainly makes for speed and intensity.

Jack Biles's *Talk* sets out to get answers to questions that any enthusiast might ask.[64] How does Golding write? (or does he type?); how long does it take? (the several drafts of *Lord of the Flies* occupied Golding "three or four months"; the single draft of *The Inheritors* took only three weeks). In addition, a fuller picture of Golding appears. He seems to have a delightful sense of humor. In response to Biles's chiding him for burning old notes (rather than saving them for literary scholars), Golding replies: "Well, somebody once told me that there is a university somewhere in America which is so rich that on Sundays it puts up rockets, but on weekdays it buys the lunch bills and the train tickets and all the rest from authors. Now this is the university I've been looking for" (p. 22). Leighton Hodson was the first critic to mention Golding's sense of humor. Biles displays it in their conversations. And Golding's sense of humor is relevant to an assessment of the novels.

Of more immediate value to the scholar are comments by Golding upon his own art (in such chapters as "The Teller versus the Tale") and upon art in general. He says, for instance: "Writing is not reportage, but imagination. Therefore, I don't think you ever write about what you know about. You write about what you guess about and what you imagine about" (p. 16). This illustrates Biles's method and his best results. Biles wants to know what Golding thinks and what he thinks with, particularly when his thought is germane to a crux in the novels. This is nowhere more important than in the division over the type and quality of the morality in *Lord of the Flies*. Thus when Biles engages Golding in discussion about moral questions, and when the talk sharpens for an instant so that Golding shares with Biles a pithy, resonant idea, the critics and the general reader are enriched.

Golding's preface to the book dramatizes his misgivings over its form. He warns the reader against expecting too much, and of course he is right. Nevertheless, the mental set of this author is more fully and sympathetically put forward here than anywhere else.

John S. Whitley provides a smaller book which presents nothing very new, but does provide a synthesis. He places the novel in historical perspective and then examines the text, dealing suggestively with such matters as characterization, fable, and closure.[65]

Eugene Hollahan demonstrates that Golding utilizes the circle as a controlling motif in his intricate story.[66] He finds that the word *circle*, with variations like circular, encircled, and cirque, together with "the semantically-related word *ring*," occurs in the novel forty-two times. Such words, linking in various contexts with setting, plot, and theme, help provide the dense symbolic background. Furthermore, "Golding's novel is arranged around the concept of two important kinds of circles, the first being the socio-political circle where the assembled boys engage in rational discussion in order to plan their way out of their difficulties, and the second being the tribal circle where the regressive boys dance ritually and kill savagely." Thus the circle is Golding's "main device for showing the shape of the two societies."

In another criticism, David Spitz suggests that Golding's novel is "a direct and incisive work in political theory" and that the characters are symbols of "diverse responses to the question of authority."[67] In addressing questions of power placement and legitimacy, Golding works through his character-symbols to show that: (1) men do not heed the seer (Simon the Christ figure) as he reveals God's message; (2) Socratic man, the voice of reason, goes equally unheeded; (3) democratic man (Ralph the symbol of assent) is likewise abandoned as a principle of authority; (4) having rejected God, man is thrown back upon himself; having rejected reason, man is left with only savagery and force—with Jack the authoritarian man. Spitz carefully marshals his evidence to suggest that Golding is only partially right in *Lord of the Flies*. Evil, he concludes, resides not only in man but also in institutions. What surprises him is not that there is evil or that power and authority are seldom brought together with justice, but that there is any good or justice at all—ever.

In a slighter article, John Oakland argues that Golding's criticism of modern life has a sharper point if it is considered satire.[68] "It is the liberal humanist tradition of rationalist orthodoxy, man's presumption of possible perfection, his human self-sufficiency, and (in John Wain's term) 'his belief that the untutored human being is naturally good,' which Golding satirizes" (p. 15).

In an article titled "The Decline of *Lord of the Flies*," James R. Baker returns to lament the passing of the vogue.[69] The big wave of popularity is over and Golding's later, more difficult novels, he says, "have not caught on." Inasmuch as Baker views *Lord of the Flies* as a "vital fable for our time," he regrets its declining readership and popularity. The force of Golding's prophecy has been misspent and diffused for various unhappy reasons. Nay-sayers (specifically R. C. Townsend, although his article appeared in 1964) have undercut the novel's popularity, Baker claims, and they "indicate the prevailing feeling of surfeit among those who have seen years of tireless explication and analysis of every detail of the all-too-familiar story, so that one has to become a veritable Lord of the Files to keep up with it all" (p. 447). Other reasons for the decline are academia's lust for novelty and the disinclination to look squarely at Golding's frightening parable. More serious is criticism from the Radical Right and the New Left, which maintains that the Beast is the system rather than an inherent defect in Man. Most serious—and here we reach the heart of Baker's unhappiness—is the seductive nature of culture critics who "are now lords of the campus." Critics like Erich Fromm and Herbert Marcuse seem to put forward new solutions for contemporary problems, but for Baker theirs is a mistaken view—they only prescribe as an antidote "social action and manipulation."

After Baker's article, Golding criticism seems to reach a plateau. As an anonymous reviewer of *The Scorpion God* put it, Golding has reached "an age when a man has made his life, done the best of his work."[70] His first novel forms a case in point. Although some of the best criticism may yet be written, one can say that the basic guidelines are complete. With Jack Biles's earlier *Checklist* of criticism and his bibliography in this volume, full access to it is open to everyone.

Much of the criticism is of generally high quality, and it seems traditional, giving off reminders of nineteenth-century encounters between the humanities and science. One can almost envision two forces (one generaled by F. R. Leavis, the other by C. P. Snow) contending for supremacy. At first the "humanists" hold the field. Indeed, the preponderance of commentary has appeared in quarterly reviews rather than in journals like *PMLA*.

The novel clearly answered the call of the 1960s for relevance. With its reactionary or illiberal view of man, *Lord of the Flies* struck deeply into a variety of twentieth-century ganglia. It was immediately applicable to the contemporary situation. But the novel was traditional as well as modern, and it was well written. Thus, as humanist critics came to base their texts to ever greater degrees on the novel itself, the forces of science (formalism) may be said to have encroached upon the field, providing criticism of technique and content. The technique-oriented critics and the moralists stand clearly defined in the field of Golding criticism, with the moralists carrying an edge.

It may not come as a surprise, then, to discover that the major crux thus far in Golding scholarship has been over what one might call Golding's religion. To date, the response to the novel has been to ask Is Golding religious? In all Golding's novels the same concerns are present: free will versus necessity, the Fall from innocence, the origin and manifestation of evil, the search for meaning. Although later critics have resisted any interpretation of *Lord of the Flies* based upon one discipline—religious, political, psychological, or economic— earlier critics who scoffed at complacently Christian readings ("Original Sin, of course") must have been somewhat embarrassed by the religious turn Golding's work took with *Pincher Martin*.

It is fair to say that most critics have granted a religious dimension to *Lord of the Flies*. The two best approaches have been Hynes's and Elmen's. Hynes found Golding to be that rarity in English literature, a religious novelist. His concerns are the eternal religious questions, and he is distinctive both for his depth of concern and for the form it takes. Elmen would add that Golding's unresolved problem, the problem of "good," stems from the fact that he can believe in Beelzebub, but not in Beelzebub's master.

It is this dwelling upon evil, this narrow "Calvinistic" form of Golding's religion, which is primarily responsible for the view of certain later critics, such as Kenneth Watson: they feel that the most vital understanding of Golding's fable is probably in moral rather than in theological terms.[71] Thus, while most critics grant the novel a religious dimension, all find it deeply moral. For most, and this includes Golding himself, the moral is transmitted by a fabulistic, rather than a traditionally novelistic, method.[72] However, the logical conjunction of the critical terms *moral* and *fable* has caused uneasiness. In Golding criticism generally, there has been concern with form, which began with *Lord of the Flies*. The first term used to describe Golding's method, *allegory*, was discarded early. The novel was found to be too complex for an easy assignment of one-to-one relationships between elements inside and outside the story. The term *fable* was found by John Peter to be more suitable. *Moral fable* is a key term in Arnold Kettle's criticism, and it has been given recent currency by Robert Scholes and others. Given Golding's admitted purpose, the term is functional—especially in the light of Margaret Walters's definition of this novelistic mode with relevance to Golding. " 'Fable,' " writes Bernard Dick, "comes closest to being the one technical term to cover the Golding *corpus*" (p. 102).

Despite the usefulness of the designation, several critics have been chary about it, preferring instead the word *patterned*, as in "patterned quality" or "heavily patterned."[73] Babb puts it this way: "As for Golding's method . . . there is some difference of critical opinion, his books being called fables, allegories, symbolic structures, or even romances. But the critics agree that his method . . . is radically conditioned by meaning: that the entire fictional structure . . . is created with a view to its significance."[74]

This unease may stem in part from difficulty in reading Golding's fable. Various readings have met the novel's religious, moral, and social implications head on, but there is such complexity of implication that division has been inevitable over such matters as tone and orthodoxy. What kind of fable is it whose moral cannot be read aright? One group of critics, in general the most recent, denies the possibility of one best reading: for them the novel is too complex. Another

group deals with the novel's rich resonance by comparing it
with works ranging from *The Bacchae* to *Duelo in Paraiso*—
comparing it with, in short, any work seriously addressing itself to the question What is Man?

Confining such resonance under one rubric is impossible,
and no critic has attempted it. But it is as traditional fable and
relevant prophecy that *Lord of the Flies* has caused such di-
visiveness. Although a good deal of agreement has been
reached about the reading of specific scenes, characters, and
symbols, a deep division still exists.

R. C. Townsend has spoken best, perhaps, for the "nay-
sayers." [75] In his view, thousands of students have been exploited because Golding's wrongheaded and "facile comment
on the human situation" has become holy writ proving the
text "Man is inherently evil."

This kind of critical disagreement is not new. The moral of
the fable (and the use of the moral) is a subject for sincere
argument, whereas the story/storyteller facet is above re-
proach. I call this aspect of Golding criticism the "second-
reading premise," and it, like other central issues, appears
early. As Douglas Hewitt observed in 1954, "Reservations
come only on reflection when the book is subjected to the
most exacting scrutiny" (p. 4). To date, whether the book is
praised or derided, almost no one has been able to avoid being caught up in the story. As Walter Allen has said: "There
is an intriguing gap between the initial receptions of Golding's
books and the critics' second thoughts." [76]

Some of the second reading of *Lord of the Flies* has been
initiated by Golding himself. Much critical ink has been
spilled because Golding jiggled the inkwell. His comments,
both in and out of print, have fueled fires that still smolder. In
the religious controversy, in the matter of form, in more sin-
gular topics (history, Simon, Piggy, gimmick, etc.), Golding
has in one way or another influenced criticism of his book.
The resultant cleavage says as much about Golding's critics,

no doubt, as about Golding's novel; and yet the second-reading premise represents an important crux in ranking *Lord of the Flies*. If the novel cannot bear rereading, can it be a classic?

The best and most loyal critics provide ample basis for faith in the permanence of Golding's achievement—especially *Lord of the Flies*. In a review of Babb's and Hodson's studies, Dick placed the novel solidly in its tradition. Although not in Dick's estimation a cosmic work, *Lord of the Flies* is an excellent novel because "symbolism is *welded* to the narrative" (my italics). "Golding's ability to align action and symbol is precisely why the novel is such a good introduction to literature."[77]

What has emerged from twenty years of commentary? On the one hand, it is easy to praise the rapid formation of a body of criticism which has made more accessible the difficult work of this "ideas-man," William Golding. On the other hand, these years have been jumbled by attempts to apply biography and history in order to assess intention. Succeeding interviewers built upon what earlier interviewers said that Golding said, and then later commentators came along to fit these remarks to the novel. This situation has caused several critics to decry the criticism and declare that it is time to stop haggling. For me, the outstanding factors of Golding scholarship to date have been threefold: (1) the rapid mobilization of critical forces, (2) the relatively clear drawing of battle lines, and (3) the quickened maturity of the forces in the field.

James Baker's 1970 obituary for the Golding vogue has at this distance a nice ring of prophecy. That year's work in many ways marks the end of the first exciting phase of *Lord of the Flies* criticism. To be sure, familiar names like Baker and Biles still appear in Golding scholarship, but they are not narrowly associated with the phenomenon of Golding's first novel. Others of Golding's works have demanded critical at-

tention. As in Gabriel Josipovici's chapter on Golding, all of
Golding's fables are made relevant to a critical insight concerning the works as a whole.[78]

What has happened since the *Lord of the Flies* vogue is a
broadening of critical perspective—and critical enterprise.
Perhaps, it has been suggested, *Lord of the Flies* is not Golding's best novel. *The Inheritors* has its supporters, as does
The Spire.[79]

Whether or not Golding's first novel is his best, its fame
continues to spread, judging from recent criticism in many
countries and in many languages. In addition, dissertations,
appearing at the rate of two or three a year, seem to be on the
increase. One of these, Virginia Tiger's, recently appeared as
a book-length study.[80]

Tiger's book is the most important recent addition to *Lord
of the Flies* scholarship. Accepting Golding as a fabulist, she
focuses upon what she calls the "ideographic structure" of the
novels in order to examine linkages between Golding's fictional worlds and readers' real ones. Ideographic structure,
defined in her introduction, unites the matter of the fable and
its form—new in each novel, yet bred by the same mytho-
poeia. In her chapter on *Lord of the Flies*, she reviews the
main lines of criticism, then finds the novel "ideographically
suggestive" rather than "allegorically simple." This suggestiveness she locates formally in "confrontation scenes," colli-
sions between the boys' disintegrating society and the adult
world. Such confrontations are elements of ideographic structure by which the novel "portrays its thematic meaning."

Her chapter on *Lord of the Flies* evidently required some
courage. Looking at "some twenty years of narcissistic, repetitive exegesis," Tiger wondered whether too much commentary had appeared already. And certainly in sheer weight
(and sometimes perversity)—the critical quest for the essential *Lord of the Flies* has had its comic side—a fact Gold-

ing has more than once pointed out. And yet *Lord of the Flies* needed, and has received, much clarification. True, not all of the needed studies called for by Arthur Ziegler in the 1964 casebook edition have been done, but much necessary work has, and Virginia Tiger's is a case in point. Not the last, nor even the latest, but certainly one of the important links in the critical chain.

---

1. *The Novel Now* (New York: Norton, 1967), 205.

2. "The Decline of *Lord of the Flies*," *South Atlantic Quarterly*, 69 (1970), 447.

3. William Nelson, ed., *William Golding's "Lord of the Flies": A Source Book* (New York: Odyssey, 1963), 3; *The Modern Novel in Britain and the United States* (Harmondsworth: Penguin, 1965), 291.

4. *Source Book*, 5

5. Ibid., 4.

6. 22 October 1954, 669.

7. Peter, "The Fables of William Golding," *Kenyon Review*, 19 (1957), 577–92; Freedman, "The New Realism: The Fancy of William Golding," *Perspective*, 10 (1958), 118–28.

8. In James R. Baker, *William Golding: A Critical Study* (New York: St. Martin's, 1965), 101.

9. Ibid., 100. Baker calls it a "somewhat obscure commentary on the first four novels."

10. Drew, "Second Reading," *Cambridge Review*, 27 October 1956, 79; MacLure, "William Golding's Survivor Stories," *Tamarack Review*, 4 (Summer 1957), 60–67. V. S. Pritchett's "Secret Parables" (*New Statesman*, 2 August 1958) praising Golding as an "Austere Romancer" is also worthy, as is John Bowen's *TLS* notice (7 August 1959, xii–xiii).

11. His work includes "Coral Islands," *Spectator*, 22 August 1958, 257; "The Meaning of It All," *Books and Bookmen*, 5 (October 1959), 9–10; and "The Novels of William Golding," *International Literary Annual*, 3 (1961) 11–29. This last essay was reprinted in his *Puzzles and Epiphanies* (London: Routledge and Kegan Paul, 1962) and, with "Postscript, 1964," in *On Contemporary Literature*, ed. Richard Kostelanetz (New York: Avon Books, 1964). The BBC interview was broadcast 28 August 1959. It was printed in *Books and Bookmen* (October 1959) and reprinted in part in James R. Baker and Arthur P. Ziegler, eds., *William Golding's "Lord of the Flies,"* casebook ed. (New York: Putnam's, 1964). Other interviews available are: with James Keating (1962, casebook edition), with Douglas M. Davis (*New Republic*, 4 May 1963), with Leslie Hannon (*Cavalier*, December 1963),

with Bernard Dick (*College English*, March 1965), with Jack I. Biles (*Talk: Conversations with William Golding* [New York: Harcourt, 1970]). Excepting Hannon's piece, in which everything of value comes from the Kermode/Golding exchange, which Hannon does not cite, these interviews all contain valuable comments by the artist on his work.

12. "The World of William Golding," *Review of English Literature*, 1 (April 1960), 62–72.

13. "Lord of the Flies," *Critical Quarterly*, 2 (Summer 1960), 112–17.

14. " 'Gimmick' and Metaphor in the Novels of William Golding," *Modern Fiction Studies*, 6 (Summer 1960), 145–52.

15. "Distaste for the Contemporary," *Nation*, 21 May 1960, 451–54.

16. "Novels of a Religious Man," *Commonweal*, 18 March 1960, 673–75.

17. MacLure, "Allegories of Innocence," *Dalhousie Review*, 40 (Summer 1960), 145–56.

18. "Two Fabulists: Golding and Camus," *Melbourne Critical Review*, 4 (1961), 18–19. Walters pays a necessary debt to Arnold Kettle, whose application of the term "moral fable" to writers from Defoe to Graham Greene goes back many years (see his *An Introduction to the English Novel* [London: Hutchinson's University Library, 1957], 1:17f). No other critic mentions Kettle.

19. " 'Men of a Smaller Growth': A Psychological Analysis of William Golding's *Lord of the Flies*," *Literature and Psychology*, 11 (1961), 93–101.

20. Wasserstrom, "Reason and Reverence in Art and Science," ibid., 12 (1962), 2–5; Rosenfield, "Reply by Miss Rosenfield," ibid., 12 (1962), 11–12.

21. Pendry, "William Golding and 'Mankind's Essential Illness,' " *Moderna Språk*, 55 (1961), 1–7; Niemeyer, "*The Coral Island* Revisited," *College English*, January 1961, 241–45.

22. Trilling, "*Lord of the Flies*," *Mid-Century*, October 1962, 10–12; Fuller, "Behind the Vogue, a Rigorous Understanding," *New York Herald Tribune Book Week*, 4 November 1962, 3; Davis, "Golding, the Optimist, Belies His Somber Pictures and Fiction," *National Observer*, 17 September 1962, 17.

23. Karl, *A Reader's Guide to the Contemporary English Novel* (New York: Noonday Press, 1962); Marcus, "The Novel Again," *Partisan Review*, 29 (Spring 1962), 171–95.

24. Williams, "The Art of William Golding," *Bulletin of the Department of English* (Calcutta University), 3 (1962), 20–31; MacShane, "The Novels of William Golding," *Dalhousie Review*, 42 (1962), 171–83; Michel-Michot, "The Myth of Innocence," *Revue des Langues Vivantes*, 28 (1962), 510–20.

25. "Concepts and Technique in William Golding," *New Left Review*, May–June 1962, 63–71.

26. "Lord of the Agonies," *Aspect*, April 1963, 56–67. In another way

this criticism by a fellow novelist is of great concern. Golding's later work, Baker says, "has not caught on." Does the problem lie with Golding or with his art form? Ronald Stone asserted that the movies, "Being Image . . . are necessarily true—Image affective in all our lives, inheritor of the power once the Word's. So the novel must be a Lie, nowise affective in our lives, relative to nothing but itself. *Sui Generis*" ("The Novel in the Age of the Movies," *Modern Occasions* 1 [1971], 547–72). The fable, welcomed back into popularity by such critics as Robert Scholes, has been held to be a minor form of fiction by such critics as Steven Marcus. With regard to Ronald Stone's overwritten attack on the novel—especially concerning application of these remarks to Golding—see Robin Lee's comments on *Lord of the Flies* as film, "Where Has All the Meaning Gone?" *New Nation*, 1 (January 1967), 18–19.

27. Kearns, "Salinger and Golding: Conflict on the Campus," *America*, 26 January 1963, 136–39; Egan, "Golding's View of Man," ibid., 140–41.

28. "The Appeal of Golding," *Commonweal*, 25 January 1963, 457–59.

29. "Behind the Vogue, a Rigorous Understanding," *New York Herald Tribune Book Week*, 4 November 1962, 3.

30. See "An Exchange of Views," *Commonweal*, 22 February 1963, 569–71.

31. "Is Golding Calvinistic?" *America*, 6 July 1963, 18–20.

32. "*Lord of the Flies:* Beelzebub Revisited," *College English*, November 1963, 90–99.

33. Irwin, "The Serpent Coiled Within," *Motive*, May 1963, 1–5; Sullivan, "William Golding: The Fables and the Art," *Sewanee Review*, 71 (1963), 660–64.

34. Baker and Ziegler, *William Golding's "Lord of the Flies,"* casebook ed.; Bufkin, "The Novels of William Golding: A Descriptive and Analytic Study (Ph.D. diss., Vanderbilt University, 1969); Warner, "Mr. Golding and Marryat's *Little Savage*," *Review of English Literature*, 5 (1964), 51–55; Baker, "Why It's No Go: A Study of William Golding's *Lord of the Flies*," *Arizona Quarterly*, 19 (1963), 293–305.

35. White, "Butterfly and Beast in *Lord of the Flies*," *Modern Fiction Studies*, 1 (1964), 163–70; Townsend, "*Lord of the Flies:* Fool's Gold?" *Journal of General Education*, 16 (July 1964), 153–160.

36. Called by Oldsey and Weintraub "a specious denigration of *Lord of the Flies* through a working out of proposed parallels with *A High Wind in Jamaica*," Townsend's article is not the first to compare the two books. However, Golding says that he read Hughes's book only after he had written *Lord of the Flies*. See James Keating, "Interview with William Golding," (casebook ed.), and Jack I. Biles, "Literary Sources and William Golding," *South Atlantic Bulletin*, 37 (May 1972), 29–36.–Eds.

37. Veidemanis, "*Lord of the Flies* in the Classroom—No Passing Fad," 569–74; Lederer, "Student Reactions to *Lord of the Flies*," 575–79.

38. "A Reading of *Lord of the Flies*," *English*, 15 (Spring 1964), 2–7.

39. *A Critical Commentary on William Golding: "Lord of the Flies"* (London: Macmillan, 1966).

40. *William Golding*, Columbia Essays on Modern Writers, no. 2 (New York: Columbia University Press, 1964).

41. *The Art of William Golding* (New York: Harcourt, 1965).

42. *William Golding: A Critical Study* (New York: St. Martin's, 1965).

43. "Golding and Salinger: A Clear Choice," *Wiseman Review*, no. 502 (Winter 1964–1965), 309–22.

44. Babb, "Four Passages from William Golding's Fiction," *Minnesota Review*, 5 (1965), 50–58; Davis, "Mr. Golding's Optical Delusion," *English Language Notes*, 3 (1965), 125–26; Hampton, "An Error in *Lord of the Flies*," *Notes and Queries*, July 1965, 275; Malin, "The Elements of William Golding," in *Contemporary British Novelists*, ed. Charles Shapiro (Carbondale: Southern Illinois University Press, 1965), 37–47; Bufkin, "*Lord of the Flies*: An Analysis," *Georgia Review*, 19 (Spring 1965), 40–57.

45. "The Case against William Golding's Simon-Piggy," *Contemporary Review*, September 1966, 155–60.

46. "Mute Choirboys and Angelic Pigs: The Fable in *Lord of the Flies*," *Texas Studies in Literature and Language*, 7 (1966), 411–20.

47. Gordon, "Classical Themes in *Lord of the Flies*," *Modern Fiction Studies*, 11 (1965–1966), 424–27; Gulbin, "Parallels and Contrasts in *Lord of the Flies* and *Animal Farm*," *English Journal*, January 1966, 86; Díaz-Plaja, "Náufragos en dos islas," *Insula*, October 1965, 6; Cixous-Berger, "L'allégorie du mal dans l'oeuvre de William Golding," *Critique*, no. 227, April 1966, 309–20; Cohn, "The Berengaria Allusion in *Lord of the Flies*," *Notes and Queries*, November 1966, 419–20; Mitchell, "The *Lord of the Flies* and the Escape from Freedom," *Arizona Quarterly*, 22 (Spring 1966), 27–40.

48. *William Golding*, no. 57 (New York: Twayne, 1967).

49. *William Golding: A Critical Study* (London: Faber, 1967).

50. *Arizona Quarterly*, 25 (1969), 77–80.

51. *William Golding: A Critical Essay* (Grand Rapids, Mich.: Eerdmans, 1967).

52. Ely, "The Adult Image in Three Novels of Adolescent Life," *English Journal*, November 1967, 1127–31; Rosenberg, "Lord of the Fireflies," *Centennial Review*, 11 (1967), 128–39.

53. Gaskin, "Beelzebub," *Hibbert Journal*, 66 (1968), 58–61; Lee, "Where Has All the Meaning Gone?" *New Nation*, 1 (January 1967), 18–19; Nossen, "The Beast-Man Theme in the Work of William Golding," *Ball State University Forum*, 9 (1968), 60–69.

54. Sternlicht, "Songs of Innocence and Songs of Experience in *Lord of the Flies* and *The Inheritors*," *Midwest Quarterly*, 9 (1968), 383–90; Talon, "Irony in *Lord of the Flies*," *Essays in Criticism*, 18 (1968), 296–309; Nichols, "Nathanael West, Sinclair Lewis, Alexander Pope, and Satiric Contrasts," *Satire Newsletter*, 5 (1968), 119–22.

55. "Piggy: *Apologia Pro Vita Sua*," *Studies in the Literary Imagination*, 1 (1968), 83–109.

56. *Talk: Conversations with William Golding* (New York: Harcourt, 1970), 11–14.

57. Hodson, *William Golding*, no. 61 (Edinburgh: Oliver and Boyd, 1969); Pemberton, *William Golding*, no. 210 (London: Longmans, 1969).

58. "Two William Golding Novels: Two Aspects of His Work," *Queen's Quarterly*, 76 (1969), 92–100.

59. Thomson, "William Golding: Between God-Darkness and God-Light," *Cresset*, June 1969, 8–12; Mužina, "William Golding: Novels of Extreme Situations," *Studia Romanica et Anglica*, nos. 27–28 (1969), 43–66; Broberg, "Connections between William Golding's First Two Novels," *Moderna Språk*, 63 (1969), 1–24.

60. "Symbol Hunting: Golding's *Lord of the Flies*," *English Journal*, March 1969, 408–13.

61. "*African Genesis* and *Lord of the Flies:* Two Studies of the Beastie Within," *English Journal*, December 1969, 1316.

62. "Trust the Tale: A Second Reading of *Lord of the Flies*," *English Journal*, April 1969, 521.

63. *The Novels of William Golding* (Columbus: Ohio State University Press, 1970).

64. *Talk.* See above, note 56.

65. *Golding: "Lord of the Flies*," Studies in English Literature, no. 42 (London: Edward Arnold, 1970).

66. "Running in Circles: A Major Motif in *Lord of the Flies*," *Studies in the Novel*, 2 (Spring 1970), 22–30.

67. "Power and Authority: An Interpretation of Golding's *Lord of the Flies*," *Antioch Review*, 30 (Spring 1970), 21–33.

68. "Satiric Technique in *Lord of the Flies*," *Moderna Språk*, 64 (1970), 14–18.

69. *South Atlantic Quarterly*, 69 (1970), 446–60.

70. "Origins of the Species," *Times Literary Supplement*, 5 November 1971, 1381.

71. The term *Calvinistic* has been seriously applied to Golding's thought in *Lord of the Flies* only once, so far as I know; but, although the picture of Golding as Calvinistic was found by other religious critics to be egregious, Golding has come to see that the label is not totally inappropriate (see Biles, *Talk*, p. 86).

72. See "Fable," *The Hot Gates* (London: Faber, 1965), 85–101.

73. The term is used by Samuel Hynes. Unhappy with the overtones of "fable" (*Lord of the Flies* does not possess *all* the formal properties of fable), Hynes falls back upon this neutral term, which is picked up by Kinkead-Weekes and Gregor.

74. *Novels of William Golding*, p. 7. Babb's note to the first sentence of the quotation traces briefly the changes in critical nomenclature, but omits

Ralph Freedman's "new realism" and Kingsley Amis's description of Golding's method as that of science fiction (*New Maps of Hell*, [New York: Harcourt, 1960], 24).

75. These include Walter Allen, Martin Green, Juliet Mitchell, and J. D. O'Hara. Bernard Dick's summary is mildly surprising for its low ranking of the novel. One nay-sayer not yet mentioned is Kenneth Rexroth, whose superficial assessment of Golding as a careless writer seems best forgotten (*Atlantic*, May 1965, 96–98). On the other hand, the defensive critic who assumes that anyone questioning Golding's proficiency is "egregiously harsh and willful" or "specious" is also suspect (see Oldsey and Weintraub, *Art of William Golding*, 16, 25).

76. *The Modern Novel in Britain and the United States* (Harmondsworth: Penguin, 1965), 288.

77. *Journal of Modern Literature*, 1 (1970), 810–12. Dick seems somewhat to reverse his opinion of the novel here.

78. *The World and the Book* (Stanford, Calif.: Stanford University Press, 1971).

79. Frederick Karl in the "Postscript" of his revised edition of *A Reader's Guide to the Contemporary English Novel* decides that *Lord of the Flies* is Golding's most important work (although flawed), while Virginia Tiger favors *The Spire;* I am sure they are both wrong.

80. *William Golding: The Dark Fields of Discovery* (London: Calder and Boyars, 1974).

Jack I. Biles

WILLIAM GOLDING: BIBLIOGRAPHY OF PRIMARY AND SECONDARY SOURCES

THIS BIBLIOGRAPHY has two major divisions: the first lists the works of William Golding, with reviews; the second lists criticism and commentary. Listing of Golding's books is limited to initial English and American publication. The limitation for short works is to first publication, with the exception of the Leningrad speech, which is entered for both the original Italian publication ("Una Terribile Malattia") and the English version.

Following is the organization of the bibliography:

WORKS BY WILLIAM GOLDING
  I. Books and Parts of Books
 II. Short Works
     A. Short Fiction
     B. Occasional Pieces
     C. Book Reviews
     D. British Broadcasting Corporation Programs

CRITICISM AND COMMENTARY
   I. Bibliographical Sources
  II. Biographical Sources
 III. Books and Other Separate Publications
  IV. Parts of Books
   V. Theses and Dissertations
  VI. Articles, Review-Articles, Interviews, Notes
 VII. Letters to the Editor
VIII. British Broadcasting Corporation Programs

The success of *Lord of the Flies* has been spectacular. The novel has become familiar in many countries and has been published in numerous languages. As long ago as 18 April 1964, *The Bookseller* could report it in print in English, Norwegian, French, German, Portuguese, Spanish, Finnish, Danish, Dutch, Serbo-Croatian, Hungarian, Swedish, and Italian; also noted were contracts for its translation into Hebrew, Icelandic, Japanese, and Polish. Entries in this bibliography indicate the availability of *Lord of the Flies* in still other languages and some translation of other Golding titles as well. These data suggest that a bibliography of all editions of *Lord of the Flies* and the other books may never be compiled, and to catalog more than a portion of the reviews and other criticism of the works seems impossible. I have tried, nevertheless, to be as comprehensive as was compatible with these restrictions: I have entered the items from the documents themselves or I have verified the bibliographical data from several sources. Items I know of from only one reference are marked by asterisks, and such entries have been minimized.

Reviews are of special importance in establishing critical reputation; reviews of an author's books over a period of years provide an index to the response of readers and critics alike and afford a valuable adjunct to formal criticism. I have listed reviews immediately below each work. Reviews and comment concerning the motion picture version of *Lord of the Flies*, directed by Peter Brook, follow the reviews of the novel.

In addition to the checklists recorded in Section I of "Criticism and Commentary," there are, of course, others in books about Golding; also, in newspaper stories, there are biographical items which amplify those in Section II. Those interviews with Golding published in periodicals are entered under the interviewer's name in Section VI.

Titles of periodicals have been shortened; because of variations in their titles, I have regularized those of three periodicals: *New Statesman, New York Herald Tribune Book Week*, and *Contemporary Literature*.

Five special notations are used:

1. (THG) marks the twenty short pieces collected with a preface in *The Hot Gates and Other Occasional Pieces* by William Golding (1965).

2. (NSB) marks the thirty-one "Articles on William Golding" collected with a preface and eleven "Related Readings" in *William Golding's "Lord of the Flies": A Source Book* by William Nelson (1963).

3. (CBE) marks the "Foreword," "Introduction," two interviews with Golding, and twelve critical items collected with the text of *Lord of the Flies* and a short checklist in the casebook edition by James R. Baker and Arthur P. Ziegler, Jr. (1964).

4. (OLF) marks the twelve reviews and articles collected in the study guide *An Outline of "Lord of the Flies"* by Frederick Jackson (1968).

5. (WGM) marks the six critical essays collected with an "Editor's Comment" in "A William Golding Miscellany," a special number of *Studies in the Literary Imagination*, by Jack I. Biles (1969).

Note: Parts of this bibliography appeared in a different form in *Twentieth Century Literature* and are reprinted with permission.

WORKS BY WILLIAM GOLDING

I. *BOOKS AND PARTS OF BOOKS*

POEMS.   London: Macmillan, 1934.   New York: Macmillan, 1935.
LORD OF THE FLIES.   London: Faber, 1954.   New York: Coward-McCann, 1955.
   REVIEWS:
      Booklist, 15 September 1955, 26.
      British Book News, November 1954, 636.
      British Book News, October 1958, 697.
      British Book News, November 1960, 831.
      Kirkus Bulletin, 1 August 1955, 560.
      Kirkus Bulletin, 1 September 1955, 659.
      New Yorker, 15 October 1955, 189.
      Reporter, 17 November 1955, 48.
      Times (London), 18 September 1954, 9.
      Times Literary Supplement, 22 October 1954, 669.
      Allen, Walter. *New Statesman*, 25 September 1954, 370. (NSB) (OLF)
      Allsop, Kenneth. *Daily Mail* (London), 27 June 1963.
      Bennis, Warren G. *Contemporary Psychology*, June 1963, 231–32.
      Cooperman, Stanley. *Nation*, 19 November 1955, 446.
      F., B.P. *Irish Times*, 29 June 1963.
      Fuller, Edmund. *Chicago Sunday Tribune Magazine of Books,* 9 September 1962, 6.
      Garlington, Jack. *Western Humanities Review*, 14 (Spring 1960), 233–34.
      Halle, Louis J. *Saturday Review*, 15 October 1955, 16. (NSB) (OLF)
      Hewitt, Douglas. *Manchester Guardian*, 28 September 1954, 4. (NSB) (OLF)
      Hughes, Riley. *Catholic World*, December 1955, 230.
      Metcalf, John, *Spectator*, 1 October 1954, 418–22.
      Moon, Eric. *Library Journal*, 1 October 1962, 3466–67.
      Moore, Reginald. *Time and Tide*, 18 September 1954, 1241–42.
      Moran, John. *Library Journal*, 1 September 1955, 1815.
      Painter, George D. *Listener*, 21 October 1954, 687.
      Stern, James. *New York Times Book Review*, 23 October 1955, 38. (NSB) (OLF)
      Walker, Peregrine. *Tablet*, 2 October 1954, 328.

Wickenden, Dan. *New York Herald Tribune Book Week*, 23 October 1955, 6. (NSB) (OLF)

Wyndham, Francis. *London Magazine*, December 1954, 90.

LORD OF THE FLIES (motion picture directed by Peter Brook).

REVIEWS AND COMMENT:

Esquire, February 1964, 28.

Evening Standard (London), 30 July 1964.

Newsweek, 26 August 1963, 76.

People (London), 2 August 1964.

Sunday Mirror (London), 2 August 1964.

Time, 23 August 1963, 68–69.

Times (London), 30 July 1964.

Alpert, Hollis. "Boys Will Be Boys." *Saturday Review*, 17 August 1963, 14.

Barker, Felix. *Evening News and Star* (London), 30 July 1964.

Brook, Peter. "Filming a Masterpiece." *Observer*, 26 July 1964, 21.

Burgess, Jackson. *Film Quarterly*, 17 (Winter 1963–64), 31–32.

Cecil, Norman. *Films in Review*, June–July 1963, 439–40.

Coleman, John. *New Statesman*, 31 July 1964, 159.

Crist, Judith. *New York Herald Tribune*, 20 August 1963.

Crowther, Bosley. "Agitating Fable of Wild Boys; Savagery Is Depicted in *Lord of the Flies*." *New York Times*, 20 August 1963, 37.

———. "*Lord of the Flies*: Film of Golding Novel about Castaway Boys Falls Wide of the Mark." *New York Times*, 25 August 1963, 1.

Dinhofer, Al. "Shooting 'Flies.' " *New York Times*, 23 July 1961, 5.

Ford, Charles. *Films in Review*, June–July 1963, 341.

Gibbs, Patrick. *Daily Telegraph* (London), 31 July 1964.

Gilliatt, Penelope. *Observer*, 2 August 1964.

Harman, Carter. "Making a Movie with an All–Small-Boy Cast." *Island Times* (San Juan, P.R.), 22 June 1961, 13.

Hart, Henry. *Films in Review*, January 1964, 1–2.

Hartung, Philip T. *Commonweal*, 27 September 1963, 16–17.

———. "Following the Films." *Senior Scholastic*, 11 October 1963, 27–28.

Kauffmann, Stanley. "Gold, Golding, Gilt." *New Republic*, 17 August 1963, 27–28.

*Lee, Robin. "Where Has All the Meaning Gone?" *New Nation*, 1 (January 1967), 18–19.

Lewis, Jack. *Sunday Citizen* (London), 2 August 1964.

Miller, Jonathan. "Trailing Clouds of Glory." *New Yorker*, 31 August 1963, 56.

Oakes, Philip. *Sunday Telegraph* (London), 2 August 1964.

Powell, Dilys. *Sunday Times* (London), 2 August 1964.

Richards, Dick. *Daily Mirror* (London), 31 July 1964.

Roud, Richard. *Manchester Guardian*, 31 July 1964.

Thornton, Michael. *Sunday Express* (London), 2 August 1964.
Wallace, Robert. "A Gamble on Novices Works Almost Too Well."
    Life, 25 October 1963, 100.
————. "A Gamble on Novices Works Almost Too Well." *Life International*, 2 December 1963, 70–80.
Walsh, Moira. *America*, 5 October 1963, 398–99.
"Whitefriar." *Smith's Trade News*, 1 June 1963.
Woods, Eddie. *Daily Worker* (London), 1 August 1964.

THE INHERITORS.   London: Faber, 1955.   New York: Harcourt, 1962.
    REVIEWS:
    Booklist, 1 September 1962, 30.
    British Book News, December 1955, 1454.
    Kirkus Bulletin, 15 July 1962, 643–44.
    Newsweek, 30 July 1962, 77.
    New York Herald Tribune Book Week, 23 September 1962, 12.
    Time, 27 July 1962, 70.
    Times (London), 22 September 1955, 11.
    Times Literary Supplement, 21 October 1955, 617.
    Bannon, Barbara A. *Publishers Weekly*, 19 August 1963, 113–19.
    Blakeston, Oswell. *Time and Tide*, 17 September 1955, 1205.
    Davenport, Guy. *National Review*, 9 October 1962, 273–74.
    Davenport, John. *Observer*, 18 September 1955, 11.
    Day, Philip. *Sunday Times* (London), 25 September 1955, 51.
    Dolbier, Maurice. *New York Herald Tribune*, 27 July 1962, 15.
    Fraser, G. S. *Encounter*, November 1955, 90.
    Grundy, Priscilla. *Christian Century*, 28 November 1962, 1451–52.
    Hewitt, Douglas. *Manchester Guardian*, 27 September 1955, 5.
    Hyman, Stanley Edgar. *New Leader*, 20 August 1962, 18–19.
    Lehiste, Ilse. *Current Anthropology*, 6 (April 1965), 232.
    Mann, Charles W. *Library Journal*, 1 September 1962, 2916.
    Plimpton, George. *New York Times Book Review*, 29 July 1962, 4.
    Preece, Warren E. *Chicago Sunday Tribune Magazine of Books*, 5
        August 1962, 8.
    Prescott, Orville. *New York Times*, 25 July 1962, 31.
    Quigly, Isabel. *Spectator*, 30 September 1955, 428.
    Rogers, W. G. *Saturday Review*, 25 August 1962, 25–26.
    Smith, William James. *Commonweal*, 28 September 1962, 19.
    Southern, Terry. *Nation*, 17 November 1962, 330–33.
PINCHER MARTIN.   London: Faber, 1956.   New York: Harcourt, 1957
(under the title THE TWO DEATHS OF CHRISTOPHER MARTIN).
    REVIEWS:
    British Book News, December 1956, 762.
    British Book News, June 1962, 457.
    Newsweek, 2 September 1957, 91.
    Time, 9 September 1957, 118.

Times (London), 1 November 1956, 13.
Times Literary Supplement, 26 October 1956, 629.
Virginia Quarterly Review, 34 (Winter 1958), xi–xii.
Amis, Kingsley. *Spectator*, 9 November 1956, 656.
Bensen, Donald R. *Saturday Review*, 31 August 1957, 15–16.
Bryden, Ronald. *Listener*, 29 November 1956, 891.
Davies, Robertson. *Saturday Night*, 2 February 1957, 16.
Mayne, Richard. *New Statesman*, 27 October 1956, 524.
Miller, Nolan. *Antioch Review*, 17 (Winter 1957), 519–24.
Moore, Reginald. *Time and Tide*, 3 November 1956, 1340.
Podhoretz, Norman. *New Yorker*, 21 September 1957, 189–90.
Solomon, Harold. *Isis*, 31 October 1956, 25.
Stallings, Sylvia. *New York Herald Tribune Book Week*, 1 September
    1957, 3.
Stern, James. *New York Times Book Review*, 1 September 1957, 16.
Wyndham, Francis. *London Magazine*, December 1956, 79.
ENVOY EXTRAORDINARY (in *Sometime, Never: Three Tales of Imagina-
tion by William Golding, John Wyndham, Mervyn Peake*).   London: Eyre
& Spottiswoode, 1956.   New York: Ballantine Books, 1957.
    REVIEWS:
    British Book News, February 1957, 138.
    Kirkus Bulletin, 15 May 1957, 358.
    Times (London), 29 November 1956, 13.
    Times Literary Supplement, 21 December 1956, 761.
    Yorkshire Post, 10 January 1957.
    Bowen, John. *Truth*, 23 November 1956, 1360.
    Green, Peter. *Daily Telegraph* (London), 30 November 1956.
    Holmes, H. H. *New York Herald Tribune Book Week*, 28 July
        1957, 9.
    Lardner, Rex. *New York Times Book Review*, 8 September 1957, 33.
    Metcalf, John. *Sunday Times* (London), 23 December 1956.
    Richardson, Maurice. *New Statesman*, 1 December 1956, 718.
    Shrapnel, Norman. *Manchester Guardian*, 4 December 1956, 4.

THE BRASS BUTTERFLY.   London: Faber, 1958.   New York: New American Library, 1962 (in *The Genius of the Later English Theater*, eds. Sylvan
Barnet, Morton Berman, and William Burto).
    REVIEWS:
    British Book News, September 1958, 616.
    Times (London), 15 April 1958, 3.
    Times (London), 18 April 1958, 3.
    Times Literary Supplement, 1 August 1958, 432.
    Barnes, Clive. *New York Times*, 31 January 1970, 34.
    Benedict, Stewart H. *Jersey Journal*, 31 January 1970, 26.
    Brukenfeld, Dick. *Village Voice*, 5 February 1970.

Findlater, Richard. *Sunday Dispatch* (London), 20 April 1958, 31.
Hope-Wallace, Philip. *Time and Tide*, 26 April 1958, 520.
Keown, Eric. *Punch*, 23 April 1958, 556.
Mavor, Ronald. *Scotsman*, 25 March 1958, 8.
Stasio, Marilyn. *Cue*, 14 February 1970, 10.
Trewin, J. C. *Illustrated London News*, 3 May 1958, 748.
Tynan, Kenneth. *Observer*, 20 April 1958, 15.
Worsley, T. C. *New Statesman*, 26 April 1958, 530.
FREE FALL.   London: Faber, 1959.   New York: Harcourt, 1960.
  REVIEWS:
  British Book News, January 1960, 62.
  Kirkus Bulletin, 1 January 1960, 27–28.
  Publishers Weekly, 17 April 1967, 59.
  Times (London), 29 October 1959, 15.
  Times Literary Supplement, 23 October 1959, 608. (NSB)
  Baldanza, Frank. *Minnesota Review*, 1 (Spring 1961), 378–85.
  Bradbury, Malcolm. *Punch*, 4 November 1959, 411.
  Cosman, Max. *New Leader*, 18 April 1960, 25.
  Elliott, George P. *Hudson Review*, 13 (Summer 1960), 298–303.
  Green, Peter. *Bookman*, October 1959, 13–14.
  Gregor, Ian. *Tablet*, 7 November 1959, 964.
  Hough, Graham. *Listener*, 5 November 1959, 793.
  Kermode, Frank. *Spectator*, 23 October 1959, 564.
  ———. *Partisan Review*, 27 (Summer 1960), 551–57.
  Lewis, R. W. B. *New York Herald Tribune Book Week*, 14 February 1960, 5.
  Miller, Nolan. *Antioch Review*, 20 (Summer 1960), 248–56.
  Mizener, Arthur. *Sewanee Review*, 69 (Winter 1961), 155–64.
  Owen, Patricia. *Tamarack Review*, 15 (Spring 1960), 87–94.
  Parker, Dorothy. *Esquire*, April 1960, 36–42.
  Pattison, Andrew. *Isis*, 18 November 1959, n.p.
  Perrott, Roy. *Manchester Guardian*, 23 October 1959, 8.
  ———. *Manchester Guardian*, 29 October 1959, 10.
  Pippett, Aileen. *New York Times Book Review*, 14 February 1960, 4.
  Price, Martin. *Yale Review*, 49 (Summer 1960), 618–27.
  Rees, David. *Time and Tide*, 31 October 1959, 1196.
  Rees, Goronwy. *Encounter*, January 1960, 84–85.
  Renault, Mary. *Saturday Review*, 19 March 1960, 21.
  Scott, J. D. *Sunday Times* (London), 25 October 1959, 16.
  Smith, Peter Duval. *New Statesman*, 24 October 1959, 550–51.
  Thompson, Donald E. *Library Journal*, 15 February 1960, 779.
  Toynbee, Philip. *Observer*, 25 October 1959.
  Webster, Owen. *John o' London's*, 28 January 1960, 90.
  West, Anthony. *New Yorker*, 30 April 1960, 170.
  Wyndham, Francis. *London Magazine*, January 1960, 70–73.

THE SPIRE.   London: Faber, 1964.   New York: Harcourt, 1964.
REVIEWS:
 Aldershot News, 8 May 1964.
 Booklist, 15 April 1964, 776.
 British Book News, July 1964, 543.
 Choice, September 1964, 241.
 Church Times, 10 April 1964.
 Doncaster Gazette, 28 May 1964.
 Kirkus Bulletin, 1 March 1964, 250.
 Manchester Guardian, 22 May 1964, 7.
 Newsweek, 27 April 1964, 105–6.
 New Yorker, 13 June 1964, 142.
 Publishers Weekly, 24 February 1964, 156.
 Time, 24 April 1964, 104.
 Time and Tide, 14 May 1964.
 Times (London), 16 April 1964, 17.
 Times Education Supplement, 22 May 1964, 1409.
 Times Literary Supplement, 16 April 1964, 310.
 Allsop, Kenneth. *Daily Mail* (London), 9 April 1964.
 "Astragal." *Architects' Journal*, 22 April 1964.
 Baker, James R. *Arizona Quarterly*, 20 (Autumn 1964), 268–69.
 Barrett, William. *Atlantic*, May 1964, 135–36.
 Boston, Richard. *Peace News*, 10 April 1964.
 Bowen, John. *New York Times Book Review*, 24 May 1964, 33.
 Brickner, Richard P. *New Republic*, 23 May 1964, 18–20.
 Buckmaster, Henrietta. *Christian Science Monitor*, 23 April 1964, 11.
 Bufkin, E. C. *Georgia Review*, 18 (Winter 1964), 480–82.
 Church, Richard. *Bookman*, April 1964, 35.
 Davenport, Guy. *National Review*, 19 May 1964, 409–10.
 Dennis, Nigel. *New York Times Book Review*, 19 April 1964, 1.
 Dolbier, Maurice. *New York Herald Tribune*, 22 April 1964, 27.
 Downing, John. *Socialist Leader* (Glasgow), 16 May 1964.
 Elmen, Paul. *Christian Century*, 3 June 1964, 740.
 Fane, Vernon. *Sphere*, 25 April 1964, 133.
 Fleischer, Lenore. *Publishers' Weekly*, 9 May 1966, 81.
 Fuller, Edmund. *Wall Street Journal*, 23 April 1964, 16.
 Gable, Sister Mariella. *Critic*, 23 (August-September 1964), 63–64.
 Gardiner, Harold C. *America*, 16 May 1964, 679.
 Greene, A. C. *Times Herald* (Dallas), 12 April 1964.
 Gregor, Ian. *Manchester Guardian*, 10 April 1964.
 ———. *Manchester Guardian*, 16 April 1964, 11.
 Grigson, Geoffrey. *Country Life*, 16 April 1964, 944–45.
 Halio, Jay L. *Southern Review*, 4 (Winter 1968), 236–47.
 Haskell, Douglas. *Life*, 24 April 1964, 12.

Hicks, Granville. *Saturday Review*, 18 April 1964, 35–36.
Highet, Gilbert. *Book-of-the-Month Club News*, July 1964, 7.
Hyman, Stanley Edgar. *New Leader*, 8 June 1964, 24–25.
Igoe, W. J. *Books Today*, 10 May 1964, 1.
Jennings, Elizabeth. *Listener*, 9 April 1964, 601.
Jillett, Neil. *Age*, 16 May 1964.
Johnson, Lucy. *Progressive*, July 1964, 40–41.
Kermode, Frank. *New York Review of Books*, 30 April 1964, 3–4.
Kinnaird, Clark. *New York Journal-American*, 19 April 1964.
Leone, Arthur T. *Catholic World*, October 1964, 56–57.
Lewis, R. W. B. *New York Herald Tribune Book Week*, 26 April 1964, 1.
———. *Washington Post*, 26 April 1964.
Lickes, W. G. *Methodist Recorder*, 23 April 1964, 9.
Lister, Richard. *Evening Standard* (London), 14 April 1964.
Lodge, David. *Spectator*, 10 April 1964, 489–90.
McDonnell, Thomas P. *Commonweal*, 12 June 1964, 377–79.
McNay, M. G. *Oxford Mail*, 9 April 1964.
Mann, Charles W. *Library Journal*, 15 May 1964, 2114.
Millar, Ruby. *Oldham Chronicle*, 9 May 1964.
Murray, Isobel. *Scotsman*, 18 April 1964.
Norrie, Ian. *Hampstead and Highgate Express*, 15 May 1964.
Nowell, Robert. *Tablet*, 11 April 1964, 408.
Nye, Robert. *Tribune*, 17 April 1964.
Paul, Leslie. *Kenyon Review*, 26 (Summer 1964), 568–71.
Pickrel, Paul. *Harper's*, May 1964, 119–20.
Pollock, Venetia. *Punch*, 29 April 1964, 651.
Prescott, Orville. *New York Times*, 11 May 1964, 29.
Pritchett, V. S. *New Statesman*, 10 April 1964, 562–63.
Quinn, John J. *Best Sellers*, 1 May 1964, 45–46.
Salvesen, Christopher. *Dubliner*, 3 (Summer 1964), 90–91.
Thompson, Richard J. *Cross Currents*, 15 (Winter 1965), 107–9.
Wain, John. *Observer*, 12 April 1964.
Walsh, George. *Cosmopolitan*, May 1964, 9–11.
West, Rebecca. *Sunday Telegraph* (London), 12 April 1964.
"Whitefriar." *Smith's Trade News*, 21 March 1964.
———. *Smith's Trade News*, 18 April 1964, 22.
Wood, Frederick T. *English Studies*, 46 (August 1965), 360–66.
Woodward, Anthony. *Sunday Chronicle* (Johannesburg), 28 June 1964.
Wyndham, Francis. *Sunday Times* (London), 12 April 1964, 36.
THE HOT GATES AND OTHER OCCASIONAL PIECES. London: Faber, 1965. New York: Harcourt, 1966.
REVIEWS:
Booklist, 1 May 1966, 858.

Booklist, 15 June 1966, 996.
British Book News, January 1966, 55–56.
Choice, September 1966, 519.
Kirkus Bulletin, 15 January 1966, 97.
Library Journal, July 1966, 3556.
Observer, 31 October 1965, 28.
Publishers Weekly, 13 February 1967, 78.
Publishers Weekly, 16 October 1967, 61.
Times (London), 28 October 1965, 16.
Times Literary Supplement, 4 November 1965, 972.
Virginia Quarterly Review, 42 (Summer 1966), cii.
Burgess, Anthony. *Listener*, 4 November 1965, 717–18.
Connolly, Brendan. *America*, 16 April 1966, 560.
Daniel, John. *Spectator*, 5 November 1965, 588.
Dolbier, Maurice. *New York Herald Tribune*, 23 March 1966, 27.
Fuller, Edmund. *Wall Street Journal*, 23 March 1966, 18.
Griffin, Lloyd W. *Library Journal*, 1 March 1966, 1226–27.
Harvey, David D. *Southern Review*, 5 (Winter 1969), 259–72.
Kitching, Jessie. *Publishers Weekly*, 17 January 1966, 131.
Levitas, Gloria. *Book World*, 27 November 1967, 19.
Nowell, Robert. *Tablet*, 15 January 1966, 103.
Quinn, John J. *Best Sellers*, 1 April 1966, 4–5.
Ricks, Christopher. *New Statesman*, 5 November 1965, 699–700.
Schroth, Raymond A. *Catholic World*, June 1966, 185–86.
Shrapnel, Norman. *Manchester Guardian*, 9 December 1965, 10.
Stafford, Jean. *New York Herald Tribune Book Week*, 27 March 1966,
    2.
Stevens, Elizabeth. *Books and Bookmen*, December 1965, 13.
Tanner, Tony. *New Society*, 2 December 1965, 35–36.
Thomson, George H. *Dalhousie Review*, 46 (Summer 1966), 256–58.
Weintraub, Stanley. *New York Times Book Review*, 27 March 1966,
    5.
THE PYRAMID.   London: Faber, 1967.   New York: Harcourt, 1967.
  REVIEWS:
    Booklist, 1 September 1967, 47.
    British Book News, August 1967, 648.
    Choice, June 1968, 482.
    Kirkus Bulletin, 1 August 1967, 900.
    Manchester Guardian, 21 December 1967, 11.
    Publishers Weekly, 31 July 1967, 53.
    Quest, 56 (January–March 1968), 96–98.
    Time, 13 October 1967, 113.
    Times Literary Supplement, 1 June 1967, 481.
    Virginia Quarterly Review, 44 (Summer 1968), cii.

Baker, James R. *Arizona Quarterly*, 23 (Winter 1967), 372–74.

Baldick, R. *Daily Telegraph* (London), 1 June 1967, 21.

Barker, Paul. *Times* (London), 1 June 1967, 7.

Bayley, John. *Manchester Guardian*, 2 June 1967, 7.

———. *Manchester Guardian*, 8 June 1967, 11.

Byatt, A. S. *New Statesman*, 2 June 1967, 761.

Cixous, Hélène. *Le Monde des Livres*, 26 July 1967, 1–2.

Clements, Robert J. *Saturday Review*, 1 July 1967, 19.

Cook, Roderick. *Harper's*, November 1967, 129–30.

Corke, Hilary. *Listener*, 8 June 1967, 761–62.

Curtin, Anne. *Progressive*, February 1968, 50–51.

Daniels, Judith G. *Book-of-the-Month Club News*, special fall selection issue, 1967, 11.

Dick, Bernard F. *Catholic World*, February 1968, 236–37.

Donoghue, Denis. *New York Review of Books*, 7 December 1967, 21–24.

E., A. *Saturday Night*, November 1967, 71.

Fuller, Edmund. *Wall Street Journal*, 30 October 1967, 18.

Grumbach, Doris. *America*, 9 December 1967, 720–21.

Hall, Mary. *Christian Century*, 27 March 1968, 402.

Haltrecht, Montague. *Sunday Times* (London), 4 June 1967, 28.

Hicks, Granville. *Saturday Review*, 14 October 1967, 25–26.

Hill, William B. *America*, 25 November 1967, 666.

Mann, Charles W. *Library Journal*, August 1967, 2805.

Nordell, Roderick. *Christian Science Monitor*, 19 October 1967, 11.

Nowell, Robert. *Tablet*, 10 June 1967, 641.

O'Neill, John. *Atlanta Journal and Constitution*, 15 October 1967.

Quinn, John J. *Best Sellers*, 15 October 1967, 276.

Sale, Roger. *Hudson Review*, 20 (Winter 1967–68), 666–74.

Seymour-Smith, Martin. *Spectator*, 30 June 1967, 768–69.

Sheed, Wilfrid. *Life*, 13 October 1967, 10.

Shuttleworth, Martin. *Punch*, 14 June 1967, 888.

Stevens, Elizabeth. *Books and Bookmen*, July 1967, 48.

Thompson, John. *Commentary*, January 1968, 68–69.

Thorpe, Michael. *English Studies*, 49 (June 1968), 271.

Trickett, Rachel. *Yale Review*, 57 (March 1968), 438–52.

Wain, John. *Observer*, 4 June 1967.

Wakeman, John. *New York Times Book Review*, 15 October 1967, 4.

West, Paul. *Book World*, 8 October 1967, 3.

Whitehead, John. *London Magazine*, June 1967, 100–104.

THE SCORPION GOD.   London: Faber, 1971.   New York: Harcourt, 1972.

REVIEWS:

British Book News, January 1972, 82–83.

Kirkus Bulletin, 15 December 1971, 1329.
New Yorker, 29 January 1972, 94.
Playboy, March 1972, 20.
Publishers Weekly, 13 December 1971, 36.
Times Literary Supplement, 5 November 1971, 1381.
Adams, Phoebe. *Atlantic*, February 1972, 109.
Blakeston, Oswell. *Books and Bookmen*, January 1972, 57.
Bodart, Joni. *Library Journal*, 15 April 1972, 1625.
Bradbury, Malcolm. *New Statesman*, 29 October 1971, 594.
Feinstein, Elaine. *London Magazine*, February–March 1972, 177–
    80.
Furbank, P. N. *Listener*, 28 October 1971, 579–80.
Gordon, David J. *Saturday Review*, 5 February 1972, 72.
Hoagland, Edward. *New York Times Book Review*, 6 February 1972,
    6.
Mann, Charles W. *Library Journal*, 1 March 1972, 898.
Marsh, Pamela. *Christian Science Monitor*, 3 February 1972, 11.
Pritchett, V. S. *New York Review of Books*, 24 February 1972,
    12–13.
Quick, Jonathan. *Los Angeles Times Book Review*, 27 February 1972,
    2.
Skow, John. *Time*, 21 February 1972, 78.
Wall, Stephen. *Observer Review*, 22 October 1971.
Waugh, Auberon. *Spectator*, 30 October 1971, 621.
West, Paul. *Book World*, 23 January 1972, 4.
Wood, Scott. *America*, 9 September 1972, 159–60.

II. *SHORT WORKS*

A. SHORT FICTION

THE ANGLO-SAXON. Queen, 22 December 1959, 27–30.
MISS PULKINHORN. Encounter, August 1960, 27–32.
INSIDE A PYRAMID. Esquire, December 1966, 165. (Part 3 of *THE
    PYRAMID*)
ON THE ESCARPMENT. Kenyon Review, 29 (June 1967), 311–400. (Part 1
    of *THE PYRAMID*)

B. OCCASIONAL PIECES

CONTRIBUTION to "The Writer in His Age." *London Magazine*, May
    1957, 45–46.
PINCHER MARTIN. Radio Times, 21 March 1958, 8.
THE LADDER AND THE TREE. Listener, 24 March 1960, 531–33. (THG)
ON THE CREST OF THE WAVE. Times Literary Supplement, 17 June
    1960, 387. (THG)

BILLY THE KID. Spectator, 25 November 1960, 808. (THG)
THE WELL BUILT HOUSE in *Authors Talking*. London: British Broadcasting Corp., 1961.
IT'S A LONG WAY TO OXYRHYNCHUS. Spectator, 7 July 1961, 9.
THINKING AS A HOBBY. Holiday, August 1961, 8.
A TOUCH OF INSOMNIA. Spectator, 27 October 1961, 569. (THG)
THE ENGLISH CHANNEL. Holiday, November 1961, 32. (THG)
THE GLASS DOOR. Spectator, 24 November 1961, 732–33. (THG)
THROUGH THE DUTCH WATERWAYS. Holiday, January 1962, 58.
BODY AND SOUL. Spectator, 19 January 1962, 65–66. (THG)
SHAKESPEARE'S BIRTHPLACE. Holiday, May 1962, 82. (THG)
THERMOPYLAE—A WALK THROUGH HISTORY. Holiday, September 1962, 50–51. (THG: under the title *THE HOT GATES*)
GRADUS AD PARNASSUM. Spectator, 7 September 1962, 327. (THG)
INTRODUCTION to *THE BRASS BUTTERFLY*, Faber School Eds. London: Faber, 1963, 1–4.
MISS PULKINHORN in *An Introduction to Literature*. Boston: Little, Brown, 1963. 2d ed., eds. Sylvan Barnet, Morton Berman, and William Burto.
DIGGING FOR PICTURES. Holiday, March 1963, 86. (THG)
EXILE, POVERTY, HOMECOMING: THE HAUNTING THEMES OF IRISH POETRY. Holiday, April 1963, 10.
ADVICE TO A NERVOUS VISITOR. Holiday, July 1963, 42.
UNA TERRIBILE MALATTIA. L'Europa Letteraria, 4 (July–December 1963), 124. (English version: untitled CONTRIBUTION to "The Condition of the Novel." *New Left Review*, January–February 1965, 34–35.)
A DISTINGUISHED AUTHOR RUEFULLY REVIEWS SOME CROSSES— GRAND AND LITTLE—THAT HE BEARS. Holiday, December 1963, 12. (THG: under the title *CROSSES*)
COPERNICUS: A UNIVERSE REVEALED. Holiday, January 1964, 56. (THG: under the title *COPERNICUS*)
THE BEST OF LUCK. Holiday, May 1964, 12.
AN AFFECTION FOR CATHEDRALS. Holiday, December 1965, 35.
EGYPT AND I. Holiday, April 1966, 32. (THG: under the title *EGYPT FROM MY INSIDE*)
*WILTSHIRE: THE RURAL RETREAT. Venture, 7 (September–December 1966), 19–26.
DELPHI: THE ORACLE REVEALED. Holiday, August 1967, 60.
FOREWORD to Jack I. Biles, *Talk: Conversations with William Golding*. New York: Harcourt, 1970.

C. Book Reviews

CHILDREN'S BOOKS: SENIOR BOOKSHELF. Listener, 5 December 1957, 953. (Twenty-odd books.)

IN RETREAT. Spectator, 25 March 1960, 448–49. (*A Hermit Disclosed* by Raleigh Trevelyan.)

RAIDER. Spectator, 20 May 1960, 741. (*John Paul Jones* by Samuel Eliot Morison.)

ISLANDS. Spectator, 10 June 1960, 844–46. (*The Swiss Family Robinson* by Johann Wyss and *Treasure Island* by Robert Louis Stevenson.) (THG)

HEADMASTERS. Spectator, 12 August 1960, 252–53. (*Thomas Arnold* by T. W. Bamford.) (THG)

IN MY ARK. Spectator, 16 September 1960, 409. (*The Ring of Bright Water* by Gavin Maxwell.) (THG)

MAN OF GOD. Spectator, 7 October 1960, 530. (*The Sabres of Paradise* by Lesley Blanch.)

PROSPECT OF ETON. Spectator, 25 November 1960, 856–57. (*Eton* by Christopher Hollis.)

THIN PARTITIONS. Spectator, 13 January 1961, 49. (*Some Reflections on Genius, and Other Essays* by Russell Brain.)

THE RISE OF LOVE. Spectator, 10 February 1961, 194. (*The Characters of Love* by John Bayley.)

ANDROIDS ALL. Spectator, 24 February 1961, 263–64. (*New Maps of Hell* by Kingsley Amis.)

ALL OR NOTHING. Spectator, 24 March 1961, 410. (*The Faithful Thinker*, ed. A. C. Harwood.)

BEFORE THE BEGINNING. Spectator, 26 May 1961, 768. (*World Prehistory* by Grahame Clark.)

ASTRONAUT BY GASLIGHT. Spectator, 9 June 1961, 841–42. (*Journey to the Centre of the Earth, 20,000 Leagues under the Sea, From the Earth to the Moon, Round the Moon, Five Weeks in a Balloon, At the North Pole, The Wilderness of Ice*, and *Propellor Island* by Jules Verne.) (THG)

TOLSTOY'S MOUNTAIN. Spectator, 8 September 1961, 325–26. (*War and Peace* by Leo Tolstoy.) (THG)

SURGE AND THUNDER. Spectator, 14 September 1962, 370. (*The Odyssey*, trans. Robert Fitzgerald.)

NO-NONSENSE VERSE. Manchester Guardian, 17 February 1967, 8. (*Selections from the Greek Anthology*, trans. Andrew Sinclair.)

THE VINLAND QUEST. Manchester Guardian, 15 June 1967, 11. (*Vinland Voyage* by J. R. L. Anderson.)

HAVE BROOM, WILL TRAVEL. Manchester Guardian, 8 March 1975, 21. (*Europe's Inner Demons* by Norman Cohn.)

THE OTHER SIDE OF THE LENS. Manchester Guardian, 17 May 1975, 17. (*Lighthouse* by Tony Parker.)

RICH AND STRANGE. Manchester Guardian, 14 June 1975, 22. (*Full Fathom Five: Wrecks of the Spanish Armada* by Colin Martin.)

CASTLE SEMBLANCE. Manchester Guardian, 21 June 1975, 22. (*Capability Brown* by Dorothy Stroud and *The Gothick Taste* by Terence Davis.)

LAST INFIRMITY. Manchester Guardian, 28 June 1975, 22. (*Francis Chichester* by Anita Leslie.)

TACKING UP THE ANDES. Manchester Guardian, 27 September 1975, 20. (*Ice Bird* by David Lewis.)

THE LOVE CHILDREN. Manchester Guardian, 4 October 1975, 21. (*The Gentle Tasaday* by John Nance.)

CRABBED YOUTH AND AGE. Manchester Guardian, 30 November 1975, 26. (*The Great War and Modern Memory* by Paul Fussell.)

NOTHING BUT THE BEST. Manchester Guardian, 4 January 1976, 22. (*Sailing: A Course of My Life* by Edward Heath.)

SHAKESPEAR IN ARABY. Manchester Guardian, 9 May 1976, 22. (*Captain Shakespear: A Portrait* by H. V. F. Winstone.)

THE SEA AFFAIR. Manchester Guardian, 11 July 1976, 22. (*The Rise and Fall of British Naval Mastery* by Paul M. Kennedy, *Naval Policy between the Wars, Vol. II*, by Stephen Roskill, and *Command at Sea* by Oliver Warner.)

WE ARE LOVED. Manchester Guardian, 22 August 1976, 22. (*The Purpose Watcher* by Kenneth S. Norris.)

THE ICEMAN COMETH. Manchester Guardian, 5 September 1976, 22. (*Karluck* by William Laird McKinlay.)

D. British Broadcasting Corporation Programs

ENVOY EXTRAORDINARY: A FABLE FOR BROADCASTING. Third Programme Play. Produced by Peter Duval Smith. Transmission 16 April 1956.

THE MODERN NOVEL. BBC West of England Home Service Talks Feature, with R. H. Ward. Produced by Robert Waller. Transmission 23 October 1956.

*OUR WAY OF LIFE. Third Programme Feature. Transmission 15 December 1956.

THE MEANING OF IT ALL. Third Programme Interview, with Frank Kermode. Produced by George MacBeth. Transmission 28 August 1959.

MONITOR. BBC Television Interview. Transmission 25 October 1959.

THE BRAINS TRUST. BBC Television Panel Discussion, Norman Fisher, Chairman. Transmission 14 January 1960.

THE LADDER AND THE TREE. Third Programme Short Story Reading. Produced by Owen Leeming. Transmission 13 March 1960.

MISS PULKINHORN. Third Programme Play. Produced by David Thomson. Transmission 20 April 1960.

REVIEW:
   Times (London), 21 April 1960, 16.

BREAK MY HEART. BBC Home Service Play. Produced by Nesta Pain. Transmission 19 March 1961.
BILLY THE KID. Third Programme Short Story Reading. Produced by Nesta Pain. Transmission 4 August 1963.
READING FROM THE SPIRE: BEFORE PUBLICATION. Third Programme Reading. Produced by Nesta Pain. Transmission 15 March 1964.

CRITICISM AND COMMENTARY

I. *BIBLIOGRAPHICAL SOURCES*

Adelman, Irving, and Rita Dworkin. *The Contemporary Novel: A Checklist of Critical Literature on the British and American Novel since 1945.* Metuchen, N.J.: Scarecrow Press, 1972, 205–17.
Biles, Jack I. "A William Golding Checklist," *Twentieth Century Literature*, 17 (April 1971), 107–21.
Boyd, George N., and Lois A. Boyd. *Religion in Contemporary Fiction: Criticism from 1945 to the Present.* San Antonio, Tex.: Trinity University Press, 1973, 23.
Bufkin, E. C. *The Twentieth-Century Novel in English: A Checklist.* Athens: University of Georgia Press, 1967, 48.
Drescher, Horst W., and Bernd Kahrmann. *The Contemporary English Novel: An Annotated Bibliography of Secondary Sources.* Frankfurt a/M: Athenäum-Verlag, 1973, 95–114.
Mellown, Elgin W. *A Descriptive Catalogue of the Bibliographies of 20th Century British Writers.* Troy, N.Y.: Whitston, 1972, 136–37.
Palmer, Helen H., and Anne Jane Dyson. *English Novel Explication: Criticisms to 1972.* Hamden, Conn.: Shoe String Press, 1973, 122–28.
Pownall, David E. *Articles on Twentieth Century Literature: An Annotated Bibliography 1954 to 1970.* New York: Kraus-Thomson, 1973, 3: 1296–1312.
Vann, J. Don. "William Golding: A Checklist of Criticism." *Serif*, 8 (June 1971), 21–26.
Wiley, Paul L. *The British Novel: Conrad to the Present.* Goldentree Bibliographies in Language and Literature. Northbrook, Ill.: AHM Publishing Corp., 1973, 50–52.

II. *BIOGRAPHICAL SOURCES*

ANONYMOUS:
  Britannica Book of the Year, 1963. Chicago: William Benton, 1964, 414–15.

Contemporary Authors: A Bio-Bibliographical Guide to Current Authors and Their Works, ed. Barbara Harte and Carolyn Riley, rev. ed. (vols. 5–8 in 1). Detroit: Gale, 1969, 449–51.

200 Contemporary Authors: Bio-Bibliographies of Selected Leading Writers of Today with Critical and Personal Sidelights, eds. Barbara Harte and Carolyn Riley. Detroit: Gale, 1969, 126–29.

Current Biography, March 1964, 12–14.

Current Biography Yearbook 1964, ed. Charles Moritz. New York: Wilson, 1964–65, 152–54.

"Golding on Golding." *Manchester Guardian*, 15 January 1960, 7.

The Reader's Adviser: A Layman's Guide to Literature, 12th ed., ed. Sarah L. Prakken. New York: Bowker, 1974, 474–75.

Who's Who 1969–70: An Annual Biographical Dictionary. New York: St. Martin's, 1969, 1192.

Who's Who 1972–1973: An Annual Biographical Dictionary. New York: St. Martin's, 1972, 1228.

Aldridge, John W. "Mr. Golding's Own Story." *New York Times Book Review*, 10 December 1961, 56–57.

Colby, Vineta. "William Golding." *Wilson Library Bulletin*, February 1963, 505. (NSB)

Hebert, Hugh. "Lord of the Tenace." *Manchester Guardian*, 14 July 1967, 7.

Watts, Harold H. "Golding, William (Gerald)." In *Contemporary Novelists*, ed. James Vinson. New York: St. Martin's, 1972, 491–94.

III. BOOKS AND OTHER SEPARATE PUBLICATIONS

ANONYMOUS:
A Critical Commentary: "Lord of the Flies." Study-Master Critical Commentaries, no. 451. New York: American R. D. M. Corp., 1964.

Notes on William Golding's "Lord of the Flies." Study-Aid Series. London: Methuen, 1966.

Babb, Howard S. *The Novels of William Golding*. Columbus: Ohio State University Press, 1971; Columbus: Ohio State University Press, 1973.

REVIEWS:
Booklist, 1 September 1970, 27.

Choice, November 1970, 1228.

Baker, James R. *South Atlantic Quarterly*, 70 (Winter 1971), 127–28.

DeVitis, A. A. *Modern Fiction Studies*, 18 (Winter 1972–1973), 618–23.

Dick, Bernard F. *Journal of Modern Literature*, 1971 Supplement, 1 (1971), 810–12.

Gray, David B. *Modern Language Quarterly*, 32 (1971), 335–38.

Mann, Charles W., Jr. *Library Journal*, 1 November 1970, 3777.

Mayhew, George P. *Books Abroad*, 45 (Summer 1971), 518.

Baker, James R. *William Golding: A Critical Study.* New York: St. Martin's, 1965.
REVIEWS:
    Arizona Quarterly, 21 (Autumn 1965), 288.
    Booklist, 1 September 1965, 26.
    Choice, December 1965, 681.
    Kirkus Bulletin, 1 June 1965, 561.
    Hough, Graham, *Saturday Review*, 31 July 1965, 17–18.
    Mellown, Elgin W. *South Atlantic Quarterly*, 65 (Spring 1966), 292–93.
    Moseley, Virginia. *College English*, May 1966, 651.
    Thomson, George H. *Dalhousie Review*, 46 (Summer 1966), 256–58.
    Ziegler, Arthur P., Jr. *Western Humanities Review*, 20 (Spring 1966), 174–75.
Beston, John. *A Comprehensive Outline of William Golding's "Lord of the Flies."* New York: Harvard Outline Co., 1963.
Biles, Jack I. *Talk: Conversations with William Golding.* New York: Harcourt, 1970.
REVIEWS:
    Choice, May 1971, 384.
    Boyle, Ted E. *Panorama—Chicago Daily News*, 6–7 February 1971, 8.
    Bufkin, E. C. *South Atlantic Bulletin*, 36 (May 1971), 72–73.
    Dick, Bernard F. *Progressive*, March 1971, 50–51.
    Gibbs, Jeanne. *Georgia Magazine*, May 1971, 39.
    Hutchinson, Harry T., Jr. *Library Journal*, 15 December 1970, 4262.
    Maddocks, Melvin. *Christian Science Monitor*, 15 October 1970, 12.
    Oldsey, Bernard S. *Studies in the Novel*, 3 (Fall 1971), 346–48.
    Smith, Don. *Atlanta Journal and Constitution*, 8 November 1970.
———, ed. "A William Golding Miscellany." *Studies in the Literary Imagination*, 2 (October 1969).
Calandra, Denis M. *"Lord of the Flies": Notes.* Rev. ed. Lincoln, Nebr.: Cliff's Notes, 1971.
Dewsnap, Terence. *William Golding's "The Inheritors" and "Free Fall."* Monarch Literature Notes. New York: Monarch Press, 1966.
———. *William Golding's "Lord of the Flies" and "The Inheritors," "Pincher Martin," "Free Fall."* Monarch Literature Notes. New York: Monarch Press, 1964.
———. *William Golding's "Pincher Martin."* Monarch Literature Notes. New York: Monarch Press, 1966.
Dick, Bernard F. *William Golding.* Twayne's English Authors Series, no. 57. New York: Twayne, 1967.
REVIEWS:
    Booklist, 1 June 1968, 1123.

Choice, September 1968, 774.
Elmen, Paul. *William Golding: A Critical Essay*. Contemporary Writers in Christian Perspective. Grand Rapids, Mich.: Eerdmans, 1967.
Handley, Graham. *William Golding: "Lord of the Flies."* Notes on Chosen English Texts. Bath: James Brodie, n.d.
Hodson, Leighton. *William Golding*. Writers and Critics, no. 61. Edinburgh: Oliver and Boyd, 1969; New York: Capricorn, 1971.
REVIEW:
   Dick, Bernard F. *Journal of Modern Literature*, 1971 Supplement, 1 (1971), 810–12.
Hynes, Samuel. *William Golding*. Columbia Essays on Modern Writers, no. 2. New York: Columbia University Press, 1964.
REVIEW:
   Choice, May 1965, 159.
Jackson, Frederick. *An Outline of "Lord of the Flies."* Toronto: Forum House, 1968.
*Keene, Dennis. *William Golding and Jehovah*. Kyoto, Japan: University of Kyoto Press, 1963.
Kinkead-Weekes, Mark, and Ian Gregor. *William Golding: A Critical Study*. London: Faber, 1967; New York: Harcourt, 1968; London: Faber, 1970.
REVIEWS:
   Booklist, 1 September 1968, 33.
   British Book News, August 1967, 628.
   Choice, July–August 1968, 624.
   Quest, 57 (April–June 1968), 110–11.
   Times Literary Supplement, 1 June 1967, 481.
   Baker, James R. *Arizona Quarterly*, 25 (Spring 1969), 77–80.
   Burroway, Janet. *Books and Bookmen*, June 1967, 26.
   Dick, Bernard F. *Catholic World*, December 1968, 139–40.
   Donoghue, Denis. *New York Review of Books*, 7 December 1967, 21–24.
   Green, Martin. *Manchester Guardian*, 21 April 1967, 7.
   Hough, Graham. *Saturday Review*, 31 July 1965, 17–18.
   Talon, Henri-A. *Essays in Criticism*, 18 (January 1968), 74–78.
   Whitehead, John. *London Magazine*, June 1967, 100–104.
Livingston, James C. *Commentary on William Golding's "The Spire."* Religious Dimensions in Literature, no. 3. New York: Seabury Press, 1967.
Medcalf, Stephen. *William Golding*. Writers and Their Work, no. 243. London: Longman, 1975.
Milch, Robert. *"Lord of the Flies": Notes*. Lincoln, Nebr.: Cliff's Notes, 1964.
Moody, Philippa. *A Critical Commentary on William Golding: "Lord of the Flies."* Critical Commentaries for Australian Schools. North Adelaide:

Australian Letters Publications, 1964; London: Macmillan, 1966 (Macmillan's Critical Commentaries); Toronto: Macmillan, 1967 (Macmillan's Critical Commentaries).

Nelson, William, ed. *William Golding's "Lord of the Flies": A Source Book*. New York: Odyssey, 1963.
REVIEW:
> *Choice*, October 1964, 313.

Oldsey, Bernard S., and Stanley Weintraub. *The Art of William Golding*. New York: Harcourt, 1965; Bloomington: Indiana University Press, 1968.
REVIEWS:
> *Choice*, December 1965, 681.
> *Kirkus Bulletin*, 1 June 1965, 552.
> Donoghue, Denis. *New York Review of Books*, 7 December 1967, 21–24.
> Gindin, James. *Modern Fiction Studies*, 15 (Summer 1969), 318–22.
> Hough, Graham. *Saturday Review*, 31 July 1965, 17–18.
> Kirvan, John J. *Catholic World*, January 1966, 253–54.
> Lerner, Arthur. *Books Abroad*, 40 (1966), 460–61.
> Mellown, Elgin W. *South Atlantic Quarterly*, 65 (Spring 1966), 292–93.
> Thomson, George H. *Dalhousie Review*, 46 (Summer 1966), 256–58.

Pemberton, Clive. *William Golding*. Writers and Their Work, no. 210. London: Longmans, 1969.

Talon, Henri-A. "Le Mal dans l'oeuvre de William Golding." *Archives des Lettres Modernes*, 6 (1966), 1–88.

Tiger, Virginia. *William Golding: The Dark Fields of Discovery*. London: Calder & Boyars, 1974.

Tristram, Philippa. See Moody, Philippa.

Whitley, John S. *Golding: "Lord of the Flies."* Studies in English Literature, no. 42. London: Edward Arnold, 1970.
REVIEW:
> *British Book News*, October 1970, 798.

IV. *PARTS OF BOOKS*

ANONYMOUS:
> "Fiction of 1967: (e) William Golding: *The Pyramid*." In *T.L.S.: Essays and Reviews from The Times Literary Supplement*, ed. Times Newspapers. London: Oxford University Press, 1968.
> "Fiction of 1971: (b) William Golding: *The Scorpion God*." In *T.L.S.: Essays and Reviews from The Times Literary Supplement*, ed. Times Newspapers. London: Oxford University Press, 1972.
> "*Free Fall*." In *Masterplots 1961 Annual: Essay-Reviews of 100 Out-*

standing Books Published in the United States during 1960, ed. Frank
N. Magill. New York: Salem Press, 1961.

"*The Inheritors.*" In *Masterplots 1963 Annual: Essay-Reviews of 100
Outstanding Books Published in the United States during 1962*, ed.
Frank N. Magill. New York: Salem Press, 1963.

Longman Companion to English Literature. Hong Kong: Longman,
1972.

"Novels of 1964: (a) William Golding, *The Spire.*" In *T.L.S.: Essays and
Reviews from The Times Literary Supplement*, ed. Times News-
papers. London: Oxford University Press, 1965.

The Penguin Companion to English Literature, ed. David Daiches.
New York: McGraw-Hill, 1971.

Allen, Walter. *The Novel To-day.* Rev. ed. London: Longmans, 1960.

———. *Tradition and Dream: The English and American Novel from the
Twenties to Our Time.* London: Phoenix House, 1964; New York: Dut-
ton, 1964 (under the title *The Modern Novel in Britain and the United
States*); Harmondsworth: Penguin, 1965.

Allsop, Kenneth. *The Angry Decade: A Survey of the Cultural Revolt of
the Nineteen-Fifties.* New York: British Book Center, 1958.

Amis, Kingsley. *New Maps of Hell.* New York: Harcourt; New York: Ballantine Books, 1960; London: Gollancz, 1961.

Anderson, David. *The Tragic Protest: A Christian Study of Some Modern
Literature.* London: SCM Press, 1969; Richmond, Va.: John Knox
Press, 1970.

Anderson, James R. *British Novels of the Twentieth Century.* Reader's
Guides, 3d Series, 7. Folcroft, Pa.: Folcroft Library Editions,1970.

Axthelm, Peter M. *The Modern Confessional Novel.* New Haven: Yale
University Press, 1967.

Baker, James R., and Arthur P. Ziegler, Jr., eds. *William Golding's "Lord
of the Flies."* Casebook ed. New York: Putnam's, 1964.

Barnes, Clive. "Golding Premiere Given by Chelsea Center." In *The New
York Times Theater Reviews 1920–1970*, vol. 8. New York: *New York
Times* and Arno Press, 1971.

Barnet, Sylvan, Morton Berman, and William Burto. Introduction to *The
Brass Butterfly.* In *The Genius of the Later English Theater.* New York:
New American Library, 1962.

Barrows, Marjorie Wescott, et al. *The English Tradition: Nonfiction.* Macmillan Literary Heritage. New York: Macmillan, 1968.

Bell, Michael. *Primitivism.* The Critical Idiom, no. 20. London: Methuen,
1972.

Benét, William Rose. *The Reader's Encyclopedia.* 2d. ed. New York:
Crowell, 1965.

Bergonzi, Bernard. *The Situation of the Novel.* London: Macmillan, 1970.

Blamires, Harry. *A Short History of English Literature.* London: Methuen, 1974.

Bohannan, Paul. *Social Anthropology*. New York: Holt, 1963.

Bradbury, Malcolm. "The Novel." In *The Twentieth-Century Mind: History, Ideas, and Literature in Britain*, 3:1945–1965, ed. C. B. Cox and A. E. Dyson. London: Oxford University Press 1972.

Broes, Arthur T. "The Two Worlds of William Golding." In *Lectures on Modern Novelists*, ed. A. Fred Sochatoff, Beekman W. Cottrell, and Ann L. Hayes. Pittsburgh: Carnegie Institute of Technology, 1963.

Buckley, Jerome Hamilton. *Season of Youth: The Bildungsroman from Dickens to Golding*. Cambridge, Mass.: Harvard University Press, 1974.

Burgess, Anthony. *English Literature: A Survey for Students*. London: Longman, 1974.

————. *The Novel Now: A Guide to Contemporary Fiction*. London: Faber; New York: Norton, 1967.

————. *The Novel Now: A Student's Guide to Contemporary Fiction*. New ed. London: Faber, 1971.

————. *The Novel Today*. London: Longmans, 1963.

————. *Urgent Copy: Literary Studies*. New York: Norton, 1968.

Campbell, Archie. "William Golding: *Pincher Martin*." In *From the Fifties*, ed. Michael Bakewell and Eric Evans. London: British Broadcasting Corp., 1961.

Capey, Arthur. "The Post War English Novel." In *Literature and Environment: Essays and Readings in Social Studies*, ed. Fred Inglis. London: Chatto and Windus, 1971.

Clark, George. "An Illiberal Education: William Golding's Pedagogy." In *Seven Contemporary Authors: Essays on Cozzens, Miller, West, Golding, Heller, Albee and Powers*, ed. Thomas B. Whitbread. Austin: University of Texas Press, 1966.

Cook, Albert. *Prisms: Studies in Modern Literature*. Bloomington: Indiana University Press, 1967.

Cox, C. B. *The Free Spirit*. London: Oxford University Press, 1963.

Daiches, David. *A Critical History of English Literature*. 2d ed., 2 vols. New York: Ronald, 1970.

Day, Martin S. *History of English Literature, 1837 to the Present: A College Course Guide*. New York: Doubleday, 1964.

Dillard, R. H. W. "*The Pyramid*." In *Masterplots 1968 Annual . . . Essay-Reviews of 100 Outstanding Books Published in the United States during 1967*, ed. Frank N. Magill. New York: Salem Press, 1969.

Dillistone, Frederick W. "The Fall: Christian Truth and Literary Symbol." In *Mansions of the Spirit: Essays in Literature and Religion*, ed. George A. Panichas. New York: Hawthorn Books, 1969.

Earnshaw, H. G. *Modern Writers: A Guide to Twentieth-Century Literature in the English Language*. Edinburgh: W. & R. Chambers, 1968.

Epstein, E. L. "Notes on *Lord of the Flies*." In William Golding, *Lord of the Flies*. New York: Capricorn Books, 1959. (CBE)

————. "Notes on William Golding and *Pincher Martin*." In William Gold-
ing, *Pincher Martin*. New York: Capricorn Books, 1962.
Esch, Arno. "William Golding: *Lord of the Flies*." In *Der moderne
englische Roman: Interpretationen* ed. Horst Oppel. Berlin: Erich
Schmidt Verlag, 1965.
Fairman, Marion A. *Biblical Patterns in Modern Literature*. Cleveland,
Ohio: Dillon/Liederbach, 1972.
Faulkner, Peter. *Humanism in the English Novel*. London: Elek/
Pemberton, 1975.
Fiedler, Leslie. *The Collected Essays of Leslie Fiedler*. 2 vols. New York:
Stein and Day, 1971.
————. "The Eye of Innocence." In *Salinger: A Critical and Personal
Portrait*, ed. Henry Anatole Grunwald. New York: Harper, 1962.
————. *No! in Thunder: Essays on Myth and Literature*. Boston: Beacon
Press, 1960.
Fleck, A. D. "The Golding Bough: Aspects of Myth and Ritual in *The Lord
of the Flies*." In *On the Novel: A Present for Walter Allen on his 60th
Birthday from His Friends and Colleagues*, ed. B. S. Benedikz. Lon-
don: Dent, 1971.
Fleischmann, Wolfgang Bernard, ed. *Encyclopedia of World Literature in
the 20th Century*. 3 vols. New York: Ungar, 1967–71.
Fleishman, Avrom. *The English Historical Novel: Walter Scott to Virginia
Woolf*. Baltimore: Johns Hopkins University Press, 1971.
Forster, E. M. Introduction to William Golding, *Lord of the Flies*. New
York: Coward-McCann, 1962. (CBE)
Fraser, G. S. *The Modern Writer and His World*. Harmondsworth: Pen-
guin, 1964; New York: Praeger, 1965.
Fricker, Robert. "Das Kathedralenmotiv in der modernen englischen
Dichtung." In *Festschrift Rudolf Stamm: zu seinem sechzigsten
Geburtstag*, ed. Eduard Kolb and Jörg Hasler. Bern: Francke, 1969.
Friedman, Norman. *Form and Meaning in Fiction*. Athens: University
of Georgia Press, 1975.
Gifford, Denis. *The British Film Catalogue 1895–1970: A Guide to
Entertainment Films*. Newton Abbot, Devon: David & Charles; New
York: McGraw-Hill, 1973.
Gindin, James. *Harvest of a Quiet Eye: The Novel of Compassion*.
Bloomington: Indiana University Press, 1971.
————. *Postwar British Fiction: New Accents and Attitudes*. Berkeley:
University of California Press; London: Cambridge University Press,
1962.
Golding, J. T. C. "A World of Violence and Small Boys." In *William Gold-
ing's "Lord of the Flies,"* ed. James R. Baker and Arthur P. Ziegler, Jr.
Casebook ed. New York: Putnam's, 1964. (CBE)
Gray, David B. Introduction to William Golding, *The Spire*. Educational
ed. London: Faber, 1971.

Green, Peter. "The World of William Golding." In *Essays by Divers Hands* (*Transactions and Proceedings of the Royal Society of Literature*), vol. 32, ed. Joanna Richardson. London: Oxford University Press, 1963. (NSB)

Gregor, Ian, and Mark Kinkead-Weekes. Introduction to William Golding, *The Inheritors*. Educational ed. London: Faber, 1964.

————. Introduction to William Golding, *Lord of the Flies*. Educational ed. London: Faber, 1962. (CBE)

Grigson, Geoffrey, ed. *The Concise Encyclopedia of Modern World Literature*. New York: Hawthorn Books, 1963.

Hall, James. *The Lunatic Giant in the Drawing Room: The British and American Novel since 1930*. Bloomington: Indiana University Press, 1968.

Halliday, M. A. K. *Explorations in the Functions of Language*. Explorations in Language Study. London: Edward Arnold, 1973.

————. "Linguistic Function and Literary Style: An Inquiry into the Language of William Golding's *The Inheritors*." In *Literary Style: A Symposium*, ed. Seymour Chatman. London: Oxford University Press, 1971.

Hardy, Barbara. *The Appropriate Form: An Essay on the Novel*. London: Athlone Press, 1964.

Hartt, Julian N. *The Lost Image of Man*. Baton Rouge: Louisiana State University Press, 1963.

Hillegas, Mark R. *The Future as Nightmare: H. G. Wells and the Anti-Utopians*. New York: Oxford University Press, 1967.

Hunter, Jim, ed. *The Modern Novel in English: Studied in Extracts*. London: Faber, 1966.

Hyman, Stanley Edgar. *Standards: A Chronicle of Books for Our Time*. New York: Horizon Press, 1966.

Johnson, J. W., ed. *Utopian Literature: A Selection*. New York: Modern Library, 1968.

Josipovici, Gabriel. *The World and the Book: A Study of Modern Fiction*. Stanford, Calif.: Stanford University Press; London: Macmillan, 1971.

Kahrmann, Bernd. *Die idyllische Szene in zeitgenössischen englischen Roman*. Berlin: Verlag Gehlen, 1969.

Karl, Frederick R. *A Reader's Guide to the Contemporary English Novel*. New York: Noonday Press, 1962; London: Thames and Hudson, 1963. Rev. ed. New York: Farrar; Toronto: Doubleday Canada, 1972.

Kearns, Francis E. "Golding Revisited." In *William Golding's "Lord of the Flies": A Source Book*, ed. William Nelson. New York: Odyssey, 1963. (NSB)

Keating, James. "Interview with William Golding." In *William Golding's "Lord of the Flies,"* ed. James R. Baker and Arthur P. Ziegler, Jr. Casebook ed. New York: Putnam's, 1964. (CBE)

Kennard, Jean E. *Number and Nightmare: Forms of Fantasy in Contemporary Fiction*. Hamden, Conn.: Archon Books, 1975.

Kermode, Frank. *Continuities*. London: Routledge and Kegan Paul; New York: Random House, 1968.
————. *Modern Essays*. London: Collins, 1971.
————. *Puzzles and Epiphanies*. London: Routledge and Kegan Paul; New York: Chilmark Press, 1962.
————. "William Golding." In *On Contemporary Literature*, ed. Richard Kostelanetz. New York: Avon Books, 1964. (NSB) (CBE)
————. "William Golding." In *Writing in England Today: The Last Fifteen Years*, ed. Karl Miller. Harmondsworth: Penguin, 1968. (NSB) (CBE)
Knight, Damon. *In Search of Wonder: Essays on Modern Science Fiction*. Chicago: Advent Publishers, 1967.
Kort, Wesley A. *Narrative Elements and Religious Meanings*. Philadelphia: Fortress Press, 1975.
Larson, Richard L. *Rhetorical Guide to The Borzoi College Reader and the Shorter Edition*. New York: Knopf, 1967.
Lass, Abraham H., ed. *A Student's Guide to 50 British Novels*. New York: Washington Square Press, 1966.
Lewis, C. S., Brian W. Aldiss, and Kingsley Amis. "Unreal Estates." In *Spectrum IV: A Science Fiction Anthology*, ed. Kingsley Amis and Robert Conquest. New York: Harcourt, 1965,
Lodge, David. *Language of Fiction*. London: Routledge and Kegan Paul, 1966.
————. *The Novelist at the Crossroads and Other Essays on Fiction and Criticism*. Ithaca, N.Y.: Cornell University Press, 1971.
M., R. "Lord of the Flies." In *The Novelist on Organization and Administration: An Inquiry into the Relationship between Two Worlds*, ed. Dwight Waldo. Berkeley: University of California Press, 1968.
MacNeice, Louis. *Varieties of Parable*. Cambridge: Cambridge University Press, 1965.
Malin, Irving. "The Elements of William Golding." In *Contemporary British Novelists*, ed. Charles Shapiro. Carbondale: Southern Illinois University Press, 1965.
Marcus, Steven. "The Novel Again." In *The Novel: Modern Essays in Criticism*, ed. Robert Murray Davis. Englewood Cliffs, N.J.: Prentice-Hall, 1969.
————. *Representations: Essays on Literature and Society*. New York: Random House, 1975.
Matlaw, Myron. *Modern World Drama: An Encyclopedia*. New York: Dutton, 1972.
McCombie, Frank. Introduction to William Golding, *Free Fall*. Educational ed. London: Faber, 1968.
Merivale, Patricia. *Pan the Goat-God: His Myth in Modern Times*. Cambridge, Mass.: Harvard University Press, 1969.
Monod, Sylvere. *Histoire de la littérature anglaise: De Victoria à Elisabeth II*. Paris: Colin, 1970.

Moody, William Vaughn, and Robert Morss Lovett. *A History of English Literature*. 8th ed., rev., ed. Fred B. Millett. New York: Scribner's, 1964.

Mueller, William R. *Celebration of Life: Studies in Modern Fiction*. New York: Sheed and Ward, 1972.

Neill, S. Diana. *A Short History of the English Novel*. Rev. ed. London: Collier-Macmillan; New York: Collier Books, 1964.

Padovano, Anthony T. *The Estranged God: Modern Man's Search for Belief*. New York: Sheed and Ward, 1966.

Parry, John. *A Guide through English Literature*. London: University of London Press, 1963.

Pérez Minik, Domingo. *Introducción a la novela inglesa actual*. Madrid: Ediciones Guadarrama, 1968.

Peter, John. "Postscript." In *William Golding's "Lord of the Flies": A Source Book*, ed. William Nelson. New York: Odyssey, 1963. (NSB) (OLF)

Prescott, Peter S. *Soundings: Encounters with Contemporary Books*. New York: Coward-McCann, 1972.

Pritchett, V. S. *The Living Novel and Later Appreciations*. New York: Random House, 1964; New York: Vintage Books, 1967.

———. *The Working Novelist*. London: Chatto and Windus, 1965.

Raban, Jonathan. *The Technique of Modern Fiction: Essays in Practical Criticism*. London: Edward Arnold, 1968.

Rabinovitz, Rubin. *The Reaction against Experiment in the English Novel, 1950–1960*. New York: Columbia University Press, 1967.

Ratcliffe, Michael. *The Novel Today*. London: Longmans, 1968.

Rexroth, Kenneth. *With Eye and Ear*. New York: Herder, 1970.

Richardson, Kenneth, and R. Clive Willis, eds. *Twentieth Century Writing: A Reader's Guide to Contemporary Literature*. London: Newnes Books, 1969; Levittown, N.Y.: Transatlantic Arts, 1971.

Richter, David H. *Fable's End: Completeness and Closure in Rhetorical Fiction*. Chicago: University of Chicago Press, 1974.

Riley, Carolyn, ed. *Contemporary Literary Criticism*. Vols. 1 & 3. Detroit: Gale, 1973, 1975.

Riley, Carolyn, and Barbara Harte, eds. *Contemporary Literary Criticism*. Vol. 2. Detroit: Gale, 1974.

Rippier, Joseph S. *Some Postwar English Novelists*. Studien zur Sprache und Literatur Englands 1. Frankfurt a/M: Verlag Moritz Diesterweg, 1965.

Robson, W. W. *Modern English Literature*. London: Oxford University Press, 1970.

Rodway, Allan. *The Truths of Fiction*. New York: Schocken Books, 1971.

Rosenfield, Claire. "'Men of a Smaller Growth': A Psychological Analysis of William Golding's *Lord of the Flies*." In *Hidden Patterns: Studies in*

Psychoanalytic Literary Criticism, ed. L. F. and E. B. Manheim. New York: Macmillan, 1966. (NSB) (CBE)

Ross, Stephen D. *Literature & Philosophy: An Analysis of the Philosophical Novel*. New York: Appleton, 1969.

Ruotolo, Lucio P. *Six Existential Heroes: The Politics of Faith*. Cambridge, Mass.: Harvard University Press, 1973.

Sampson, George. *The Concise Cambridge History of English Literature*. 3d ed., rev., ed. R. C. Churchill. London: Cambridge University Press, 1970.

Scholes, Robert. *Elements of Fiction*. New York: Oxford University Press, 1968.

Scott-James, R. A. *Fifty Years of English Literature 1900–1950: With a Postscript 1951 to 1955*. London: Longmans, 1956.

Seymour-Smith, Martin. *Who's Who in Twentieth Century Literature*. New York: Holt, 1976.

Sheed, Wilfrid. *The Morning After: Selected Essays and Reviews*. New York: Farrar, 1971.

Smith, Eric. *Some Versions of the Fall*. London: Croom Helm; Pittsburgh: University of Pittsburgh Press, 1973.

Spangler, Donald R. "Simon." In *William Golding's "Lord of the Flies,"* ed. James R. Baker and Arthur P. Ziegler, Jr. Casebook ed. New York: Putnam's, 1964. (CBE)

Spector, Robert Donald, ed. "Islands of Good and Evil: *Tom Sawyer* and *Lord of the Flies*." In Mark Twain, *The Adventures of Tom Sawyer*. New York. Bantam Books, 1966.

Spender, Stephen. "Is There No More Need to Experiment?" In *Opinions and Perspectives from the "New York Times Book Review,"* ed. Francis Brown. Boston: Houghton, 1964.

―――. "Traditional vs. Underground Novels." In *Great Ideas Today, 1965*. Chicago: Encyclopedia Britannica, 1965.

―――. *The Writer's Dilemma*. London: Oxford University Press, 1961.

Steiner, George. *Language and Silence: Essays on Language, Literature, and the Inhuman*. New York: Atheneum, 1967.

Stern, James. "English Schoolboys in the Jungle." In Louise E. Rorabacher, *Assignments in Exposition*. 4th ed. New York: Harper, 1970. (NSB) (OLF)

Stevenson, Lionel. *The History of the English Novel*, vol. 11, *Yesterday and After*. New York: Barnes & Noble, 1967.

Sullivan, Walter. "The Long Chronicle of Guilt: William Golding's *The Spire*," "Afterword," "About William Golding," and "Books by William Golding." In *The Sounder Few: Essays from the Hollins Critic*, ed. R. H. W. Dillard, George Garrett, and John Rees Moore. Athens: University of Georgia Press, 1971.

Swinden, Patrick. *Unofficial Selves: Character in the Novel from Dickens to the Present Day*. New York: Barnes & Noble, 1973.

Temple, Ruth Z., and Martin Tucker, eds. *A Library of Literary Criticism: Modern British Literature*, vol. 1. New York: Ungar, 1966.

Thornley, G. C. *An Outline of English Literature*. Longmans' Background Books. London: Longmans, 1968.

Tiger, Lionel. *Men in Groups*. London: Nelson; New York: Random House, 1969; New York: Vintage Books, 1970.

Townsend, R. C. "Golding, William." In *Encyclopedia of World Literature in the 20th Century*, ed. Wolfgang Bernard Fleischmann. New York: Ungar, 1969.

Tyre, Richard H. "A Note to Teachers and Parents." In *Sometime, Never: Three Tales of Imagination by William Golding, John Wyndham, Mervyn Peake*. New York: Ballantine Books, 1971.

Vinson, James, ed. *Contemporary Novelists*. New York: St. Martin's, 1972.

Wain, John. *Essays on Literature and Ideas*. London: Macmillan; New York: St. Martin's, 1963.

———. "From 'The Conflict of Forms in Contemporary English Literature.'" In *The Novel: Modern Essays in Criticism*, ed. Robert Murray Davis. Englewood Cliffs, N.J.: Prentice-Hall, 1969.

Wall, Stephen. "Aspects of the Novel 1930–1960." In *Sphere History of Literature in the English Language*, vol. 7, *The Twentieth Century*, ed. Bernard Bergonzi. London: Sphere Books, 1970.

Ward, A. C. *Longman Companion to Twentieth Century Literature*. London: Longman, 1970.

———. *Twentieth-Century English Literature, 1901–1960*. New York: Barnes & Noble, 1964.

Webster, Harvey Curtis. *After the Trauma: Representative British Novelists since 1920*. Lexington: University Press of Kentucky, 1970.

———. "The Spire." In *Masterplots 1965 Annual: Essay-Reviews of 101 Outstanding Books Published in the United States during 1964*, ed. Frank N. Magill. New York: Salem Press, 1965.

West, Paul. *The Modern Novel*. London: Hutchinson, 1963.

Wilpert, Gero von, and Ivar Ivask, eds. *Moderne Weltliteratur: Die Gegenwartsliteraturen Europas und Amerikas*. Stuttgart: Alfred Kroner Verlag, 1972; (under the title *World Literature since 1945: Critical Surveys of the Contemporary Literatures of Europe and the Americas*) New York: Ungar, 1973.

Wilson, Angus. "The Dilemma of the Contemporary Novelist." In *Approaches to the Novel*, ed. John Colmer. Adelaide: Rigby, 1966.

Yuill, W. L. "Tradition and Nightmare: Some Reflections on the Postwar Novel in England and Germany." In *Affinities: Essays in German and English Literature*, ed. R. W. Last. London: Oswald Wolff, 1971.

Ziegler, Arthur P., Jr. Foreword to *William Golding's "Lord of the Flies,"* ed. James R. Baker and Arthur P. Ziegler, Jr. Casebook ed. New York: Putnam's, 1964. (CBE)

V. THESES AND DISSERTATIONS

Abel, Charlsie M. "Desire and Reality in William Golding's *Lord of the Flies:* A Psychological Study." M.A. thesis, University of Virginia, 1965.

Bartley, Seward K. "Levels of Allegory in William Golding's *Lord of the Flies.*" M.A. thesis, University of Florida, 1963.

Botting, G. N. A. "Dualism in the Novels of William Golding." M.A. thesis, Memorial University of Newfoundland, 1970.

Briggs, Jane Ann. "Children in Contemporary Novels: Studies in Richard Hughes, J. D. Salinger, and William Golding." M.A. thesis, Auburn University, 1964.

Campbell, Mary Lavinia. "The Cornerstone of *The Spire.*" M.A. thesis, Emory University, 1967.

Chase, Kathryn Isabel. "A Study of Discord and Harmony in the Novels of William Golding." M.A. thesis, University of Manitoba, 1968.

Crook, Bernard. "The Use of Music Vocabulary in William Golding's Novels." M.A. thesis, Georgia State University, 1971.

Dickens, Denise Cross. "Success and Failure: 'Envoy Extraordinary' and *The Brass Butterfly.*" M.A. thesis, Georgia State University, 1975.

Dodson, Diane M. "William Golding: A Process of Discovery." M.A. thesis, North Texas State University, 1970.

Duncan, Judith G. "Death and Judgment in *Pincher Martin.*" M.A. thesis, Georgia State University, 1975.

Feinstein, Michael D. "The Innocent, the Wicked, and the Guilty in the Novels of William Golding." M.A. thesis, Miami University, 1965.

Fox, Stephen D. "William Golding: The Experiment in the Contemporary Novel." M.A. thesis, Emory University, 1966.

Hayhow, M. "The Element of Fable in the Novels of William Golding and Albert Camus." M.A. thesis, University of Nottingham, 1970.

Keiss, Sister Walter Mary. "Symbolic Object as Organizing Principle in William Golding's *The Spire.*" M.A. thesis, Catholic University of America, 1966.

Lloyd, Gayle Ponder. "The Ironic Myth of *Free Fall:* A Study in the Works of William Golding." A.B. Honors Essay, University of North Carolina at Chapel Hill, 1962.

McClendon, Sara. "The Nature of Man in William Golding's Novels." M.A. thesis, Vanderbilt University, 1964.

Mužina, Matej. "William Golding De Miseria Humanae Conditionis." M.A. thesis, University of Sussex, 1968.

Parker, Helen Nethercutt. "William Golding's *The Brass Butterfly:* An Analysis." M.A. thesis, University of North Carolina at Chapel Hill, 1970.

Poole, Mary Ann. "The Imagery of Vision in William Golding's *The Spire.*" M.A. thesis, Georgia State University, 1976.

Ray, Joel Weir. "Myth and Method in William Golding's *The Inheritors*."
    M.A. thesis, University of North Carolina at Chapel Hill, 1963.
Reid-Thomas, H. C. "Myth in Twentieth Century Theology and Literature,
    with Special Reference to Bultmann, Kafka, and Golding." M.A. thesis,
    University of Manchester, 1969.
Schneider, Mary Wheeler. "William Golding's *The Inheritors:* Structure,
    Point of View, and Theme." M.A. thesis, University of North Carolina
    at Chapel Hill, 1965.
Smith, Catherine C. "Chronology and Theme in William Golding's *Free
    Fall*." M.A. thesis, Georgia State University, 1971.
Smith, Ronnie Kay. "Three Kinds of Golding Characters." M.A. thesis,
    University of North Carolina at Chapel Hill, 1969.
Wilson, Norma Clark. "A Study of the Nature of Man as Presented in the
    Novels of William Golding." M.A. thesis, Austin Peay State University,
    1970.
Witherspoon, Marvin Lynn. "The 'Other' Societies: A Study of William
    Golding's *Lord of the Flies* and *The Inheritors*." M.A. thesis, Univer-
    sity of North Carolina at Chapel Hill, 1970.

Alterman, Peter Steven. "A Study of Four Science Fiction Themes and
    Their Function in Two Contemporary Novels." Ph.D. diss., University
    of Denver, 1974.
Bowen, Roger. "Isolation, Utopia, and Anti-utopia: The Island Motif in the
    Literary Imagination." Ph.D. diss., Harvard University, 1972.
Bufkin, Ernest Claude, Jr. "The Novels of William Golding: A Descriptive
    and Analytic Study." Ph.D. diss., Vanderbilt University, 1964.
Cammarota, Richard Stephen. "'Like the Appletree': Symbolism and the
    Fable in the Prose Works of William Golding." Ph.D. diss., Pennsyl-
    vania State University, 1972.
Dickson, Larry Lee. "Allegory in the Novels of William Golding." Ph.D.
    diss., Miami University, 1975.
Hasan, Ruqaiya. "A Linguistic Study of Contrasting Features in the Style of
    Two Contemporary English Prose Writers, William Golding and Angus
    Wilson." Ph.D. diss., University of Edinburgh, 1964.
Johnston, Arnold. "The Novels of William Golding." Ph.D. diss., Univer-
    sity of Delaware, 1970.
Khera, Sunit Bala. "Ethical Epistemology in the Novels of William Gold-
    ing." Ph.D. diss., Bowling Green State University, 1969.
LaChance, Paul R. "Man and Religion in the Novels of William Golding
    and Graham Greene." Ph.D. diss., Kent State University, 1970.
Latimer, Paula Ann. "William Golding's View of Man: A Study of Six of His
    Novels." Ph.D. diss., Texas Christian University, 1972.
Lipson, Carol Sharon. "The Influence of Egyptology on the Novels of
    William Golding." Ph.D. diss., University of California, Los Angeles,
    1971.

Popkin, David S. "Flake of Fire: Peak-Experiences in the Fiction of William Golding." Ph.D. diss., Pennsylvania State University, 1973.

Putnam, Stephen Hoyt. "'The Colors of the Spirit': Man and Nature in the Novels of William Golding." Ph.D. diss., University of North Carolina at Chapel Hill, 1975.

Rabinovitz, Rubin. "The Reaction against Experiment: A Study of the English Novel 1950–1960." Ph.D. diss., Columbia University, 1966.

Sanders, Joseph Lee. "Fantasy in the Twentieth Century British Novel." Ph.D. diss., Indiana University, 1972.

Sorensen, Eugene C. "Definition of Character in William Golding." Ph.D. diss., University of Denver, 1974.

Stinson, John Jerome. "The Uses of the Grotesque and Other Modes of Distortion: Philosophy and Implication in the Novels of Iris Murdoch, William Golding, Anthony Burgess, and J. P. Donleavy." Ph.D. diss., New York University, 1971.

Tiger, Virginia Marie. "An Analysis of William Golding's Fiction." Ph.D. diss., University of British Columbia, 1971.

Wight, Marjorie. "An Analysis of Selected British Novelists between 1945 and 1966, and Their Critics." Ph.D. diss., University of Southern California, 1968.

VI. ARTICLES, REVIEW-ARTICLES, INTERVIEWS, NOTES

ANONYMOUS:

"The British Imagination: The Workaday World That the Novelist Never Enters." *Times Literary Supplement*, 9 September 1960, vii.

"Lord of the Campus." *Time*, 22 June 1962, 64. (NSB) (CBE) (OLF)

Aarseth, Inger. "Golding's Journey to Hell: An Examination of Prefigurations and Archetypal Pattern in *Free Fall*." *English Studies*, 56 (August 1975).

Adriaens, Mark. "Style in W. Golding's *The Inheritors*." *English Studies*, 51 (February 1970), 16–30.

Alcantara-Dimalanta, O. "Christian Dimensions in Contemporary Literature." *Unitas*, 46 (1973), 213–23.

Ali, Nasood Amjad. "*The Inheritors:* An Experiment in Technique." *Venture*, 5 (April 1969), 123–30.

Allen, Walter. "Recent Trends in the English Novel." *English*, 18 (Spring 1969), 2–5.

Anderson, Perry. "The Singleton." *Isis*, 14 May 1958, 10–11.

Anderson, Robert S. "*Lord of the Flies* on *Coral Island*." *Canadian Review of Sociology and Anthropology*, February 1967, 54–69.

Antonini, Maria. "*Free Fall* di William Golding." *Convivium*, 37 (July-August 1969), 486–93.

Babb, Howard S. "Four Passages from William Golding's Fiction." *Minnesota Review*, 5 (January-April 1965), 50–58.

Babb, Howard S. "On the Ending of *Pincher Martin*." *Essays in Criticism*, 14 (January 1964), 106–8.

Baker, James R. "The Decline of *Lord of the Flies*." *South Atlantic Quarterly*, 69 (Autumn 1970), 446–60.

———. "Golding's Progress." *Novel*, 7 (Fall 1973), 62–70.

———. "Why It's No Go: A Study of William Golding's *Lord of the Flies*." *Arizona Quarterly*, 19 (Winter 1963), 293–305. (CBE)

Banaag, Concepcion B. "Evil and Redemption in *Lord of the Flies*." *Fu Jen Studies* (Republic of China), 3 (1970), 1–13.

Biles, Jack I. "An Interview in London with Angus Wilson." *Studies in the Novel*, 2 (Spring 1970), 76–87.

———. "Literary Sources and William Golding." *South Atlantic Bulletin*, 37 (May 1972), 29–36.

———. "Piggy: *Apologia Pro Vita Sua*." *Studies in the Literary Imagination*, 1 (October 1968), 83–109.

Biles, Jack I., and Carl R. Kropf. "The Cleft Rock of Conversion: *Robinson Crusoe* and *Pincher Martin*." *Studies in the Literary Imagination*, 2 (October 1969), 17–43. (WGM)

Bird, Stephen B. "Natural Science and the Modern Novel." *English Record*, February 1966, 2–6.

Blake, Ian. "*Pincher Martin*: William Golding and 'Taffrail.' " *Notes and Queries*, August 1962, 309–10.

Bowen, John. "One Man's Meat; The Idea of Individual Responsibility." Special Insert, "British Books around the World," *Times Literary Supplement*, 7 August 1959, xii–xiii. (NSB)

Boyle, Ted E. "The Denial of the Spirit: An Explication of William Golding's *Free Fall*." *Wascana Review*, 1 (1966), 3–10.

Bradbury, Malcolm. "Recent Novels." *Critical Survey*, 1 (Summer 1964), 193–96.

Braybrooke, Neville. "The Castaways and the Mariner." *Aryan Path*, 40 (February 1969), 54–59.

———. "The Return of Pincher Martin." *Commonweal*, 25 October 1968, 115.

———. "Two William Golding Novels: Two Aspects of His Work."*Queen's Quarterly*, 76 (Spring 1969), 92–100.

Brierre, Anne. "Littérature anglo-irlandaise." *La Revue des Deux Mondes*, 1 January 1968, 84–91.

Broberg, Britta. "Connections between William Golding's First Two Novels." *Moderna Språk*, 63 (1969), 1–24.

Brockway, James. "Niet God marr Golding." *Tirade*, 8 (1964), 402–6.

Brooke-Rose, Christine. "Le Roman Expérimental En Angleterre." *Les Langues Modernes*, March-April 1969, 158–68.

Bufkin, E. C. "The Ironic Art of William Golding's *The Inheritors*." *Texas Studies in Literature and Language*, 9 (Winter 1968), 567–78.

nglish Language

ling's The Spire."

attern in William
inter 1971–1972),

ree Fall." English

Studies, 51 (De-

Fiction." Contem-

paralelo narrativo:

e." Classical World,

terview with William

Studies in the Literary

d Oedipus." Cithara,

En analyse af idé og
romaner." Extracta, 2

mans de W. Golding."
0–42.

Pro Civitate Dei: Wil-
& Literature, 1 (1972),

lose Second." New York

ss to Blackout." Anarchy,

ridge Review, 4 May 1957,

w, 27 October 1956, 79.

Study in Parallels

Georgia Review, 19 (Spring 1965),

ʒ's Morality Play." Studies in the
, 5–16. (WGM)

s: I—The Manicheans." Times
–54.

xpress, 26 July 1962, 24–25.
of Our Novelists." Books and

33 (January-February 1965),

s l'oeuvre de William Gold-

ironique." Les Langues

of the Flies." Notes and

." Critical Quarterly, 5

Encounter, February

? A More Optimistic
f the Flies." America,

Summer 1960), 112–

, 12 March 1964,

em Consciousness
Short Fiction, 6

." Rocky Moun-
136–41.

g 1967), 63–79.
rancaise, Se

g Them
968),

Davis, W. Eugene. "Mr. Golding's Optical Delusion." *E*
Notes, 3 (December 1965), 125–26.

Delbaere-Garant, Jeanne. "The Evil Plant in William Gold
Revue des Langues Vivantes, 35 (1969), 623–31.

———. "From the Cellar to the Rock: A Recurrent P
Golding's Novels." *Modern Fiction Studies*, 17 (W
501–12.

———. "Time as a Structural Device in Golding's *F*
Studies, 57 (August 1976), 353–65.

———. "William Golding's *Pincher Martin*." *Englis*
cember 1970), 538–44.

Detweiler, Robert. "The Moment of Death in Moder
porary Literature, 13 (Summer 1972), 269–94.

Díaz-Plaja, Fernando. "Náufragos en dos islas: Un
Goytisolo y Golding." *Insula*, October 1965, 6.

Dick, Bernard F. "*Lord of the Flies* and the *Baccha*
January 1964, 145–46.

———. "'The Novelist Is a Displaced Person': An I
Golding." *College English*, March 1965, 480–82.

———. "*The Pyramid*: Mr. Golding's 'New' Novel."
Imagination, 2 (October 1969), 83–95. (WGM)

Dick, Bernard F., and Raymond J. Porter. "Jocelin a
6 (November 1966), 43–48.

*Diemer, Kirsten. "William Golding's *The Spire*
struktur set i sammenhaeng med de øvrige
(1969), 67–70.

Dierickx, J. "Le Thème de la chute dans les ro
Études Anglaises, 16 (July-September 1963), 2

Ditlevsen, Torben. "Civilization and Culture, o
liam Golding's *Lord of the Flies*." *Language*
20–38.

Dolbier, Maurice. "Running J. D. Salinger a C
Herald Tribune Book Week, 20 May 1962, 6.

Drasdo, Harold. "William Golding: From Darkn
February 1965, 35–38.

rew, Philip. "Man on a Cold Wet Rock." *Camb*
538–39.

——. "Second Reading." *Cambridge Revi*
B) (OLF)

Kirby L. "William Golding and Vardis
tensions." *College English*, Decemb

M., et al. "*Lord of the Flies* Goes
, 27–28.

"Golding's View of Man." *Am*

Eller, Vernard. "Depravity or Sin?" *Christian Century*, 20 November 1963, 1440.

Ellerby, John. "Must the Good Guys Always Lose?" *Anarchy*, February 1965, 33–34.

Elmen, Paul. "Prince of the Devils." *Christianity and Crisis*, 4 February 1963, 7–10.

Ely, Sister M. Amanda. "The Adult Image in Three Novels of Adolescent Life." *English Journal*, November 1967, 1127–31.

Engelborghs, M. "Engelse letteren: De romans van William Golding." *Dietsche Warande en Belfort*, 105 (1960), 515–27.

Fackler, Herbert V. "Paleontology and Paradise Lost: A Study of Golding's Modifications of Fact in *The Inheritors*." *Ball State University Forum*, 10 (1969), 64–66.

Fiedler, Leslie. "The Profanation of the Child." *New Leader*, 23 June 1958.

Filipi, Živan. "Moralna deterioracija u romanima Williama Goldinga." *Izraz*, 23 (1968), 576–85.

———. "William Golding: *Pincher Martin*." *Hrvatsko kolo*, N.S., 5 (1967), 1911–50.

Fox, Dorothy. "William Golding's Microcosms of Evil." *Innisfree*, 1 (1974), 30–37.

Freedman, Ralph. "The New Realism: The Fancy of William Golding." *Perspective*, 10 (Summer-Autumn 1958), 118–28. (NSB)

Freehof, Solomon B. "Nostalgia for the Middle Ages: William Golding's *The Spire*." *Carnegie Magazine*, 39 (January 1965), 13–16.

Freese, Peter. "Verweisende Zeichen in William Goldings *Lord of the Flies*." *Die Neueren Sprachen*, March 1972, 160–72.

Fuller, Edmund. "Behind the Vogue, a Rigorous Understanding." *New York Herald Tribune Book Week*, 4 November 1962, 3. (NSB)

Furbank, P. N. "Golding's Spire." *Encounter*, May 1964, 59–61.

Gallagher, Michael P. "The Human Image in William Golding." *Studies*, 54 (Summer-Autumn 1965), 197–216.

———. "Human Values in Modern Literature." *Studies*, 57 (Summer 1968), 142–52.

Gaskin, J. C. A. "Beelzebub." *Hibbert Journal*, 66 (Winter 1967–1968), 58–61.

Gibson, Catherine, "Hunters and Builders." *Anarchy*, February 1965, 38–40.

Gindin, James. "The Fable Begins to Break Down." *Contemporary Literature*, 8 (Winter 1967), 1–18.

———. "'Gimmick' and Metaphor in the Novels of William Golding." *Modern Fiction Studies*, 6 (Summer 1960), 145–52. (NSB)

Goldberg, Gerald Jay. "The Search for the Artist in Some Recent British Fiction." *South Atlantic Quarterly*, 62 (Summer 1963), 387–401.

Gordon, Robert C. "Classical Themes in *Lord of the Flies*." *Modern Fiction Studies*, 11 (Winter 1965–1966), 424–27.

Grande, Luke M., "The Appeal of Golding." *Commonweal*, 25 January 1963, 457–59. (NSB)

Green, Martin. "Distaste for the Contemporary." *Nation*, 21 May 1960, 451–54. (NSB)

Green, Peter. "The World of William Golding." *Review of English Literature*, 1 (April 1960), 62–72. (NSB)

Greenberg, Alvin. "Breakable Beginnings: The Fall into Reality in the Modern Novel." *Texas Studies in Literature and Language*, 10 (Spring 1968), 133–42.

———. "The Death of the Psyche: A Way to the Self in the Contemporary Novel." *Criticism*, 8 (1966), 1–18.

Gregor, Ian, and Mark Kinkead-Weekes. "The Strange Case of Mr. Golding and His Critics." *Twentieth Century*, February 1960, 115–25. (NSB)

Gulbin, Suzanne. "Parallels and Contrasts in *Lord of the Flies* and *Animal Farm*." *English Journal*, January 1966, 86.

Gutwillig, Robert. "*Lord of the Flies*." *Vogue*, May 1963, 154.

Hainsworth, J. D. "William Golding." *Hibbert Journal*, 64 (Spring 1966), 122–23.

Hamilton, Alex. "First Lord of the Novel." *Manchester Arts Guardian*, 20 December 1971, 8.

Hampton, T. "An Error in *Lord of the Flies*." *Notes and Queries*, July 1965, 275.

Hannon, Leslie. "William Golding: Spokesman for Youth." *Cavalier*, December 1963, 10.

Harris, Wendell V. "Golding's *Free Fall*." *Explicator*, May 1965, Item 76.

Harvey, W. J. "The Reviewing of Contemporary Fiction." *Essays in Criticism*, 8 (April 1958), 182–87.

Henry, Avril. "William Golding: *The Pyramid*." *Southern Review: An Australian Journal of Literary Studies*, 3 (1968), 5–31.

Hentig, Hartmut von. "'Jus' you wait!' Beobachtungen zu William Goldings 'Herr der Fliegen.'" *Neue Sammlung*, 5 (1967), 413–29.

Herndl, George C. "Golding and Salinger: A Clear Choice." *Wiseman Review*, no. 502 (Winter 1964–1965), 309–22.

Hollahan, Eugene. "Running in Circles: A Major Motif in *Lord of the Flies*." *Studies in the Novel*, 2 (Spring 1970), 22–30.

Hollinger, Alexandru, and Corina Cojan. "William Golding: Un Mesaj Umanist." *Viata Românească*, December 1967, 155–56.

Hurt, James R. "Grendel's Point of View: *Beowulf* and William Golding." *Modern Fiction Studies*, 13 (Summer 1967), 264–65.

Hynes, Sam[uel]. "Novels of a Religious Man." *Commonweal*, 18 March 1960, 673–75. (NSB)

Irwin, Joseph J. "The Serpent Coiled Within." *Motive*, May 1963, 1–5.

Ivasheva, V. "Uil'yam Golding ta ekzistentsialists' kii roman." *Vsesvit*, 4 (1967), 73–79.

Johnston, Arnold. "Innovation and Rediscovery in Golding's *The Pyramid.*" *Critique: Studies in Modern Fiction*, 14 (1972), 97–112.

Kearns, Francis E. "Salinger and Golding: Conflict on the Campus." *America*, 26 January 1963, 136–39. (NSB)

Kearns, Francis E., and Luke M. Grande. "An Exchange of Views." *Commonweal*, 22 February 1963, 569–71. (NSB)

Kermode, Frank. "The British Novel Lives." *Atlantic*, July 1972, 85–88.

———. "Coral Islands." *Spectator*, 22 August 1958, 257. (NSB) (OLF)

———. "The Meaning of It All." *Books and Bookmen*, October 1959, 9–10. (CBE)

———. Contribution to "The New Novelists: An Enquiry." *London Magazine*, November 1958, 21–25.

———. "The Novels of William Golding." *International Literary Annual*, 3 (1961), 11–29. (NSB) (CBE)

Kiely, Robert. "The Craft of Despondency—The Traditional Novelists." *Daedalus*, 92 (Spring 1963), 220–37.

Koestler, Arthur. "Books of the Year." *Sunday Times* (London), 23 December 1956.

Kort, Wesley. "The Groundless Glory of Golding's Spire." *Renascence*, 20 (Winter 1968), 75–78.

Kvam, Ragnar. "William Golding." *Vinduet*, 13 (Autumn 1959), 292–98.

LaChance, Paul R. "*Pincher Martin:* The Essential Dilemma of Modern Man." *Cithara*, 8 (May 1969), 55–60.

Lederer, Richard H. "Student Reactions to *Lord of the Flies.*" *English Journal*, November 1964, 575–79.

Lederer, Richard H., and Paul Hamilton Beattie. "*African Genesis* and *Lord of the Flies:* Two Studies of the Beastie Within." *English Journal*, December 1969, 1316.

Leed, Jacob R. "Golding's *Lord of the Flies*, Chapter 7." *Explicator*, September 1965, Item 8.

———. "*Lord of the Flies.*" *Dimension*, Supplement to *Daily Northwestern*, January 1963, 9–10.

Lehmann, John. "English Letters in the Doldrums? An Editor's View." *Texas Quarterly*, 4 (Autumn 1961), 56–63.

Levine, Paul. "Individualism and the Traditional Talent." *Hudson Review*, 17 (Autumn 1964), 470–77.

Levitt, Leon. "Trust the Tale: A Second Reading of *Lord of the Flies.*" *English Journal*, April 1969, 521.

Lewis, C. S., Brian W. Aldiss, and Kingsley Amis. "Unreal Estates." *Encounter*, March 1965, 61–65.

Lodge, David. "The Novelist at the Crossroads." *Critical Quarterly*, 11 (Summer 1969), 105–32.

———. "Le roman contemporain en Angleterre." *La Table Ronde*, December 1962, 80–92.

Lueders, Edward. "Entr'acte." *Reporter,* 16 November 1967, 49–52.

McGuinness, Frank. "*The Spire* by William Golding." *London Magazine,* August 1964, 84–88.

McKeating, H. "The Significance of William Golding." *Expository Times,* August 1968, 329–33.

MacLure, Millar. "Allegories of Innocence." *Dalhousie Review,* 40 (Summer 1960), 145–56.

————. "William Golding's Survivor Stories." *Tamarack Review,* 4 (Summer 1957), 60–67.

MacShane, Frank. "The Novels of William Golding." *Dalhousie Review,* 42 (Summer 1962), 171–83.

Mansfield, Joy. "Anthroposophy and the Writer: A Symposium." *Golden Blade,* (1966), 113–18.

Marcus, Steven. "The Novel Again." *Partisan Review,* 29 (Spring 1962), 171–95.

Marković, Vida. "U potrazi za autentičnim ljudskim likom." *Forum,* 1967, 11.

Marsden, Arthur. "The Novels of William Golding." *Delta: The Cambridge Literary Review,* no. 10 (Autumn 1956), 26–29.

Martin, Jerome. "Symbol Hunting: Golding's *Lord of the Flies.*" *English Journal,* March 1969, 408–13.

Massey, Irving. "An End to Innocence." *Queen's Quarterly,* 72 (Spring 1965), 178–94.

Mathewson, Joseph. "The Hobbit Habit." *Esquire,* September 1966, 130.

Merren, John. [Abstract of] "*Lord of the Flies* as an Anatomy." *Proceedings of the Conference of College Teachers of English of Texas,* 31 (September 1966), 28–29.

Michel-Michot, Paulette. "The Myth of Innocence." *Revue des Langues Vivantes,* 28 (1962), 510–20.

Michelmore, Cliff. "Books." *Punch,* 1 September 1971, 290–91.

Miller, Jeanne C. "Elusive and Obscure." *Virginia Quarterly Review,* 40 (Autumn 1964), 668–71.

Millgate, Michael. "Contemporary English Fiction: Some Observations." *Venture,* 2 (September-December 1961), 214–20.

Mitchell, Charles. "*The Lord of the Flies* and the Escape from Freedom." *Arizona Quarterly,* 22 (Spring 1966), 27–40.

Mitchell, Juliet. "Concepts and Technique in William Golding." *New Left Review,* May-June 1962, 63–71.

Moody, Philippa. "In the Lavatory of the Athenaeum—Post-war English Novels." *Melbourne Critical Review,* 6 (1963), 83–92.

Morgan, Edwin. "*Pincher Martin* and *The Coral Island.*" *Notes and Queries,* April 1960, 150.

Mueller, William R. "An Old Story Well Told: Commentary on William Golding's *Lord of the Flies.*" *Christian Century,* 2 October 1963, 1203–6. (CBE)

Mužina, Matej. "William Golding: Novels of Extreme Situations." *Studia Romanica et Anglica*, nos. 27–28 (July-December 1969), 43–66.

———. "William Golding: The World of Perception and the World of Cognition." Ibid., 107–27.

Nichols, James W. "Nathanael West, Sinclair Lewis, Alexander Pope and Satiric Contrasts." *Satire Newsletter*, 5 (Spring 1968), 119–22.

Niemeyer, Carl. "*The Coral Island* Revisited." *College English*, January 1961, 241–45. (NSB) (CBE)

Nordell, Roderick. "Book Report." *Christian Science Monitor*, 27 December 1962, 9.

Nossen, Evon. "The Beast-Man Theme in the Work of William Golding." *Ball State University Forum*, 9 (1968), 60–69.

Oakland, John. "Satiric Technique in *Lord of the Flies*." *Moderna Språk*, 64 (1970), 14–18.

O'Hara, J. D. "Mute Choirboys and Angelic Pigs: The Fable in *Lord of the Flies*." *Texas Studies in Literature and Language*, 7 (Winter 1966), 411–20.

Oldsey, Bern[ard S.], and Stanley Weintraub. "*Lord of the Flies:* Beelzebub Revisited." *College English*, November 1963, 90–99.

Oliphant, Robert. "Public Voices and Wise Guys." *Virginia Quarterly Review*, 37 (Autumn 1961), 522–37.

Page, Norman. "*Lord of the Flies*." *Use of English*, 16 (Autumn 1964), 44.

Pearson, Anthony. "H. G. Wells and *Pincher Martin*." *Notes and Queries*, July 1965, 275–76.

Pendry, E. D. "William Golding and 'Mankind's Essential Illness.'" *Moderna Språk*, 55 (1961), 1–7.

Pérez Minik, Domingo. "William Golding de *La pirámide a Martin el náufrago*." *Insula*, June 1970, 5.

Peter, John. "The Fables of William Golding." *Kenyon Review*, 19 (Autumn 1957), 577–92. (NSB) (CBE) (OLF)

Pira, Gisela. "Die Macht des Bösen in Goldings Roman *Lord of the Flies*." *Die Neueren Sprachen*, February 1969, 67–73.

Pittock, M. J. W., and J. G. Roberts. "Michael Roberts and William Golding." *English Studies*, 52 (October 1971), 442–43.

Pritchett, V. S. "Secret Parables." *New Statesman*, 2 August 1958, 146–47. (NSB) (OLF)

Quinn, Michael. "An Unheroic Hero: William Golding's *Pincher Martin*." *Critical Quarterly*, 4 (Autumn 1962), 247–56.

Raphaël, André. "La Pesanteur et la Grâce dans *Lord of the Flies*." *Les Langues Modernes*, 66 (1972), 449–68.

Rexroth, Kenneth. "William Golding." *Atlantic*, May 1965, 96–98.

Richter, Irmgard. "Betrachtungen zu William Goldings *Lord of the Flies*." *Die Neueren Sprachen*, July 1965, 332–36.

Richter, Richard H. "William Golding." *Praxis des Neusprachlichen Unterrichts*, 17 (1970), 62–68.

*Rocco-Bergera, Niny. "William Golding." *Rivista di Letterature Moderne e Comparate*, 22 (1969), 204–29.

Roper, Derek. "Allegory and Novel in Golding's *The Spire*." *Contemporary Literature*, 8 (Winter 1967), 19–30.

Rose, W. K. "An Interview with Iris Murdoch." *Shenandoah*, 19 (Winter 1968), 3–22.

Rosenberg, Bruce A. "Lord of the Fire-flies." *Centennial Review*, 11 (Winter 1967), 128–39.

Rosenfield, Claire. "'Men of a Smaller Growth': A Psychological Analysis of William Golding's *Lord of the Flies*." *Literature and Psychology*, 11 (Autumn 1961), 93–101. (NSB) (CBE)

―――. "Reply by Miss Rosenfield." *Literature and Psychology*, 12 (Winter 1962), 11–12.

Ryan, J. S. "The Two Pincher Martins: From Survival Adventure to Golding's Myth of Dying." *English Studies*, 55 (1974), 140–51.

Sasso, Laurence J., Jr. "A Note on the Dwarf in *Pincher Martin*." *Massachusetts Studies in English*, 1 (1968), 66–68.

Scott-Kilvert, Ian. "English Fiction 1967." *British Book News*, March 1968, 165–69.

Seehase, Georg. "Kapitalistiche Entfremdung und humanistische Integration. Bemerkungen zum englischen proletarischen Gegenwartsroman." *Zeitschrift für Anglistik und Amerikanistik*, 15 (1967), 383–400.

Servotte, Herman. "Sterfelijkheid en Licht." *Dietsche Warande en Belfort*, 109 (1964), 590–95.

―――. "William Golding, religieus romancier zonder dogma's." *Dietsche Warande en Belfort*, 108 (1963), 437–44.

Simpson, Arthur. "Sacco and Vanzetti: On Trial Again." *Mainstream*, March 1963, 3–9.

Skilton, David. "Golding's *The Spire*." *Studies in the Literary Imagination*, 2 (October 1969), 45–56. (WGM)

Sklar, Robert. "Tolkien and Hesse: Top of the Pops." *Nation*, 8 May 1967, 598–601.

Small, Martin. "Beelzebub Rides Again." *Anarchy*, February 1965, 41–45.

Spender, Stephen. "British Culture & Co.: The 'T.L.S.' Submits a Company Report." *Encounter*, November 1960, 56–61.

Spitz, David. "Power and Authority: An Interpretation of Golding's *Lord of the Flies*." *Antioch Review*, 30 (Spring 1970), 21–33.

Spivack, Charlotte K. "The Journey to Hell: Satan, the Shadow, and the Self." *Centennial Review*, 9 (Fall 1965), 420–37.

Steiner, George. "Building a Monument." *Reporter*, 7 May 1964, 37–39.

Stephane, N. "Deux Anglais Aliénés." *Europe*, September 1966, 220–26.

Sternlicht, Sanford. "Pincher Martin: A Freudian Crusoe." *English Record*, April 1965, 2–4.

―――. "The Sin of Pride in Golding's *The Spire*." *Minnesota Review*, 5 (January 1965), 59–60.

———. "Songs of Innocence and Songs of Experience in *Lord of the Flies* and *The Inheritors.*" *Midwest Quarterly*, 9 (July 1968), 383–90.

———. "A Source for Golding's *Lord of the Flies:* Peter Pan?" *English Record*, December 1963, 41–42.

———. "Two Views of the Builder in Graham Greene's *A Burnt-Out Case* and William Golding's *The Spire.*" *Calcutta Review*, March 1970, 401–4.

Stevens, Elizabeth. "Man Is Born to Sin." *Books and Bookmen*, April 1964, 7–11.

Stevick, Philip. "The Limits of Anti-Utopia." *Criticism*, 6 (1964), 233–45.

Stinson, John J. "Trying to Exorcise the Beast: The Grotesque in the Fiction of William Golding." *Cithara*, 11 (1971), 3–30.

Sullivan, Tom R. "The Uses of a Fictional Formula: The Selkirk Mother Lode." *Journal of Popular Culture*, 8 (Summer 1974), 35–52.

Sullivan, Walter. "The Long Chronicle of Guilt: William Golding's *The Spire.*" *Hollins Critic*, 1 (June 1964), 1–12.

———. "William Golding: The Fables and the Art." *Sewanee Review*, 71 (Autumn 1963), 660–64.

Sutherland, Raymond Carter. "Mediaeval Elements in *The Spire.*" *Studies in the Literary Imagination*, 2 (October 1969), 57–65. (WGM)

Talon, Henri-A. "Irony in *Lord of the Flies.*" *Essays in Criticism*, 18 (July 1968), 296–309.

Taylor, Harry H. "The Case against William Golding's Simon-Piggy." *Contemporary Review*, September 1966, 155–60.

Temple, E. R. A. "William Golding's *The Spire:* A Critique." *Renascence*, 20 (Summer 1968), 171–73.

Thomson, George H. "The Real World of William Golding." *Alphabet*, 9 (November 1964), 26–33.

———. "William Golding: Between God-Darkness and God-Light." *Cresset*, June 1969, 8–12.

Thorpe, Peter. "Thinking in Octagons: Further Reflections on Norms in Satire." *Satire Newsletter*, 7 (Spring 1970), 91–99.

Townsend, R. C. "*Lord of the Flies:* Fool's Gold?" *Journal of General Education*, 16 (July 1964), 153–60.

Trilling, Lionel. "*Lord of the Flies.*" *Mid-Century*, October 1962, 10–12.

Tristram, Philippa. See Moody, Philippa.

Tynan, Kenneth. "Books of the Year." *Observer*, 23 December 1956.

Veidemanis, Gladys. "*Lord of the Flies* in the Classroom—No Passing Fad." *English Journal*, November 1964, 569–74.

Vizioli, Paulo. "Paráiso perdido de William Golding." *O Estado de São Paulo, Suplemento Literário*, 6 January 1968, 1.

Vogel, A. W. "William Golding on the Nature of Man." *Educational Theory*, 15 (April 1965), 130–34.

Wain, John. "The Conflict of Forms in Contemporary English Literature: Part II." *Critical Quarterly*, 4 (Summer 1962), 101–19.

Wain, John. "Lord of the Agonies." *Aspect*, April 1963, 56–67.

Walker, Marshall. "William Golding: From Paradigm to Pyramid." *Studies in the Literary Imagination*, 2 (October 1969), 67–82. (WGM)

Walters, Margaret. "Two Fabulists: Golding and Camus." *Melbourne Critical Review*, 4 (1961), 18–29. (NSB)

Warner, Oliver. "Mr. Golding and Marryat's *Little Savage*." *Review of English Literature*, 5 (January 1964), 51–55.

Wasserstrom, William. "Reason and Reverence in Art and Science." *Literature and Psychology*, 12 (Winter 1962), 2–5.

Watson, Kenneth. "A Reading of *Lord of the Flies*." *English*, 15 (Spring 1964), 2–7.

Webster, Owen. "Living with Chaos." *Books and Art*, March 1958, 15–16.

White, Robert J. "Butterfly and Beast in *Lord of the Flies*." *Modern Fiction Studies*, 10 (Summer 1964), 163–70.

Whitehead, Lee M. "The Moment out of Time: Golding's *Pincher Martin*." *Contemporary Literature*, 12 (Winter 1971), 18–41.

Wicht, Wolfgang. " '*Oh, the continent of a man!*': Das Menschenbild in William Goldings Romanen *Free Fall*, *The Spire* und *The Pyramid*." *Zeitschrift für Anglistik und Amerikanistik*, 18 (1970), 59–70.

Williams, H. M. "The Art of William Golding." *Bulletin of the Department of English* (Calcutta University), 3 (1962), 20–31.

Williams, Melvin G. "Beelzebub Comes to Church." *Christian Advocate*, 13 August 1964, 9–10.

Willingham, John R., et al. "Class of '67: The Gentle Desperadoes." *Nation*, 19 June 1967, 775–81.

Wilson, Angus. "Evil in the English Novel: Evil and the Novelist Today." *Listener*, 17 January 1963, 115–17.

———. "Evil in the English Novel." *Books and Bookmen*, June 1963, 3.

———. "Evil in the English Novel." *Kenyon Review*, 29 (March 1967), 167–94.

Wöhler, Günter. "Ein Beitrag zur Klärung der Wortbedeutung des englischen Farbadjectivs *pink*." *Die Neueren Sprachen*, March 1966, 128–32.

Young, Wayland. "Letter from London." *Kenyon Review*, 19 (Summer 1957), 478–82. (NSB) (OLF)

VII. *LETTERS TO THE EDITOR*

Alcock, N. W. *Spectator*, 12 September 1958, 347.

Bittner, William. *Atlantic*, July 1965, 28.

Braham, Mark. *Atlantic*, July 1965, 28.

Cooney, Neill L. *America*, 23 February 1963, 242.

Daish, W. G. *Times Literary Supplement*, 4 September 1959, 507.

Davidson, Ellen A. *Atlantic*, July 1965, 28.

Ferrara, Frank D. *America*, 23 February 1963, 244.

Garrigan, Kristine O. *Reporter*, 18 June 1964, 6.
Gerlich, Donald G. *America*, 23 February 1963, 244.
Green, Peter. *Times Literary Supplement*, 28 August 1959, 495.
Keener, Frederick M. *America*, 23 February 1963, 244.
Lee, David A. *Atlantic*, July 1965, 28.
Lewis, John S. *Nation*, 8 December 1962, 404.
Lewis, Theodore N. *New York Times Book Review*, 19 November 1967, 86.
Maxwell, J. C. *Times Literary Supplement*, 21 August 1959, 483.
Monteith, Charles. *Reporter*, 18 June 1964, 6.
Morgan, Edwin. *Times Literary Supplement*, 28 August 1959, 495.
Reichenberger, Alfred E. *New York Times Book Review*, 2 February 1964, 28.
Schneider, Franz. *America*, 23 February 1963, 244.
Simon, S. E. *New Statesman*, 31 October 1959, 582.
Singh, Raman K. *Atlantic*, July 1965, 28.
Starinshak, Melanne. *America*, 23 February 1963, 244.
Steiner, George. *Reporter*, 18 June 1964, 8.
Vollrath, Jeanne. *Atlantic*, July 1965, 28.
Wakeman, John. *New York Times Book Review*, 19 November 1967, 86.
Webster, Owen. *Times Literary Supplement*, 11 September 1959, 519.

VIII. *BRITISH BROADCASTING CORPORATION PROGRAMS*

Alvarez, A. "On *Free Fall*." Third Programme "Comment" Critical Talk, no. 44. Produced by George MacBeth. Transmission 29 October 1959.

*Ayrton, Michael, and Ian Gregor. "The Masters: William Golding." Third Programme. Transmission 28 March 1966.

Calder-Marshall, Arthur. "Weekly Book Summary, no. 693." European Service Review. Transmission 9 January 1957.

Campbell, Archie. "*Pincher Martin*." Third Programme Play. Produced by Archie Campbell. Transmission 27 March 1958.

Cooper, Giles. "*Lord of the Flies*." Third Programme Play. Produced by Archie Campbell. Transmission 28 August 1955.
    REVIEWS:
        Croydon Advertiser, 9 September 1955.
        Manchester Guardian, 5 September 1955.
        Times (London), 29 August 1955, 10.
    Lewis, Peter. *Yorkshire Evening News*, 5 September 1955.

Evans, Lindsay. "*Lord of the Flies*: Part 1. A Place in the Forest." Home Service (Schools) "Books, Plays, Poems" Dramatization. Produced by David Lyttle. Transmission 3 November 1965.

———. "*Lord of the Flies*: Part 2. The Beast." Home Service (Schools) "Books, Plays, Poems" Dramatization. Produced by David Lyttle. Transmission 10 November 1965.

———. "*Lord of the Flies*: Part 3. A View to a Death." Home Service

(Schools) "Books, Plays, Poems" Dramatization. Produced by David Lyttle. Transmission 17 November 1965.

————. *Lord of the Flies:* Part 4. The Hunt." Home Service (Schools) "Books, Plays, Poems" Dramatization. Produced by David Lyttle. Transmission 24 November 1965.

Hough, Graham, et al. "On *Pincher Martin.*" Third Programme Panel Discussion. Transmission 21 December 1956.

Huxley, Elspeth. "Just Published." "London Calling Asia—English Writing" Review. Produced by Laurence Stapley. Transmission 12 October 1954.

Kermode, Frank. "Frank Kermode on *Pincher Martin* by William Golding." Third Programme "Comment" Critical Talk, no. 31. Produced by D. S. Carne-Ross. Transmission 1 November 1956.

Lambert, J. W., et al. "The Critics." Home Service Panel Discussion. Transmission 12 April 1964.

McWhinnie, Donald. "*Free Fall.*" Third Programme Play. Produced by Donald McWhinnie. Transmission 27 January 1960.
    REVIEWS:
        Times (London), 28 January 1960, 3.
        Ferris, Paul. *Observer*, 31 January 1960.

Pain, Nesta. "*The Spire.*" Third Programme Play. Produced by Nesta Pain. Transmission early 1965.

Powell, Dilys, et al. "The Critics." Home Service Panel Discussion. Transmission 4 May 1958.

Worsley, T. C., et al. "The Critics." Home Service Panel Discussion. Transmission 28 October 1956.

CONTRIBUTORS

DAVID ANDERSON is principal lecturer in religious studies, Hertford-
shire College of Higher Education, Aldenham, England. Among his
works are *The Tragic Protest: A Christian Study of Some Modern Literature* and *Simone Weil*.

JACK I. BILES is professor and assistant head of the Department of English, Georgia State University. His work has appeared in various scholarly journals; other publications include *Talk: Conversations with
William Golding* and "A William Golding Miscellany" and "Aspects of
Utopian Fiction," special numbers of *Studies in the Literary Imagination*.

TED E. BOYLE is professor and chairman of the Department of English,
Southern Illinois University. In addition to critical articles, he has written *Symbol and Meanings in the Writings of Joseph Conrad* and *Brendan Behan*.

E. C. BUFKIN is associate professor of English at the University of Geor-
gia. His articles on Golding have appeared in the *Georgia Review*,
Texas Studies in Literature and Language, and *Studies in the Literary
Imagination*. Other works are *The Twentieth-Century Novel in English:
A Checklist* and *P. H. Newby*.

Major RICHARD S. CAMMAROTA, a career officer in the United States
Air Force, was associate professor of English at the Air Force Academy
and currently is assigned to Wright-Patterson Air Force Base, Dayton,
Ohio. His dissertation at Pennsylvania State University treats sym-
bolism in William Golding; he has published an article on *A Passage to
India* and many film and drama reviews.

JEANNE DELBAERE-GARANT, professor of English literature at the
University of Brussels, has published essays on Golding in *Revue des
Langues Vivantes*, *English Studies*, and *Modern Fiction Studies;* other

articles concern James, Lawrence, Ford, Forster, Woolf, Joyce, Waugh, Cary, and Janet Frame. She is author of *Henry James: The Vision of France*.

ROBERT O. EVANS is professor of English and director of the Honors Program at the University of Kentucky. Besides numerous articles, he has written or edited many books, including *A Study of Milton's Elision; The Osier Cage: Rhetorical Devices in Romeo and Juliet; Graham Greene: Some Critical Considerations;* and a novel. Among recent publications are an article on the language of *A Clockwork Orange* and editions and translations of *An Introduction to American Literature* and *An Introduction to English Literature* by Jorge Luis Borges.

JAY L. HALIO, professor of English and associate provost for instruction at the University of Delaware, is author of the Angus Wilson volume in the Writers and Critics series. He has published many articles on Renaissance and on contemporary literary topics and has edited various texts of Renaissance drama, including *Volpone, Macbeth,* and *King Lear*. He also edited *Twentieth Century Interpretations of "As You Like It."*

LEIGHTON HODSON is lecturer in French at the University of Glasgow. His interests are in the modern novel and drama in both French and English. He has written on Marcel Proust and is author of *William Golding*, in the Writers and Critics series.

ARNOLD JOHNSTON is associate professor of English at Western Michigan University. "The Novels of William Golding" is his dissertation, written at the University of Delaware. He has published short stories and poems, and two of his plays have been successfully produced. His "Innovation and Rediscovery in Golding's *The Pyramid*" appeared in *Critique*.

MAURICE L. McCULLEN is professor of English at the University of the Pacific. He has written essays on Meredith, Dickens, and Thackeray, among others. At present, he is working on a book on E. M. Delafield.

DAVID SKILTON is lecturer in English literature at the University of Glasgow. Besides critical articles, he has published *Anthony Trollope and His Contemporaries*. His second book, a history of the English novel from 1700 to 1900, will soon appear.

PHILIPPA TRISTRAM holds bachelor of philosophy and master of arts degrees from Oxford University and is lecturer in English literature at the University of York. She has published on the nineteenth- and twentieth-century novel. Her book *Figures of Life and Death in Medieval Literature* appeared in 1976.

PETER WOLFE is professor of English at the University of Missouri, Saint Louis. Author of numerous articles and reviews, he also has published *The Disciplined Heart: Iris Murdoch and Her Novels; Mary Renault; Rebecca West: Artist and Thinker; Graham Greene the Entertainer;* and *John Fowles: Magus and Novelist.* He has completed a lengthy study of Ross MacDonald and a short book on Jean Rhys.

AP